RETIREMENT OF REVOLUTIONARIES IN CHINA

RETIREMENT OF REVOLUTIONARIES IN CHINA

PUBLIC POLICIES, SOCIAL NORMS,

PRIVATE INTERESTS

Melanie Manion

PRINCETON UNIVERSITY PRESS   PRINCETON, NEW JERSEY

Library of Congress Cataloging-in-Publication Data
Manion, Melanie, 1955–
Retirement of revolutionaries in China : public policies, social
norms, private interests / Melanie Manion.
p. cm.
Includes bibliographical references and index.
ISBN 0-691-08653-2 (alk. paper)
1. China—Officials and employees—Pensions. 2. China—Officials
and employees—Retirement. I. Title.
JQ1512.Z2M36   1993
354.51001′82′09048—dc20   92-32031   CIP

This book has been composed in Linotron Baskerville

Printed in the United States of America

1   3   5   7   9   10   8   6   4   2

To my parents

WITH LOVE AND GRATITUDE

Contents

Figures and Tables

FIGURES

TABLES

Acknowledgments

IT IS MY PLEASURE to acknowledge the help of a number of people without whom this book could not have been written. My first debt is to the hundreds of Chinese cadres who responded to my many questions in interviews or by self-administered questionnaire. I also thank my Chinese friends and colleagues who helped me connect with these cadres. The Ministry of Labor and Personnel was very helpful in granting interviews to clarify my understanding of cadre retirement policy. I benefited as well from the support of old friends and new at Peking University. In particular, I am grateful to people in the following offices: the Office of the President, the Department of International Politics, the Department of Political Science and Public Administration, the External Affairs Division, the Foreign Students Office, and the Veteran Cadre Division. This study was not always an easy project to support and I am fully aware and very appreciative of the extraordinary efforts made to support it.

This book began as research for my doctoral dissertation, completed in 1989 at the University of Michigan. The members of my dissertation committee contributed in different ways to its development and to my growth as a scholar throughout my years of graduate school. Robert Axelrod taught a seminar on norms which, in addition to his own exciting work, sparked an intellectual interest that grew into the research question for this book. Martha Feldman challenged basic assumptions and cautioned me about banalities. Kenneth Lieberthal prodded me with useful criticism and thoughtful suggestions on both the dissertation and book manuscript. Martin King Whyte gave constructive advice and moral support at crucial times and also inspired me, by his personal example, to try to do better work. Finally, this book owes a great deal to my dissertation committee chairman and adviser throughout graduate school, Michel Oksenberg, from whom I continue to learn about Chinese politics.

I owe a big debt of gratitude to Nina Halpern and David Weimer for their specific guidance and overall encouragement throughout the process of turning the dissertation into a book. Richard Baum, John Mueller, William Parish, Stanley Rosen, Shi Tianjian, James Tong, and Lynn White also improved the manuscript with their very helpful comments on all or parts of it. My colleagues in political science at the University of Rochester continue to provide a much appreciated mixture of intellectual stimulation, moral support, and comic relief that makes the environment for scholarship here a uniquely happy and productive one.

I thank the Joint Committee on Chinese Studies of the American Council of Learned Societies and Social Science Research Council for funding the research I conducted in the People's Republic of China in 1986–87. I also thank the Rackham Graduate School of the University of Michigan, which provided funding for a second research trip in 1988, and Mary Jarrett, the Director of Graduate Fellowships, for her support.

Chapters 2 and 3 contain material used in previous publications. I wish to thank the Association for Asian Studies, Inc., for permission to reprint material from "Policy Implementation in the People's Republic of China: Authoritative Decisions versus Individual Interests," *Journal of Asian Studies* 50, no. 2 (1991):253–79; the School of Oriental and African Studies, University of London, for permission to reprint material from "Politics and Policy in Post-Mao Cadre Retirement," *China Quarterly*, no. 129 (1992):1–25; and the University of California Press for permission to reprint material from "The Behavior of Middlemen in the Cadre Retirement Policy Process," in *Bureaucracy, Politics, and Decision Making in Post-Mao China*, edited by Kenneth G. Lieberthal and David M. Lampton, 216–44, © 1992 the Regents of the University of California.

RETIREMENT OF REVOLUTIONARIES IN CHINA

THE STUDY of mechanisms of leadership has long figured at the top of the research agenda for those who aim to describe and explain politics in the communist system. There is good reason for the interest in discovering how, and how well, leaders in such a system achieve their objectives. Communist leaders came to power with programs of massive political, economic, and social change. Compared to their counterparts in liberal democracies, communist leaders have been much less constrained in mobilizing a wide range of resources to compel and persuade citizens to participate in the realization of change.

Among communist states, the People's Republic of China has experimented more than most in penetrating deeply into society to change not only how people act, but also how they think. To be sure, Chinese communist leaders have never rejected recourse to the violent coercive instruments of rule common to all communist regimes. But a basic orientation to "peaceful coercion," a kind of manipulative leadership aimed at persuading citizens to assimilate official standards as social norms, sets off Chinese communism from that of most other states.[1]

This book is a study of peaceful coercion in the policy process. It examines an important and unusually difficult case of policy implementation under the post-Mao regime—namely, the policy to replace de facto lifelong tenure for cadres with regular age-based retirement. Policy makers in Beijing introduced cadre retirement in mid-1978. I follow its progress through more than a decade of implementation and change.

The policy to retire cadres has been a major political battleground. It has little precedent. It breaks with the dominant tradition of political purge that has stigmatized exit from office in the communist system everywhere. Not least of all, it has challenged the vested interests of the nearly 2.5 million aging veterans of the revolution alive in 1978, who had monopolized power at all levels for most of the years since the communists declared victory in 1949. Cadre retirement policy flatly contradicts the basis of their hold on power, the principle of revolutionary seniority. Its introduction and promotion by many of those with the most to lose—veteran leaders at the top who are old

[1] The term is from Lewis, *Leadership in Communist China*, 4.

and feeble and, by rights, are themselves immediate targets of the policy—have required some imaginative political maneuvering.

More generally, cadre retirement illustrates a particular orientation to policy implementation. Policy makers in Beijing did not invest heavily in continuing state enforcement of cadre retirement policy. Instead, they have treated cadre retirement as a problem of "building a norm." This orientation has a goal more grandiose than most efforts at policy implementation: to transform a public policy into a social norm, through manipulative state interventions. These interventions constitute an effort to create conditions in which ordinary members of the cadre corps take up from state agencies the task of enforcing compliance with cadre retirement policy as a social norm.

This book elaborates the idea of building a social norm as a way to implement a public policy and illustrates how it can work. In this sense, the issue of cadre retirement offers more than simply a view into post-Mao politics and policy implementation. As an example of peaceful coercion in the policy process, it adds to our understanding of leadership—its possibilities as well as its constraints.

PEACEFUL COERCION AS A PRINCIPLE OF LEADERSHIP

When, in 1963, John Wilson Lewis introduced the term "peaceful coercion" to characterize a principle of leadership practiced by the Chinese communists, he sought to draw attention to this method of persuasion as a contrast to violent means of eliciting compliance.[2] Certainly, political leaders in Beijing have employed a variety of other compliance mechanisms to further their ambitious programs—including methods of arbitrary terror and routine violence as well as material incentives and appeals to the spirit. Most ordinary Chinese citizens have not been allowed to remain mere spectators of politics under communism. Communist leaders have mobilized them to participate in a nearly continuous stream of virtually compulsory mass campaigns. Between and during campaigns, an effort to persuade people to reform their thoughts has been a regular part of life for many Chinese, especially in the cities.[3] This effort has been an insti-

[2] Lewis recognized, of course, that in Chinese communist doctrine violent coercion is quite appropriate in dealing with "enemy" classes. See ibid., 4–5.

[3] See, for example, Skinner and Winckler, "Compliance Succession in Rural Communist China"; Whyte, *Small Groups and Political Rituals in China*; Townsend, *Political Participation in Communist China*, 174–209; Chan, Madsen, and Unger, *Chen Village*; Bennett, *Yundong*; Cell, *Revolution at Work*.

tutionalized part of the peaceful coercion that Lewis and others have viewed as a key orientation of Chinese communist leadership.

Peaceful coercion is essentially a normative mechanism, but in the highly coercive context of the communist system. It aims to build new social norms to accord with official standards. As a principle of leadership, peaceful coercion resonates strongly with Leninist, Maoist, and traditional Chinese notions.

Communist states may be best distinguished from liberal and social democracies by principles of leadership devised by Lenin to gain power in a hurry and keep it. Summarized most simply, Lenin amended Marxism with the argument that the proletariat cannot be relied upon to know enough about its own historical interests to liberate all classes in a socialist revolution. For this reason, Lenin proposed denying a role in leadership to all but an exclusive vanguard of professional revolutionaries, defined by their superior grasp of communist ideology and organized into a disciplined hierarchical party. This argument and organizational solution excused communist leaders from attention to discovering and representing mass preferences. As the masses can initially be quite backward-thinking, programs that reflect popular preferences can hold back or even reverse the forward movement of history. In theory, then, Leninists lead best when they ignore popular preferences that do not reflect the "historical best interests" of the working class. At the same time, it is incumbent on Leninist leaders to shape popular preferences to bring them in line with those interests as they see them, as part of a grand effort to raise political consciousness.[4] These notions are an ideological foundation for leadership through peaceful coercion.

More particularly in the Chinese communist case, the principle of peaceful coercion also reflects a Maoist ideal of normative leadership. In the very early years of the communist revolution, Mao aired a conviction that "the key to effective action lies in first transforming the hearts of men."[5] Mao developed his version of normative rule more fully in his 1943 essay on the mass line. The essay describes mass line leadership as a process that begins with communist cadres widely soliciting opinions in society. Yet, the mass line does not abandon the Leninist principle of highly centralized power. After reporting mass opinions to higher levels for "processing," cadres propagate and implement policies issued at the top. These policies reflect a selective

[4] Good introductions to this question are in Meyer, *Leninism*, 19–56, 92–103; Kolakowski, *Main Currents of Marxism*, vol. 2, 381–412.

[5] Schram, *The Thought of Mao Tse-tung*, 16, discussing Mao's article on physical education, published in 1917. See also Schram, *The Political Thought of Mao Tse-tung*, 3–14, 94–102.

transformation of "scattered and unsystematic" mass opinions into correct ideas. Cadres explain these correct policy decisions to the masses "until the masses embrace them as their own, hold fast to them and translate them into action."[6]

The Maoist view of man as inherently educable, of political authority as the moral authority to educate, and of education as a process in which correct ideas are internalized is consistent with a centuries-old Confucian ethos. Confucianism never developed a clear concept of legitimate political authority that was not based on moral authority. And traditional Chinese rule was marked by the absence or weakness of any institutionally enforced normative system, such as law, for example.[7]

Classical Chinese and Maoist views of leadership share the assumption that education is the key to changing actions and solving political and social problems. With proper education, control becomes social control, for when people have correct ideas they will necessarily act in correct ways. The logical conclusion about appropriate methods of state control is, for both, normative leadership.[8]

Almost certainly, leaders in the post-Mao period have a diminished capacity to turn to normative mechanisms of leadership. This is partly because of revelations about politics at the top during and after the destructive Cultural Revolution and partly because of bold economic policy measures post-Mao leaders have themselves adopted since 1978. Leaders have embraced material incentives to a greater degree than before and have proclaimed economic growth as the country's top priority. They have also repudiated the idea that communist attitudes can be hastened into existence so long as people are materially poor. But post-Mao leaders have not fundamentally rejected peaceful coercion as a mechanism of leadership. A good recent example of peaceful coercion at work in society generally is the renewed attempt to curtail population growth through the one-child family policy.[9] The effort to retire cadres is a different kind of example: it is a form of peaceful coercion directed at the elite itself.

[6] From the version in Schram, *The Political Thought of Mao Tse-tung*, 315–17. See also his discussion in *The Thought of Mao Tse-tung*, 45–48, 85–86, 97–99. Mao reiterated the "processing plant" notion of the mass line in a 1962 speech. See Schram, ed., *Chairman Mao Talks to the People*, 158–87, especially 163–69.

[7] See, for example, Metzger, foreword to *Moral Behavior in Chinese Society*, xvii–xx. On the rule of propriety (*li*) and law (*fa*) in traditional China and the "Confucianization of law," see especially Ch'u, *Law and Society in Traditional China*, 226–79; Bodde and Morris, *Law in Imperial China*, 1–51.

[8] See especially the discussions in Munro, *The Concept of Man in Early China*, 160–82, and *The Concept of Man in Contemporary China*, 26–106.

[9] See especially White, "Postrevolutionary Mobilization in China."

FROM PUBLIC POLICIES TO SOCIAL NORMS

The most fundamental distinction between normative social standards and official standards issued as policies has to do with their enforcement. Agents of the state enforce compliance with policies; ordinary members of society enforce conformity to norms. The premise of compliance and conformity is, however, the same: an acknowledgment of critical views about certain actions. In the case of policies, individuals recognize that certain actions are governed by the standards of political authorities. As to norms, individuals understand that actions are socially correct or socially incorrect forms of conduct.

Political leaders can transform public policies into social norms through manipulative state interventions. Interventions to build norms are manipulative in the sense that they require changing the way people look upon the policy problem—so that official standards become understood by the general population as social standards of propriety. The interventions are also strategic, in the sense that they are designed to create the conditions for their own superfluousness. If successful, the interventions produce policy outcomes through a process that eventually transfers the task of enforcement from state agencies to civil society. This feature most distinguishes building a norm from other methods of policy implementation. It entails a planned withdrawal of the state from responsibility for ongoing enforcement and an attendant expectation that ordinary members of society will step in to enforce policy as a norm.

Building social norms to implement public policies is not unique to the Chinese communists or to the communist system generally. Although liberal democratic governments do not engage in the kind of social engineering that communist states do, policy makers in democracies do sometimes attempt to build norms. Smoking in public places, serving too much alcohol to guests, and driving without a seatbelt are only a few examples of many kinds of conduct in which liberal democratic governments have intervened recently—to prohibit with the force of law, but also to promote and support situations of normative social enforcement. A good example in the familiar American setting is the fairly widespread existing social norm against littering, to "Keep America Beautiful," a product of norm building initiated a few decades ago. Certainly, something more than mere behaviorial compliance is involved here: littering is now not simply not done, but is, in a normative sense too, "simply not done." Once a commonplace action to which people gave little thought, littering has become an incorrect way to act.

How do political leaders build norms? A point of departure for this book is the idea that general theories about how norms emerge spontaneously also describe general principles underlying how policy makers can go about getting norms to emerge through manipulative interventions. For theoretical guidance, I turned to a considerable literature on norms in several disciplines and found some of the more recent studies by political scientists and economists particularly useful. Interestingly, these studies return to questions social psychologists addressed as early as the 1930s, namely: what explains how norms emerge, are maintained, and disappear?

I used the literature on norms heuristically. I ultimately selected for presentation only the general principles that in fact describe what policy makers in Beijing did to build a norm from their policy to retire cadres. I view the case studied here as a practical illustration of those principles—adopted by leaders who were by no means necessarily conscious of them as theories.

CADRE RETIREMENT IN COMPARATIVE CONTEXT

In the People's Republic of China, as in many countries, a practice of retirement for workers was not viewed as necessarily relevant to the experience of officials. Even in noncommunist countries, retirement of officials is a relatively new idea and it has a conflictual history.

In Japan, for example, the effort to introduce retirement in the bureaucracy had to take into account a cultural tradition of seniority—one not unlike the Chinese tradition. The Japanese managed reasonably successfully to resolve the conflict between seniority and efficient personnel circulation with a system of retirement upholding both notions. Chalmers Johnson has described the system in some detail.[10] As a general rule, when a Japanese official is newly promoted to a key executive position in the ministry, officials in the cohort recruited in the same year retire to positions arranged for them by the ministry—and often in public corporations closely associated with it. This practice produces a fairly young age of retirement in the bureaucracy, but post-retirement positions are attractive enough to be considered almost a perquisite.

[10] Johnson, "The Reemployment of Retired Government Bureaucrats in Japanese Big Business," and *Japan's Public Policy Companies*, 101–14. See also Campbell, "Democracy and Bureaucracy in Japan" and Kubota, *Higher Civil Servants in Postwar Japan*, 140–59.

In the United States, efforts to introduce retirement in the federal civil service set off hot debates in and outside the government. Within the bureaucracy, sympathetic senior officials sought to protect older civil servants by exaggerating their efficiency and ability. Among likely targets of proposed retirement legislation were Civil War veterans in the bureaucracy and the idea of retiring them was politically unpopular. Despite the fundamental difference in the two systems and cultures, many of the problems addressed by American civil service retirement plans in the 1920s are similar to those that confronted Chinese communist reformers in 1978.[11] American civil servants were by no means career bureaucrats yet. William Graebner notes:

> Even in the mid-1920s, the federal bureaucracy was not yet the fully rationalized instrument that some desired. It was still laced with personal ties and informal bonds that often transcended increasing pressures for purely contractual relationships. It was the function of retirement legislation to sever these ties, break the bonds of informality, and usher in the contractual society.[12]

The Chinese communists had decades of experience with retirement—but not with retirement of cadres. In 1951 the government issued regulations on retirement for workers in the state sector. Retirement with pension was viewed as an essential part of the socialist welfare state. Regulations on retirement for officials and other personnel known collectively as cadres followed in 1955. Most women workers were eligible to retire at age fifty, most women cadres at fifty-five. Men were usually eligible to retire at sixty. Eligibility guidelines also stipulated minimum years of service. Pensions ranged from 50 to 70 percent of preretirement salary in most cases, depending on number of years worked.[13]

While age-based retirement of workers became standard practice, the retirement of cadres was neither enforced nor widely practiced. Lifelong tenure, barring political error, became the norm in the cadre corps. The dominant form of exit from office for cadres was political purge.[14] Critics of the de facto lifelong tenure system observed: "Only in two circumstances can a cadre lose his position. One is his death. . . . The other is [political] error."[15]

In its lack of a tradition of cadre retirement, the People's Republic

---

[11] See Graebner, *A History of Retirement*, 57–87.
[12] Ibid., 87.
[13] On workers see Davis-Friedmann, *Long Lives*, 15–33, and "Chinese Retirement." On cadres see Cao, *Zhonghua renmin gongheguo renshi zhidu gaiyao*, 378–413.
[14] Oksenberg, "The Exit Pattern in Chinese Politics and Its Implications."
[15] Peng and Zheng, "Shitan feizhi ganbu zhiwu zhongshenzhi," 8.

of China differed little from other communist countries. A political purge tradition of exit from office in a setting of normal lifelong tenure is common to the communist system. The approach to changes involving movement in and out of office is typically politicized and personalistic. Changes in personnel generally occur as the result of natural death, political error, or consolidation of personal power from the top. Excepting the Yugoslav system of rotation of cadres, the Chinese in 1978 had no successful precedent for the institutionalization of elite turnover in a communist country. Communist cadres able to survive the shifts in politics enjoyed de facto lifelong tenure.[16]

In the history of the first communist country, Stalin's purges ensured that the problem of aging revolutionaries did not have an opportunity to emerge. But elite purge in the People's Republic of China has usually taken the form of educative rectification rather than Stalinist-style physical purge. Chinese cadres who failed to measure up to constantly changing political standards often lost their positions and typically became targets of campaigns that had coercive aspects. But they were generally not liquidated.[17] This had important consequences. It was the context for the urgent problem of aging revolutionaries: veteran cadres survived the Cultural Revolution and returned to dominate Chinese politics in the immediate post-Mao period.

THE POLICY TO RETIRE CADRES

In the early 1930s life expectancy at birth for the Chinese was a mere twenty-four years. By the mid-1950s it had risen to approximately forty-five years and by 1978 to sixty-six years.[18] Long lives for the Chinese reflect peace and progress but they also created an enormous elderly population: 77 million over sixty years old in 1982.[19] And long lives introduced the prospect of a new problem for the state— an aging work force.

In 1978, throughout the corps of about 18 million cadres,[20] veterans of the communist revolution monopolized leadership. They had

---

[16] See Brzezinski, *The Permanent Purge*; Bialer, *Stalin's Successors*; Hough, *Soviet Leadership in Transition*; Gill, "Institutionalisation and Revolution"; Blackwell, "Cadres Policy in the Brezhnev Era"; Wesson, *The Aging of Communism*.

[17] See Teiwes, *Elite Discipline in China* and *Politics and Purges in China*.

[18] A recent report estimates Chinese life expectancy in 1989 at 70 years. *World Development Report 1991*, 204.

[19] Figures on aging are from Banister, *China's Changing Population*, 116, and "The Aging of China's Population."

[20] Song, "Renzhen jiejue gongzuo mianlin de xin keti," 2.

low levels of education and expertise and increasingly low levels of sheer physical and mental vigor. The problem of aging cadres was most serious at the top, among policy makers themselves. Consider the age composition of the twenty-six-member Politburo in 1980 after some initial post-Mao purges. The average age in this group of top communist party leaders was seventy-one years. Four members were over eighty, fifteen were over seventy, and only two were under sixty.[21]

A poorly educated and increasingly feeble corps of leaders with skills best-suited for making revolution jarred with the post-Mao regime's commitment to economic modernization. The head of the party department that manages cadres observed: "The Four Modernizations [of industry, agriculture, national defense, and science and technology] demand a large number of knowledgeable leading cadres. They demand cadres with specialized knowledge and abilities and cadres with energy. But the situation in our cadre corps is far from meeting these needs."[22]

The policy of cadre retirement was supposed to resolve this contradiction by replacing revolutionaries with younger cadres better qualified to manage the drive for modernization. But the solution was not simply to retire revolutionaries. In 1978 the cadre corps included more than 2.3 million cadres recruited in 1950–52.[23] These recruits were not young at the time policy makers introduced cadre retirement. They too were targets of retirement policy.

Indeed, all cadres were targets of the policy. Retirement was not intended as a one-time campaign. It was not an ad hoc measure to cope with a crisis or historical transition. Cadre retirement was part of a major systemic reform in cadre management generally. As Deng Xiaoping pointed out, the problem was that the party had "no regular methods" for cadres to retire or resign. Cadres could be promoted but not demoted, recruited but not discharged.[24] The regime's policy goal was to institutionalize (zhiduhua) retirement, that is, to establish age-based exit from office as a regular end to cadre careers.

Although post-Mao policy makers openly acknowledged aging cadres as a problem and regular retirement as a solution, getting cadres to retire presented an exceptionally difficult problem for a number of reasons.

[21] Fang, "The Problem of Peiping's Ageing Leadership Cadres," 28.

[22] Song, "Renzhen jiejue gongzuo mianlin de xin keti," 2.

[23] Emerson, *Administrative and Technical Manpower in the People's Republic of China*, 37. Of course, this number includes veteran revolutionaries who joined the communists before 1949 but who did not become cadres until after 1949.

[24] Deng, "On the Reform of the System of Party and State Leadership," 18.

Most obviously, cadre retirement policy threatens the vested interests of an elite—including policy makers themselves. Certainly not all veterans of the revolution became leaders after 1949, but it is fair to say that practically all leaders were veterans. Because most personnel from the old regime had been swept out of office in the early 1950s, veterans had seniority even at lower levels in the party and government.[25]

To complicate matters, revolutionary veterans could easily rationalize their interest in holding onto office in the Chinese setting. The Chinese communists had won state power through a protracted armed struggle during which material rewards for partisans had been meager and demands arduous. Most had been paid on the supply system, which had provided bare necessities for sustenance. Communist party members had taken a vow to struggle a lifetime for the communist cause. Veterans were "revolutionaries by vocation" (*zhiye gemingjia*): after the communists won national power, "for many, the distinction between [making] revolution and being a cadre was very vague."[26] As the following critique indicates, office was regarded as an entitlement:

> Many of our comrades mistakenly assume that to struggle a lifetime for the revolution necessarily implies office for a lifetime. Among them, some comrades in fact have developed the mistaken notion that contribution to the revolution merits an official position. They consider their official position and power as a well-deserved reward for participation in the revolution and their inviolable private property.[27]

These notions resonate with traditional Chinese views. For the peasant rebel: "He who conquers the country rules the country."[28] For the mandarin: "An official for a dynasty, an official's salary for a lifetime."[29]

In addition, it had been possible, acceptable, and expedient for revolutionaries to become cadres. A large proportion of the veterans had joined the revolution in their adolescence and were still relatively young in 1949. And the Chinese communists had earned a fair amount of popular support for their conduct during the war. As to expedience, in the immediate postrevolutionary period the need to consolidate political power had dictated an emphasis on personnel

[25] Vogel, "From Revolutionary to Semi-Bureaucrat."

[26] *Renmin ribao*, 28 Oct. 1980, 5.

[27] Jia, Cheng, and Wei, "Lue lun zhongshenzhi," 11.

[28] *Da tianxia jiu dei zuo tianxia*. Cited in Xiao et al., "Lun feichu ganbu lingdao zhiwu zhongshenzhi," 25.

[29] *Yi chao wei guan zhongshen shou lu*. Cited in Wu, "Ganbu zhidu shang yi xiang zhongda de gaige," 7.

committed to the communist cause. Joining the revolution before victory, especially in the early years when victory had seemed remote, was a sign of loyalty.

For all these reasons, lifelong tenure for cadres was a problem that had not posed itself naturally in the early period. It had easily evolved into something people took for granted. A Special Commentator for the party newspaper characterized it as follows: "Many things in life arise not as the result of conscious intention, but rather as a product of many factors undergoing gradual development. Therefore, it takes time for people to come to understand the problem they confront. The system of de facto lifelong tenure is precisely such a problem."[30]

The circumstances described above had fostered a notion of office as revolutionary calling and entitlement for revolutionary contributions. This was reinforced during decades of communist rule by the principle of allocating power according to seniority, which was measured by years of service since joining the party or revolution. Revolutionary seniority was a key determinant of mobility for cadres, from the top in Beijing to below the county level.[31] A. Doak Barnett notes:

> The significance of these seniority ratings was not simply that they indicated important gradations of status and prestige. To a considerable degree ... high-seniority ratings opened the door to positions of power and authority ... whether or not the cadres possessed special technical competence or experience qualifying them for such posts. One explanation for this, apparently, was the tendency of the top leaders to equate seniority with political reliability.[32]

To the extent that loyalty to the revolution was a major qualification for office, the aging of cadres was not considered a problem. If anything, for revolutionary veterans at least, age was more likely to be an asset than a liability. Seen in this perspective, retirement intro-

---

[30] *Renmin ribao*, 28 Oct. 1980, 5.

[31] This is well documented for the period up to the Cultural Revolution in 1966. See Barnett, *Cadres, Bureaucracy, and Political Power in Communist China*, 43–47, 188–89, 433; Kau, "The Urban Bureaucratic Elite in Communist China"; Oksenberg, "The Institutionalisation of the Chinese Communist Revolution" and "Local Leaders in Rural China, 1962–65"; Teiwes, *Provincial Party Personnel in Mainland China*, 10–12, 62; Vogel, "From Revolutionary to Semi-Bureaucrat." In 1966–69 the principle of revolutionary seniority (and veteran cadres personally) came under attack. But it seems that both began to be reinstated soon after 1969 and that a 1973–74 campaign on behalf of newly promoted young cadres made only small gains in limited areas. See Chang, "Political Rehabilitation of Cadres in China"; Lee, "The Politics of Cadre Rehabilitation since the Cultural Revolution."

[32] Barnett, "Social Stratification and Aspects of Personnel Management in the Chinese Communist Bureaucracy," 16.

duced a different conception of what it meant to be a cadre. It challenged revolutionary seniority as a credential for office and, by implication, the idea of office as revolutionary calling. Retirement policy inaugurated a transition to a career civil service.[33]

In appealing to cadres to retire, policy makers could not point to a pre-1949 tradition of retirement in the civil service. The imperial tradition of exit from office is not one of regular retirement at specified ages. Rather, it exhibits great variety and is connected with heritages of Confucian protest and Daoist eremitism.[34] Although imperial decrees did fix standard ages of retirement, these decrees appear to have been violated more generally than observed. For example, decrees promulgated in the Qing dynasty (1644–1911) set ages of retirement at fifty-five and sixty-five—but lifelong tenure was not in fact unusual. A sample of 567 Qing officials at three ranks indicates only 14 percent left office because of old age. Death in office was by far the most common single form of exit.[35]

In short, retirement from office because of old age was not part of any Chinese tradition—communist or precommunist. Yet another obstacle policy makers faced in 1978 was the tradition of respect for the elderly in Chinese culture. Confucian ideas about generational relationships and authority attached to old age imply that seniority in years is a credential for holding power, much like revolutionary seniority. While the communists had attacked Confucianism throughout their revolution, they had not attempted to eliminate attitudes of respect for the elderly.[36] As a result, traditional notions about age and authority remained to compound the problem of cadre retirement.

Retirement of cadres in high positions of leadership posed yet another kind of problem. If leaders had established informal relations based on personal loyalties (such as those dating back to leadership in the revolutionary field armies, for example),[37] formal retirement

[33] For other policy changes in this direction, see Manion, "The Cadre Management System, Post-Mao"; Burns, "Civil Service Reform in Contemporary China" and "Chinese Civil Service Reform."

[34] See Li, "The Changing Concept of the Recluse in Chinese Literature"; Mather, "The Controversy over Conformity and Naturalness during the Six Dynasties"; Mote, "Confucian Eremitism in the Yuan Period." See also the discussion in Lautz, "The Politics of Retirement in Republican China, 1911–1949," 4–30.

[35] Lui, "The Ch'ing Civil Service." Also on the Qing see Hsieh, *The Government of China*, 99–139. On the Song see Kracke, *Civil Service in Early Sung China, 960–1067*, 82.

[36] See Davis-Friedmann, *Long Lives*, 6–14.

[37] On factions in Chinese politics generally see Pye, *The Dynamics of Chinese Politics*. On factions in the military and factions based on field army loyalties see Whitson, "The

would not necessarily produce real disengagement from power. To the extent that power was vested in persons rather than positions, then, retirement of leading cadres was unlikely to result in a new set of managers for post-Mao modernization.

Finally, retirement of the vast majority of cadres posed difficulties because of the importance of position and workplace. The workplace is much more than a place where cadres earn a salary. It is a community, typically walled off from the rest of society, in which many of the needs of its members that will be met are met. Cadres get housing from the workplace, they eat at the workplace dining hall, and they shower at the workplace baths. Their children are usually tended in nurseries and taught in schools managed by the workplace. The workplace allocates opportunities to buy scarce and needed consumer goods. At holiday times it distributes special foods. Workplace leaders pay attention to the political growth, physical health, and personal problems of members.[38]

A position at the workplace is important for another reason too. Chinese rely greatly on informal relationships based on reciprocity to get things done. In the Chinese communist economy, goods and opportunities are scarce and may be allocated informally without ever reaching the market. Informal relations provide leverage to obtain what money cannot buy.[39] Retirement from a position entailed relinquishing the ability to reciprocate all manner of favors. Less able to reciprocate favors, retired cadres faced their old age strongly reliant on family members and pensions.

Very clearly, the policy to retire cadres presented unusual difficulties for policy makers and officials charged with implementing retirement. Building a norm of cadre retirement required challenging—in fact, literally replacing—powerful groups, established practices, and basic assumptions. These same difficulties make cadre retirement a particularly interesting and illustrative case of how public policies can become social norms.

OVERVIEW OF THE BOOK

This book is organized in the following way. Chapter 1 delves into the literature on norms for conceptual and theoretical illumination

---

Field Army in Chinese Communist Military Politics" and *The Chinese High Command, 1927–1971*.

[38] See Henderson and Cohen, *The Chinese Hospital*, 1–46, 138–48; Walder, *Communist Neo-Traditionalism*, 28–84.

[39] See especially Gold, "After Comradeship."

about how to define norms and how leaders can build norms from public policies. I present five mechanisms of norm building that policy makers in Beijing actually put into practice to build a norm of cadre retirement. Chapter 2 gives an account of the mechanisms as policy measures designed to realize the goal of regular age-based cadre retirement. I also describe the political context in which the policy was launched and how aging leaders managed to protect their own interests and promote cadre retirement too.

I then begin to address the following question: how have cadres targeted for retirement, middlemen charged with implementing the policy, and younger cadres at the workplace responded? Building a norm of cadre retirement comprised in fact three distinct policy objectives for cadres—age-based exit from office, an acceptance of retirement as a normative standard, and real disengagement from official duties after retirement. Chapters 3, 4, and 5 take up these issues, respectively.

I conclude by returning to general ideas about how norms emerge, this time in light of the empirical work presented in previous chapters. I consider how and why the process of norm building examined here did not neatly unfold as theorized, and what this tells us about politics and policy implementation after Mao and the possibilities and constraints of leadership.

PREVIEW OF FINDINGS

How and how much have policy makers in Beijing managed to build a social norm from their policy of cadre retirement? As the title of this book no doubt suggests, private interests are key to my answer and explanation. In particular, my conclusions take into account the interests of four groups in the policy process—policy makers, older cadres targeted for retirement, middlemen charged with implementing the policy, and younger cadres, who stand to gain from the retirement of their seniors. The private interests of these groups affected the policy process in different ways. Some interests delayed or encumbered cadre retirement and the emergence of a cadre retirement norm. Other interests served to hasten the realization of these objectives.

In strict terms, a policy of age-based retirement had to be directed at the powerful: the oldest generation of cadres tended also to be those in the highest positions of leadership. This presented a conflict of interest at the top. Policy makers could not be expected to come to agreement on a policy that would have them relinquish position and power. For years after 1978, policy makers disagreed on pivotal issues of cadre retirement policy.

The disagreements among policy makers were plainly evident. Middlemen at the workplace did not actively implement the policy until the contradictory signals changed in 1982. In that year policy makers resolved their conflict of interest with a program of cadre retirement that more clearly reflected the political hierarchy. The new program exempted from retirement "a few dozen leaders" at the very top and created special advisory commissions and advisory positions for leaders at lower levels. The program also clearly distinguished between veteran revolutionaries and postrevolutionaries, that is, cadres who had joined the communists only after their victory in 1949. With these program revisions, which took into account the private interests of policy makers and other powerful groups of cadres, the policy to retire cadres finally began to be widely implemented.

Interests affected policy implementation in another way too. Significant and systematic deviation from the programs designed by policy makers occurred in the course of implementation. In the words of one observer: "The top has its policies, the bottom has its countermeasures."[40] The content of deviation reflected the material interests of older cadres targeted for retirement. They bargained with middlemen for a better deal than that specified in party and government regulations. Middlemen found themselves accountable to policy makers at the top, yet subject to pressure from cadres at the bottom. Caught between pressure from above to streamline and rejuvenate the cadre corps and disinterest or resistance from below in giving up cadre positions, middlemen bent the rules and offered cadres more attractive terms. Over the years, policy makers responded to the countermeasures: prohibiting some, condoning and codifying others.

Not all private interests stood in the way of policy objectives. Policy makers successfully manipulated a conflict of interest among cadres to promote retirement and the emergence of a retirement norm. Younger cadres proved to be natural allies of policy makers and middlemen in the cadre retirement process. The reason is obvious: retirement of older cadres and promotion of younger cadres is very nearly a zero-sum game. Cadre positions, including positions of leadership at all levels, are limited in number. Without movement out of positions there cannot be movement up and into them. In short, by not enforcing compliance with the policy to retire cadres, younger cadres are only punishing themselves. As a result, there has been a

---

[40] *Shang you zhengce xia you duice*. Interview subject no. 96.

tacit and indirect, but nonetheless widespread and widely sensed, voluntary enforcement of retirement policy by younger cadres.

Almost certainly, retirement will one day be the lot of younger cadres too. Regardless of their view of the situation as zero-sum, the conflict of interest is in fact only partial. Younger cadres today are setting in motion a machinery of social enforcement that will eventually put them out of office also. And the process is self-sustaining—for there will always be younger cadres willing to enforce retirement policy, fueling the emergence of a cadre retirement norm.

A NOTE ON THE POPULATION OF INTEREST

In 1978, when the policy of cadre retirement was introduced, there were about 18 million cadres. A decade later, the cadre corps comprised more than 29 million.[41] These millions constitute my population of interest, with some exceptions as noted below.

The term cadre, *ganbu* in Chinese, has meant different things at different times.[42] Officials of the party or government who are on the state payroll have always been considered as cadres. The term lumps together political leaders and administrators, managers of state enterprises and institutes, and personnel as low-ranking as clerks in the state bureaucracies. The category has also typically included various professional groups.[43] Although cadre retirement policy was addressed to all cadres, my focus here is on cadres in the party and government bureaucracies.[44]

By any definition, top leaders of the party and government are also cadres. However, they do not figure prominently as subjects of study here (in the sense that other cadres do) mainly because to include them is to frustrate generalization. Certainly, the cadre population is diverse in ways that have an impact on the issues explored in this

[41] For an update on the growth of the cadre corps, see Lee, *From Revolutionary Cadres to Party Technocrats in Socialist China*, 206–18.

[42] An excellent discussion of the notion in Chinese is in Xu, "Ganbu yanjiu."

[43] According to a 1985 source, statistics on cadres currently refer to personnel in party or government organizations, mass organizations, enterprises, or institutions in the state sector who receive their income from the state. In addition, cadres must either have administrative ranking at or above clerk level or be professionals with specified levels of attainment in a number of designated fields (such as education, public health, scientific research). Statistics on cadres exclude all personnel working in the military (unless specified) and collective sectors. For further details see Laodong renshi bu ganbu jiaoyu ju, *Laodong renshi tongjixue*, 111–29.

[44] Some policy measures did target specific groups. In cases where cadre retirement policy focused only on higher intellectuals (*gaoji zhishi fenzi*), I have largely ignored it.

book. And precisely for this reason, my analysis considers cadres as cases in particular classes—recognizing differences between young cadres and older cadres, high-ranking cadres and ordinary cadres, for example. Top leaders are in a small class of their own, with power to shape the rules that bind them and others, so attempts to explain their behavior are bound to be highly idiosyncratic and not applicable to other classes.[45] This is not, then, a study of elite politics—except insofar as cadres on the whole constitute an elite. Consequently, I focus here on full retirement, which is the arrangement that applies to practically all of the millions in my population of interest.

While this is not a study about retirement at the top, any study of policy implementation ignores top leaders to its extreme detriment. Leaders formulate the policy that is the departure point and reference point for implementation. In the case of cadre retirement, they also reformulated policy, partly to take into account difficulties in implementation. In their role as policy makers, then, top leaders are clearly key players and they figure prominently in the chapters that follow. But leaders are also players in their role as targets of their own policy. To the extent that this latter role impinges on the retirement of the millions of cadres in other classes—and it does—I draw attention to it.

A NOTE ON SOURCES AND METHODS

I integrated a variety of sources and methods in my research for this book. Some of these are familiar to students of Chinese politics, while others are newer to the field. Here I provide a brief introduction. A detailed discussion of my survey research can be found in the appendix on survey methods.

To understand cadre retirement policy, I relied mainly on information in regulations, measures, notices, and decisions issued by top party and government organizations. By my count, the Central Committee, State Council, and subordinate departments at the national level issued about two hundred such documents on cadre retirement in 1978–88. Most are reproduced in two volumes prepared by the Central Committee's Organization Department and State Council's Ministry of Labor and Personnel as reference books for officials implementing cadre retirement policy.[46] The rest are reproduced in

[45] This is not to deny the intrinsic value of such studies of elite politics or of future work specifically about elite-level retirement and the advisory system, for example.

[46] Zhonggong zhongyang zuzhi bu lao ganbu ju laodong renshi bu lao ganbu fuwu ju, *Lao ganbu gongzuo wenjian xuanbian*, vols. 1 and 2. This book is classified as *neibu*

general and specialized collections of government documents or in government periodical publications.[47] I supplemented information obtained in documents with other sources: interviews with government officials in the Veteran Cadre Bureau and Cadre Retirement Bureau (in 1986, 1988, and 1990), recent books on the cadre system and the new civil service, and articles in newspapers and journals.[48]

Most of my information on the implementation process and its results at the workplace is from different sorts of survey work I conducted in 1986–88. I began with exploratory interviews with thirty-six retired cadres in Beijing.[49] My main concerns in these interviews were frankness and completeness. I wanted to learn about how older cadres targeted for retirement and middlemen responsible for implementation actually responded to policy directives from the top. And I wanted to turn up issues or nuances of policy I had missed when reading the documents. These considerations were particularly important in the early stages of research—before undertaking design of a questionnaire to be distributed to a much larger sample. They suggested a particular methodology: all the interviews were loosely structured, most were arranged through informal contacts, and many were conducted in private homes. I found that retired cadres make good interview subjects. They have lots of time to spare, they like to talk, and they are quite articulate. Moreover, compared to those with positions to lose, they probably feel less constrained about what they say.

With many of the exploratory interviews completed, I was able to design a self-administered questionnaire with closed-category items for a larger survey of retired cadres—one with enough observations and enough variation to merit quantitative analysis. These questionnaires were distributed to all 670 retired cadres in a city in the northeast. A total of 250 respondents completed and mailed back question-

---

and is not sold. To facilitate reference, I cite an alternative, more accessible collection as a source for a document if I know of one.

[47] The Ministry of Labor and Personnel reproduces many of its recently issued documents in a monthly *Laodong renshi zhengce zhuankan*, which I found particularly useful for the 1986–88 period. The Central Committee's Organization Department has a weekly *Zugong tongxun*, but it was unavailable to me.

[48] A list of newspapers and journals surveyed is in Works Cited. It includes six journals of provincial personnel bureaus (Henan, Hunan, Jiangxi, Shanxi, Shanghai, and Sichuan), which began to appear (or reappear) only after 1982.

[49] In order better to protect the confidentiality of interview subjects, throughout the book I refer to each by a number, which does not reflect the order in which interviews were conducted. I also refer to all subjects as male. Table A.1 in the appendix on survey methods provides an accurate breakdown of the sample by sex and other background characteristics.

naires. The response rate of 37 percent is not unusual for similarly conducted surveys in other countries, but I view it as low—taking into account the suitability of retired cadres as survey subjects. (To be sure, a bigger concern of mine was a suspiciously high response rate!)

I then conducted a second set of interviews to get another perspective on implementation. This time my subjects were younger, employed cadres. I used a questionnaire combining closed-category items and open-ended questions. I interviewed seventy-one cadres from workplaces in nearly every province, who were in Beijing for two years of special cadre study.[50] As those who stood to gain new positions with the retirement of their senior co-workers, younger cadres proved to be generally keen observers as well as willing participants in the policy implementation process.

Despite an emerging understanding of the methodology, it is difficult to do good survey research in the People's Republic of China. In my view, the most serious problem we confront is not response bias but sample bias. For some time in the future, we are likely to remain severely constrained in selecting our samples—to the extent that we are permitted to do any survey research at all. This is a problem, but not a disaster. It limits the sorts of generalizations we can make. By no means does it rule out generalizing to the larger population of interest. All my sampling in the research conducted for this book violated the principle of probability sampling. Certainly, this is not ideal. Measures of central tendency based on data from such samples are generally not considered reliable estimates of population parameters. I cannot turn to these data for a description of the retired cadre population along single dimensions—how cadres felt about retirement or even how many cadres retired late, to state a few examples. However, there is not necessarily a problem in subjecting data from nonprobability samples to inferential statistical analysis to test relationships between variables. For example, I can generalize reliably about the relationship between amount of pension and willingness to retire, between rank and time of retirement, or between willingness to retire and time of retirement. I use statistical analysis in this book to test relationships between variables. I examine hypothesized connections proposed in the theoretical literature, suggested by younger and older cadres interviewed, and, not least of all, prompted by commonsense reasoning.

---

[50] I adopted the same procedures described above to protect the confidentiality of younger cadres interviewed.

CHAPTER ONE

Building a Norm

OVER THE PAST two decades, as economists and political scientists became more interested in norms, the research agenda has shifted from a Parsonian sociological focus on how norms explain social order to the more perplexing problem of explaining norms. Recent work returns to the same questions social psychologists addressed as early as the 1930s, namely: what explains how norms emerge, are maintained, and disappear?

My concern here is with a planned process of manipulation by leaders with considerable resources, not the unfolding of social norms as some sort of "spontaneous order."[1] And my answers are empirically driven rather than theoretically derived. All the same, the literature on norms provides a useful new perspective on the subject of normative leadership. I used the literature heuristically. My point of departure was the idea that general theories about how norms can emerge spontaneously also describe general principles underlying how policy makers can go about getting norms to emerge through manipulative leadership. I ultimately selected for presentation here only those principles that in fact describe what policy makers in Beijing did to build a norm from their policy of cadre retirement. I view the case studied here as a practical illustration of those principles—adopted by leaders who were by no means necessarily conscious of them as theories. We can think of the principles as mechanisms of norm building.

WHAT ARE NORMS?

No single, shared definition of norms exists either within or across the several academic disciplines that pay attention to the concept. Further, what some have called norms others have labeled rules, institutions, customs, or conventions. These terms have also been used for related but essentially different concepts. Yet regardless of ter-

---

[1] The term is from Hayek, *Law, Legislation, and Liberty*, vol. 1, 35–54. Hayek means by the term "an equilibrium set up from within" rather than an order created by forces outside the system. Ibid., 36.

minology, work on norms has some common features. It nearly always assumes a social context (rejecting the notion of private norms) and it concerns itself with recurrent actions and some sort of critical orientation to those actions (distinguishing norms from mere reflex actions or habits, for example). I share these assumptions and concerns in this study and define a norm as *a pattern of action, accompanied by an understanding of the pattern as a social standard of propriety.*

The first part of the definition is fairly straightforward. That a pattern of action exists implies two things: actions recur and they can be described in general terms. Norms are generalizations that organize recurrent actions into some sort of comprehensible order. Clearly, norms are not the actions per se because then norms could not be motivations for those actions. And norms cannot develop around actions that seem idiosyncratic because those actions cannot be organized sensibly in a general pattern.

The second part of the definition is less obvious. Generalization about recurrent actions is essential to a norm, but there is more to it than simply a neutral perception of pattern. People view the actions critically, recognizing them as particular cases to which the generalization applies. Moreover, the generalization makes those actions binding actions. The generalization not only describes the pattern of action but also prescribes it as a correct form of conduct.

The critical evaluative orientation to the pattern is why norms essentially are not probabilistic predictions about future actions, although knowledge of norms may enable us to predict actions fairly accurately. H. L. A. Hart explains the very subtle but important distinction quite clearly in his discussion of the "internal aspect" of social rules. An external observer can

> record the regularities of observable behaviour in which conformity with the rules partly consist and those further regularities, in the form of the hostile reaction, reproofs, or punishments, with which deviations from the rules are met. After a time the external observer may, on the basis of the regularities observed, correlate deviation with hostile reaction, and be able to predict with a fair measure of success, and to assess the chances that a deviation from the group's normal behaviour will meet with hostile reaction or punishment.
>
> If, however, the observer really keeps austerely to this extreme external point of view and does not give any account of the manner in which members of the group who accept the rules view their own regular behaviour, his description of their life cannot be in terms of rules at all. . . . Instead, it will be in terms of observable regularities of conduct, predictions, probabilities, and signs. For such an observer, deviations by a

member of the group from normal conduct will be a sign that hostile reaction is likely to follow, and nothing more. His view will be like the view of one who, having observed the working of a traffic signal in a busy street for some time, limits himself to saying that when the light turns red there is a high probability that the traffic will stop. He treats the light merely as a natural *sign that* people will behave in certain ways, as clouds are a *sign that* rain will come. In so doing he will miss out a whole dimension of the social life of those whom he is watching, since for them the red light is not merely a sign that others will stop: they look upon it as a *signal for* them to stop, and so a reason for stopping in conformity to rules which make stopping when the light is red a standard of behaviour and an obligation. To mention this is to bring into the account the way in which the group regards its own behaviour. It is to refer to the internal aspect of rules seen from their internal point of view.[2]

In sum, people do not simply recognize a behaviorial regularity but also understand its rationale as "this is how things are done." To understand a pattern of actions as a social standard of propriety is to acknowledge that the standard governs those actions. In the final analysis, then, the social standard, or, more precisely, the belief that the standard exists, explains the actions. I elaborate and clarify this relationship between norms and actions below and explain how norm-guided actions are also self-interested actions.

NORMS, ACTIONS, AND INTERESTS

Beliefs explain conformity to norms in the following sense: to believe that a social standard of propriety exists is to believe that it is enforced by society and, consequently, in most cases, to engage in enforcement and self-enforcement. It is easier to grasp the logic of this relationship if we compare and contrast norms and conventions, which have been very clearly explicated by Robert Sugden.[3] Conventions are similar to norms in that they require no external intervention (such as that of the state) to maintain them. Conventions differ from norms in that conventions are not necessarily societal obligations, enforced by society.

Sugden studies conventions as repeated coordination games and finds their emergence can be understood from a perspective of evolutionary processes. In his analysis, a convention is a state of rest in an evolutionary process. It is one of two or more possible stable (or

[2] Hart, *The Concept of Law*, 87–88.
[3] Sugden, *The Economics of Rights, Co-operation and Welfare* and "Spontaneous Order."

self-enforcing) patterns of action. It is stable because "if it is generally followed in the population, any small number of people who deviate from it will do less well than the others."[4] Over the course of many encounters, a person will find it more costly to deviate from an established convention than to follow it.

Consider the convention a strategy of action, to be played when encountering others. A convention strategy is, by definition, the unique best reply to itself: against opponents who play that strategy, people who deviate do less well than those who do not deviate. Thus individual self-interest naturally dictates following a convention, but only once it is established, that is, "generally followed." When most encounters are with opponents who play the convention strategy, deviation simply does not pay. Consequently, "once a convention has started to evolve—once significantly more people are following it than are following any other convention—a self-reinforcing process is in motion."[5]

For example, stopping on red (and going on green) is a simple traffic convention that, despite its legal status, really does not require the force of law to sustain itself. As is the case with many conventions, it has no intrinsic merit until most people begin to adopt it as a strategy. At the point when significantly more people stop on red, deviation from the convention becomes generally more costly than conformity. Even if other motorists make adjustments as best they can, the deviant is more likely to have accidents over the course of many encounters. Stopping on red is a pure coordination game, in which no one cares what the convention is so long as there is a convention.[6] But the same kind of reasoning applies in mixed games, in which people prefer some kinds of outcomes over others.[7]

By Sugden's definition, it makes sense for people generally to follow an established convention. But what if, for example, out of ignorance, error, or foolishness, a person deviates from the convention strategy? Clearly, in a series of encounters, the deviant will do "less well," because of the very high probability that his opponents will be playing the convention strategy. But will the deviation matter to those opponents? And will it matter to bystanders in the population, those who do not participate in the particular encounter?

It certainly will matter once the convention is established. If a per-

---

[4] Sugden, "Spontaneous Order," 91.

[5] Ibid., 93.

[6] A good introduction to pure coordination games and extragame solutions is Schelling, *The Strategy of Conflict*, especially 53–80, 89–99.

[7] See the examples and analysis in Sugden, *The Economics of Rights, Co-operation and Welfare*, 55–144.

son expects his opponents to follow the convention, then self-interest dictates that he follow it too. And because he follows the convention, it is in his interest that his opponents do so too: the fewer deviants he encounters, the better he does. Moreover, bystanders in the population also find their interests threatened when a convention is flaunted: the deviant may turn up as their opponent in some future encounter![8] (If the logic here is not immediately evident, think again about the traffic convention of stopping on red.)

Once a convention is established, everyone is "better off" following it than deviating from it, and nearly everyone is "best off" when everyone else is following it too.[9] This is true even if the established convention always favors opponents: the underdog still does even worse by deviating. And only if he finds himself the underdog in *all* encounters is he an indifferent bystander. For example, Sugden notes of the convention of property:

> Clearly, this convention favours some people much more than others. Those who start out in life possessing relatively little would much prefer many other conventions—for example, a convention of equal division— to the one that has become established. Nevertheless, it is in each individual's interest to follow the established convention, given that almost everyone else does. And once a person has resolved to follow the convention, his interests are threatened by the existence of mavericks who are aggressive when the convention prescribes submission. Or in plainer English: provided I own *something*, thieves are a threat to me.[10]

Up to this point, Sugden's account is not one of norm-guided actions. The reason is that deviating from a convention is inherently costly. That is, the costs result from the deviant action per se.

Norms are not self-enforcing in the sense that Sugden calls conventions self-enforcing: the costs of violating a norm do not necessarily inhere in the violation. Rather, norms are socially enforced: the costs result from society's response to violation.[11] By that definition, then, a norm shares all the properties of a convention, except that doing "less well" refers not to the intrinsic cost of a strategy that deviates

[8] See ibid., 155–61; Hardin, "The Emergence of Norms."

[9] This does not mean that established conventions necessarily increase social welfare. Many do not. It refers only to the situation obtaining once any convention is established. It does not examine the possibility or comparatively evaluate the benefits of some alternative established convention. See Sugden, *The Economics of Rights, Co-operation and Welfare*, 6–8, 166–77.

[10] Ibid., 159.

[11] Of course, a convention can also be a norm. But its normativeness is not due to intrinsic costs and benefits. See below.

from an established norm but to the social disapproval that deviation can expect to encounter.[12] Costs and benefits are measured in social terms.[13] This difference between norms and conventions has two very important implications.

First, because the social enforcement of norms may be subtle and tacit, it is not very costly for opponents or bystanders to sanction deviants. Indeed, disapproval is a psychological state, which can be simply inferred: "For your ill will to cause me unease, it is not even necessary that you should choose to express it."[14] In such a situation, it is conceivable that sanctions need be no more than imagined to have an effect. For example, when climbing across the legs of fellow moviegoers ten minutes into the main show, who needs actually to see the facial expressions of those already seated to feel culpable? The possibility of merely inferred sanctions reduces maintenance costs of established norms but also points up the crucial function of beliefs, especially in getting a norm started. For once enough people believe that a norm exists, it exists in fact. They will not only conform, but are unlikely to require concrete evidence that conformity is indeed rewarded and deviation indeed punished. Obviously, the opposite is also true. Subtle or tacit disapproval may escape the notice of those who have no reason to look for it or doubt it is being expressed.

Second, if costs and benefits are measured in social terms, then the costs of disapproval are costs only insofar as membership in society is viewed as a benefit. As society is not one undifferentiated whole, it is clear that social norms are, at base, group norms. And the community or group that imposes costs and distributes benefits is, to a large extent, defined by the individual for himself. For example, juvenile delinquents are likely to care very little about what high society thinks of them and vice versa.

Conventions can also, of course, be norms. The motorist who ignores the convention of stopping on red is clearly a menace to fellow motorists. It would be surprising if actions upholding the interests of all motorists (including, of course, the deviant himself) did not emerge as standards of correct conduct. Indeed, the attachment of norms to interests structured as conventions is an important concern in recent studies on how norms emerge.[15]

[12] This differs from Sugden's definition of a norm, which I call an internalized norm. See the discussion of moral beliefs and internalized norms below.

[13] By this definition, a norm is the same as a social custom in Akerlof, "A Theory of Social Custom, of Which Unemployment May Be One Consequence."

[14] Sugden, "Spontaneous Order," 95.

[15] In addition to Sugden, *The Economics of Rights, Co-operation and Welfare*, 166–77, and "Spontaneous Order," see Lewis, *Convention*, 97–100; Ullmann-Margalit, *The Emer-*

Now there is a fairly simple answer to the question: what is the relationship between norms and actions? The core explanation is be-liefs—the belief that the action matters to a group that matters. Norm-guided actions are actions performed with the understanding that a social group to which a person cares to belong expects its members to act that way and will generally favor those who do so over those who act in other ways.

MORAL BELIEFS AND INTERNALIZED NORMS

The costs of deviation from a convention inhere in the deviant action per se; the costs of deviation from a norm inhere in the response of a social group. When a norm is internalized, however, the costs of deviation inhere in the conscience of the deviant.

Internalization is a process of preference formation, in which peo-ple develop moral beliefs that correspond to social standards. These beliefs, or acquired preferences, become an independent motivation to conform. Internalization changes the relationship between norms and actions. Expected social approval of conformity and disapproval of deviation is no longer the most relevant part in the calculation to act: the person who has internalized a norm simply would rather con-form than deviate. Deviation from an internalized norm conflicts with personal moral beliefs and causes psychological pain, commonly called guilt.

Thus an orientation to a norm can feature two kinds of "ought-ness"—a personal feeling of being obliged and a recognition of soci-etal obligation. The former results from internalization of a norm while the latter is a defining feature of all norms. Feelings of obliga-tion often accompany a recognition of societal obligation, although not necessarily. For example, the motorist who has internalized the convention and norm to stop on red feels compelled to stop at red lights and feels psychological pain if he deviates, whether he is appre-hended or not. The motorist who has not internalized that rule may feel "caught out" if apprehended running a red light at four in the morning, but lucky otherwise. Yet both will generally stop on red and both understand that they have an obligation, in this case a legal ob-

gence of Norms, 74–133. However, Lewis only looks at pure coordination games and Ullmann-Margalit only sees conventions in pure coordination games. See also Axelrod, "An Evolutionary Approach to Norms"; Opp, "The Evolutionary Emergence of Norms" for explanations of how norms may attach to interests that are structured somewhat differently than conventions.

ligation as well, to stop. The latter point is H. L. A. Hart's in his discussion of rules of obligation:

> The fact that rules of obligation are generally supported by serious social pressure does not entail that to have an obligation under the rules is to experience feelings of compulsion or pressure. Hence there is no contradiction in saying of some hardened swindler, and it may often be true, that he had an obligation to pay the rent but felt no pressure to pay when he made off without doing so. To *feel* obliged and to have an obligation are different though frequently concomitant things.[16]

Internalization is not the only issue pointed up by Hart's example. The deviant here is unlikely to care about the social group that cares about the norm of paying the rent. In fact, from the perspective of the "hardened swindler," the only costs to worry about are those that may ensue directly from failure to pay. While he may know about the existence of a norm to pay the rent, he presumably also knows that paying the rent is not a norm for swindlers. In Hart's example, what is a norm for others is a mere convention for swindlers, who are bound eventually to discover for themselves what Robert Sugden has described in general terms: crime does not pay.

While internalization adds to the costs of deviation, it does not necessarily make those costs prohibitive. People may agree to suffer the involuntary pain of guilt as the necessary price of the pleasures they choose to pursue. If internalization affects preferences, then the choice to deviate depends on how preferences are ordered. This is the same as saying that internalization is a matter of degree and that the relationship between internalized norms and actions is not altogether tautological. In terms of how internalization affects actions, however, it is clear that while it is no guarantee of established norms, the added psychological costs can certainly help to support them.

POLICY IMPLEMENTATION AS NORM BUILDING

The belief that a standard exists among a social group that matters is essentially what explains norm-guided actions. Norm building, then, is designed to elicit compliance with public policy by changing the way people look upon the policy issue. It is one approach to policy implementation—not an attribute only of political systems committed explicitly to social engineering. In the Introduction I noted smoking in public places, serving too much alcohol to guests, driving without

---

[16] Hart, *The Concept of Law*, 85–86.

a seatbelt, and littering as acts in which Western democratic governments have intervened to create and support situations of social enforcement. Similar in essence but more ambitious in scale are social transformation efforts aimed at racial desegregation and energy conservation, for example.

What distinguishes norm building from other approaches to policy implementation is the planned withdrawal of the state from responsibility for enforcement and the attendant expectation that ordinary members of society will step in to ensure compliance with policy. State intervention in this design is a short-term investment in long-term compliance. The defining feature of the intervention is that it sets in motion a process aimed at producing the eventual superfluousness of state enforcement. That is, policy makers intervene strategically in order to create the conditions for social enforcement of public policy. Under what circumstances does it make sense for policy makers to do this?

First, norm building can dominate other strategies when policy presents a serious challenge to existing norms or values. For example, in their study of protective regulation of industry, Eugene Bardach and Robert Kagan observe that regulation is viewed as "unreasonable" in many enterprises, and they propose norm building as an alternative to state enforcement.[17] They observe that the growth of aggressive and legalistic enforcement of protective regulation has produced perverse effects: diversion of effort, resentment, minimal compliance, cutting off cooperation, and outright resistance. Bardach and Kagan conclude that the only effective regulation of industry is self-regulation. They argue that self-regulation can be achieved only if government agencies "affect the consciousness, organization, or culture of the regulated enterprise in order to make it sensitive to serious sources of harm."[18] This is essentially a prescription for norm building.

Second, policy makers may choose norm building over other approaches when it is difficult to monitor compliance. Herbert Kaufman's classic study of the forest service provides an excellent illustration of this point.[19] Leaders headquartered in Washington, D.C., depend on hundreds of forest rangers, who are dispersed across the country and spend more than half their time in the woods, to execute their policies. Kaufman finds that despite a variety of centrifugal pressures, the rangers handle most situations precisely as if their su-

[17] Bardach and Kagan, *Going by the Book.*
[18] Ibid., 124.
[19] Kaufman, *The Forest Ranger.*

periors stood looking over their shoulders supervising their actions. Compliance with policies depends very little on formal sanctions. Rangers conform voluntarily to policy prescriptions because "it would not occur to them that there is any other proper way to run their areas."[20] Kaufman observes: "Often, confronted by a situation in the field, there is a course of action they would 'instinctively' like to follow, that seems 'clearly' to be the 'best' and 'proper' one; a good deal of the time, this 'happens' to be the action prescribed by the Service. That is, they are not consciously 'conforming'; they are merely doing what is 'right.' "[21] In short, Kaufman argues that forest service leaders get rangers to do what leaders want them to do, in circumstances that are impossible to monitor closely, largely by inculcating policies as norms.

Third, policy makers frequently make some effort to build norms to support policies because it is to some degree necessary. Without resorting to political terror, the state does not possess the coercive and administrative machinery to enforce policies successfully if they do not have at least the passive support of a large proportion of the population. The failure of alcohol prohibition to establish itself as a generally accepted norm in American society is a good illustration of the importance of social support for successful implementation. Ironically, prohibition began as a social movement and eventually became powerful enough to effect constitutional change. Yet prohibition proved ultimately to be unenforceable because "the essential sense of general social endorsement of the law was never established."[22] While overall drinking declined sharply, a substantial number of Americans could not be convinced there was anything wrong with it.

Finally, some effort at norm building as part of policy implementation makes sense for policy makers because norms mask vested interests and may reduce social conflict. At a minimum, it is difficult to imagine a situation in which policy makers can lose by proselytizing a public-minded rationale for their policies in an effort to build supportive social beliefs. This is particularly the case when policies clearly are (or merely appear to be) partial to certain social groups. Crucial to the efficacy of normative beliefs is their impersonal nature as matters of general principle. They are directed not for or against any particular group, although in practice they may indeed favor one group over another. Norm building can mitigate social conflict if it

[20] Ibid., 222.
[21] Ibid., 198.
[22] Kyvig, "Sober Thoughts," 13.

makes groups that must forgo immediate interests believe that doing so is the right conduct.[23]

As an approach to policy implementation, state interventions that build social norms differ from other kinds of interventions in that they produce outcomes through a process that eventually transfers responsibility for enforcement of policy from the state to society. And as social enforcement is ultimately the goal of norm building, policy makers can expect to be effective only when they adopt interventions that promise to "self-destruct"—that is, interventions that produce as a logical consequence the superfluousness of state involvement in enforcement of policy. More than anything else, this feature distinguishes norm-building interventions from the "generic policies," "policy instruments," and "implements" proposed by policy analysts to realize already formulated policies.[24]

What kinds of interventions will self-destruct? This is nearly equivalent to asking my main research question: how can policy makers build a social norm from a public policy? Before exploring this question empirically in the chapters that follow, I examine some answers culled from the literature on norms.

FIVE MECHANISMS OF NORM BUILDING

The literature on norms does not typically consider norms from a political perspective, as a question of active manipulation. Yet the various theories about how norms and similar social institutions spontaneously come into existence and maintain themselves do suggest (usually implicitly) many ideas about what kinds of manipulative interventions are likely to work in building a norm.

Here I survey five ideas I saw illustrated in the course of my empirical investigation. I make the ideas explicit where they are implicit and present them as mechanisms of norm building. The mechanisms describe principles underlying how policy makers in Beijing went about building a norm of cadre retirement. Each mechanism is an intervention that self-destructs. Each develops the capacity of ordinary members of society to enforce and self-enforce public policy as a social norm, thereby allowing the state to relinquish responsibility for supervising policy implementation.

---

[23] See the discussion of norms of inequality in Ullmann-Margalit, *The Emergence of Norms*, 134–97.

[24] See, for example, Bardach, "Implementation Studies and the Study of Implements"; Elmore, "Instruments and Strategy in Public Policy"; Weimer and Vining, *Policy Analysis*, 124–78.

Borrowing and generalizing from the relevant literature, I labeled the mechanisms of norm building as follows: association, argument, exemplary rules, exemplary conformers, and metanorms. A useful way to think about the mechanisms is to recognize them as processes of strategic manipulation by political leaders and then ask what exactly is being manipulated and how. Briefly, association and argument operate through deductive processes, by manipulating beliefs. Exemplary rules and exemplary conformers operate through inductive processes, by manipulating evidence. Metanorms operate through group interests, by manipulating conflict. I describe these processes in detail below and also preview the mechanisms at work as policy measures used to build a norm of cadre retirement.

Association

If beliefs about what the social group views as appropriate are the reason why people enforce norms and engage in self-enforcement, then an obvious way to go about building a norm is to manipulate beliefs directly. One technique policy makers in Beijing used to transform beliefs among cadres was explicitly to link up their policy with already existing beliefs and norms. They appealed to old norms to build new ones. This idea of association is a familiar theme in recent theoretical literature on norms as well as classic experimental studies in social psychology.

Theorists working in the tradition of rational choice can explain why norms sustain themselves once established: group members conform to a norm because they believe the group favors conformers over deviants. But rationality is less helpful in explaining why norms emerge or why particular norms emerge. Those who generally find game theory a useful approach often look outside the rational choice tradition to consider how norms come about spontaneously. A number of theorists build on Thomas Schelling's notion of the "prominent solution," which allows people to coordinate their actions without communication, even in games played only once.[25]

Schelling presents a number of pure coordination situations with no communication between players. For example, how does a couple who are separated in a department store find one another if there is no prior understanding on where to meet? Schelling's solution to these problems is simple, compelling, and radical from a game theoretical perspective:

[25] Schelling, *The Strategy of Conflict*, 53–80.

Most situations—perhaps every situation for people who are practiced at this kind of game—provide some clue for coordinating behavior, some focal point for each person's expectation of what the other expects him to expect to be expected to do. Finding the key, or rather finding *a* key—any key that is mutually recognized as the key becomes *the* key—may depend on imagination more than on logic; it may depend on analogy, precedent, accidental arrangement, symmetry, aesthetic or geometric configuration, casuistic reasoning, and who the parties are and what they know about each other. Whimsy may send the man and his wife to the "lost and found"; or logic may lead each to reflect and to expect the other to reflect on where they would have agreed to meet if they had had a prior agreement to cover the contingency. It is not being asserted that they will always find an obvious answer to the question; but the chances of their doing so are ever so much greater than the bare logic of abstract random probabilities would ever suggest.[26]

Building on Schelling's idea, Robert Sugden suggests that the principle of analogy might explain why particular conventions and norms appear.[27] Russell Hardin proposes the principle of generalization, which is essentially the same thing.[28] Both Sugden and Hardin argue that specific conventions (and norms eventually) come into being through an association of ideas.[29] That is, when people confront new situations, they choose how to act by applying what seems to be a relevant generalization or adopting a decision rule used in circumstances that seem analogous. This explains why norms are commonly organized in "family relationships" and are not "a chaos of arbitrary and unrelated rules."[30] An example of such a relationship is the idea of favoring first possessors and first arrivals: it lies behind the "first come, first served" queuing norm and the "last in, first out" norm for determining the order in which workers are laid off in a recession, for example.[31]

The principle of association explains not only why particular norms emerge spontaneously but also what can obstruct the emergence of norms. Analogy and generalization can produce social

[26] Ibid., 57.

[27] Sugden, *The Economics of Rights, Co-operation and Welfare*, 50–52, 94–97, and "Spontaneous Order."

[28] Hardin, *Collective Action*, 198–200.

[29] For both, norms are what I call internalized norms. However, this distinction between their definition and mine does no harm to the usefulness of their explanation here.

[30] Sugden, "Spontaneous Order," 93–94.

[31] Ibid., 94.

norms only when there is a common base of information, experience, understanding, and few conflicting principles from which to generalize.[32]

About half a century before Sugden and Hardin began their work on norms, Muzafer Sherif conducted a series of experiments in social psychology and explained the emergence of norms by the same principle.[33] Sherif set out to discover what people do in situations in which absolutely no basis of comparison for some external stimulus exists. His experiments made use of the autokinetic effect: in complete darkness a single small light appears to move. Sherif subjected individuals, alone and in groups, to this effect repeatedly, asking them to estimate the distance that the (physically stationary) light had moved. He found that without an objective scale or externally given reference point, individual subjects and groups developed their own scales and internal reference points within the scales.

Sherif's experiments reveal a general psychological tendency to experience things in terms of some frame of reference. People refer to their current inventory of frames to make sense of new situations, especially when the situations are ambiguous. Once formed, frames of reference (such as those built up for the autokinetic effect) dominate or modify later reactions. Sherif concludes that common frames of reference formed through mutual contact or common experiences are the psychological basis of social norms.

Sherif's work suggests that norms are more likely to emerge when there are generally shared frames of reference, easily accessible in the psychological inventory, and for which few conflicting frames readily present themselves. As an explanation of why some norms emerge and not others, the frame of reference is similar to the notions of analogy and generalization.

The studies surveyed above suggest we can begin to explain which new (normative) beliefs arise (and which do not) through the principle of association: new beliefs are built through their association with existing ones. If association explains how norms emerge spontaneously, then we can also expect it to boost the chances of a norm emerging when political leaders use the principle manipulatively, as a mechanism of norm building.

The principle of association can be used manipulatively by presenting compliance with policy as similar to an existing pattern of actions that is generally accepted as obligatory or as simply a specific

[32] Hardin, *Collective Action*, 199.
[33] Sherif, *The Psychology of Social Norms*.

instance of an accepted general rule. This was particularly difficult and important in the case of cadre retirement because the communist tradition of purge for political error presented an obvious association antithetical to the idea of regular age-based exit from office. Countering the purge association, policy makers in Beijing introduced three frames of reference more conducive to building a cadre retirement norm. They revived the term *lizhi xiuyang*, literally "leave of absence for convalescence," which had always connoted temporary leave and special status, and redefined it to apply to a special form of permanent retirement with full salary. At the same time, policy makers defined special retirement as quite simply a new work assignment for cadres. They took some concrete measures to persuade retired veterans that retirement was not in fact the end of a revolutionary career but the beginning of a new stage in that career. Finally, policy makers appealed to cadres as communist party members, obligated by oath to observe discipline in the hierarchical party organization. Party members were called upon to submit to organizational discipline and step down as instructed.

Argument

Exploiting existing beliefs through association is clearly not the only mechanism of norm building that operates through manipulation of beliefs. Political leaders can also appeal to reason, by presenting intellectual arguments that their policy is functional and so deserving of active social support. They can attempt to establish a logical foundation for a norm, arguing that what is socially functional is also socially obligatory.

A functionalist explanation is the core of Edna Ullmann-Margalit's game theoretical account of the spontaneous emergence of norms.[34] She reasons by rational reconstruction. That is, she tells a plausible story of how norms could have emerged in situations with certain features. Ullmann-Margalit considers three paradigmatic situations: prisoners' dilemma situations, coordination situations, and inequality situations. Each presents a different basic difficulty to some or all of the individuals involved. Three types of norms are offered as solutions to these situational problems. Ullmann-Margalit points out that a large number of real-life situations fall into one of the three paradigmatic types and that norms of the types she describes as solutions

[34] Ullmann-Margalit, *The Emergence of Norms.*

do in fact exist. This gives her her functionalist thesis that certain types of norms emerge because they are solutions to problems posed by certain types of situations.

Consider, for example, her account of norms that solve prisoners' dilemma situations, the classic problem of collective action.[35] The structure of such situations is such that the pursuit of rational self-interest by each leads to a worse outcome than is possible through cooperation. Ullmann-Margalit notes that in repeated prisoners' dilemma situations, norms of cooperation emerge to solve the collective action problem in diverse settings.[36] Simply that such norms do emerge is the crux of her argument: norms emerge because they serve the function of solving the situational problem.

If norms can emerge spontaneously simply because they are functional, then manipulative political leaders can build a logical basis for a norm by demonstrating that their policy is a socially functional solution to a problem and, consequently, deserving of social support. Policy makers in Beijing made precisely such an argument to cadres. In so doing, they had to interpret lifelong tenure in a new way, labeling as a problem what cadres took for granted as an entitlement. Policy makers also could not ignore the problem of differential costs to members of society: they argued that the contribution was a glorious mission and historic duty but acknowledged that retirement did involve a sacrifice for older cadres.

The functionalist argument for retirement was aired mainly in newspapers and journals in the early stages of norm building. It faulted lifelong tenure with all kinds of serious defects in the exercise of power and claimed no support for it in the classics of Marxism-Leninism. A generational transformation and regular renewal of personnel were promoted as necessary for a vigorous leadership and

[35] The prisoners' dilemma is so named because it features the structure of the following story: Two suspected criminals are taken into custody and separated. The district attorney tells each he has insufficient evidence to convict them in a trial and presents them with the possible outcomes. If one confesses and the other does not, the one who confesses will be released for providing evidence (the best outcome) and the other will be convicted (the worst outcome). If neither confesses, they will be booked on some minor charge (the second best outcome). If both confess, they will be prosecuted but the district attorney will recommend leniency (the third best outcome). Rationality dictates that each confess, but they could do better if neither confessed. A good introduction to the problem of collective action is Olson, *The Logic of Collective Action*. Another is Hardin, *Collective Action*.

[36] See Axelrod, *The Evolution of Cooperation*, for a fascinating sampling of a norm of cooperation in such situations.

cadre corps with the training and ability to manage the post-Mao modernization campaign.

Exemplary Rules

Manipulating beliefs through association and argument is an attempt to change beliefs by appealing to processes of deduction. Policy makers in Beijing also attempted to build a norm by manipulating evidence so as to illustrate by example an idealized version of a cadre retirement standard. This approach to norm building operates differently: it appeals to inductive processes.

Exemplary rules constitute one kind of evidence easy for policy makers to create and manipulate. Official rules such as laws and regulatory guidelines issued by the state are not the same as self-sustaining social norms, but they can promote the emergence of such norms. Exemplary rules operate to build norms in three ways: they provide clarity, they enhance salience, and they grant legitimacy. These conclusions turn up in Robert Axelrod's work on the evolution of norms.[37]

Axelrod builds on his work on the evolution of cooperation under anarchy. He uses computer simulation to discover the hardiness of norms over time. He begins his investigation with a "norms game" having the following structure: deviation from the norm is rewarding to the deviant; deviation is costly to the group; punished deviation is very costly to the deviant and somewhat less costly to the enforcer. Axelrod makes a couple of assumptions about initial levels of boldness (acceptable risk levels for deviation) and vengefulness (the probability of punishing deviation). He then runs the game in five populations, each for a hundred generations. He finds that incipient norms collapse quickly, for lack of widespread enforcement. No one has any incentive to punish deviation. This result presents Axelrod with his research question: what mechanisms can support and hurry along norms which are only partially established? Exemplary rules are one such mechanism.[38]

Axelrod does not simulate the effect of rules in getting a norm started, but he does suggest how to model it. Rules provide clarity and salience to a partially established norm. If people are expected eventually to understand and conform to official rules without fur-

---

[37] Axelrod, "An Evolutionary Approach to Norms."

[38] Axelrod specifically considers laws, but his argument applies to other kinds of rules issued by the state as well.

ther official direction or enforcement, then the rules must be intelligible and prominent enough to ensure that most of the population knows them. Exemplary rules also work to build norms by transferring some of the authoritativeness of the state to the standard, thereby providing legitimacy for enforcement. Quite apart from whether or not they can be officially enforced, such rules have substantial power of their own. For example: "Many people are likely to take seriously the idea that a specific act is mandated by the law, whether it is a requirement to use seat belts or an income tax on capital gains."[39]

In Axelrod's schema, clarity, salience, and the transfer of authoritativeness are likely to decrease boldness in the population and increase vengefulness. Not only will there be less ambiguity about what constitutes deviation but those in society who might not otherwise punish deviants will be more confident, knowing that the state is on their side. One potential problem with rules as a mechanism to build norms is, of course, that members of society may come to view enforcement as the exclusive responsibility of specialized agents of the state.

The most common form of exemplary rules in Western democracies is embodied in the law. But using law to build a norm assumes a norm of law.[40] It assumes that because something is the law people will take it seriously and comply or understand they face punishment. Neither the Chinese precommunist nor communist tradition is one of rule of law.[41] Policy makers in Beijing employed another form of exemplary rules to build a norm of cadre retirement. From 1978 through 1988 top party and government organs issued about two hundred regulations, measures, notices, and decisions on cadre retirement. These were circulated in documents (*wenjian*), a highly institutionalized and important method of communication in Chinese bureaucracies.[42] Documents flowing from Beijing down through the party and government hierarchies articulated the position of policy makers regarding cadre retirement as binding on cadres in the various bureaucracies. The flow of documents also enhanced the salience of the retirement issue because they indicated the top was paying attention and because they forced the issue onto the official agenda at lower levels.

---

[39] Axelrod, "An Evolutionary Approach to Norms," 1106.

[40] See the discussion in Hart, *The Concept of Law*, 97–120.

[41] See the discussion of leadership in the Introduction.

[42] See Oksenberg, "Methods of Communication within the Chinese Bureaucracy"; Lieberthal, *Central Documents and Politburo Politics in China*.

Exemplary Conformers

Exemplary rules can clarify, make salient, and legitimate an emerging standard, but essentially they constitute evidence of an official standard and not a social one. They direct attention to what the standard is supposed to be. A more compelling kind of evidence must present the standard as a social one already. Exemplary conformers supply this kind of evidence: they direct attention to the standard as an emerging pattern of action in society. In building a norm of cadre retirement, policy makers in Beijing promoted such models of conformity—proving that conformity existed in fact and educating cadres about the proper orientation to retirement. This mechanism of norm building through exemplary conformers resonates with a centuries-old Confucian tradition and was also an important part of mainstream Maoism.[43] It also figures prominently in a number of different accounts of how social norms emerge spontaneously, including classic experimentation in social psychology and some more recent work in sociology.

The discussion above of norm building through association introduced Muzafer Sherif's experiments with the autokinetic effect and pointed out his contribution of the frame of reference notion.[44] Sherif discovered that, left alone, subjects built up a range and internal reference points within that range to make successive distance judgments about perceived movement of a small light. Sherif also conducted group experiments. In group situations the ranges and reference points of subjects tended to converge. This was so even when a subject had first established his own peculiar reference point alone in prior experimentation. Further, the group norms carried over to individual experiments afterward.

Sherif's findings account for the emergence of norms in group situations simply by the influence of group members. Ranges and reference points are formed and transformed through the mutual contact in the group. Interpreting the findings from the group experiments, Sherif concludes that norms are formed and diffuse through a group because the actions of others provide information about what kind of conduct is correct (even if we do not know why), especially in objectively unstable situations. This is the principle of social proof, described by Robert Cialdini as follows: "We view a behavior as more correct in a given situation to the degree that we see others performing it. Whether the question is what to do with an

---

[43] See the discussion of leadership in the Introduction.
[44] Sherif, *The Psychology of Social Norms.*

empty popcorn box in a movie theater, how fast to drive on a certain stretch of highway, or how to eat chicken at a dinner party, the actions of those around us will be important in defining the answer."[45] This principle of social proof is simply about group influence, without consideration given to which kinds of groups are likely to have more or less influence. Exemplary conformers in this account help build norms by providing evidence of conduct that serves as objective information, namely: given this situation, people act this way.

Francesca Cancian's version of who exemplary conformers are and how they help build norms is somewhat different.[46] Her account comes from fieldwork on norms among the Maya in southern Mexico. In her model the group with influence is the classic reference group.[47] Cancian demonstrates that people conform to norms in order to validate an identity, that is, to make others believe they are a particular kind of person. She argues that commitment to particular identities is very resistant to change but norms validating identities can change easily. (For example, adult females may remain committed to an identity as a woman, but norms defining what conduct is appropriate for women have changed dramatically.) In Cancian's account, exemplary conformers with influence to help build norms are those with the authority to validate relevant identities. They are models other people emulate because they believe they provide the relevant and most reliable information about how to act. Their conduct is the source of norms.

In sum, Sherif's early experiments suggest simply that the actions of those around us inform us about how to act. Cancian specifies that we make distinctions and are receptive to this kind of information from certain groups only. Both accounts suggest that policy makers can promote the emergence of norms by promoting the relevant kinds of conduct among salient groups, in particular, among people who are likely to inspire emulation per se. That is, the key way to get norms started is somehow to get the action started (ideally among people who matter) and to make sure others are paying attention.

Top Chinese leaders did not make haste to provide ordinary cadres with the most salient and compelling models of retirement, namely, themselves. Instead, they used a variety of incentives and enforcement schemes to retire in one fell swoop substantial numbers of veteran cadres. Then, in hundreds of glowing biographical accounts, the communist party newspaper held up for praise some of these model

[45] Cialdini, *Influence*, 117.
[46] Cancian, *What Are Norms?*
[47] See Sherif, Sherif, and Nebergall, *Attitude and Attitude Change.*

retired revolutionaries, who (it seems) had taken the initiative to retire to make way for the younger generation and who were exemplary too in their post-retirement activities. Policy makers in Beijing created in short time a noticeable population of retired cadres, made sure others noticed, and worked to establish these conformers as models for emulation.

Metanorms

Finally, because the key to a social norm is social enforcement (or a belief that the norm is socially enforced), it may be helpful to promote social enforcement directly by setting up an incentive structure to reward enforcement and punish non-enforcement. This is the essence of Robert Axelrod's notion of metanorms.[48]

Metanorms are norms about punishing those who do not enforce the norm when faced with deviants. In Axelrod's original norms game (without metanorms) it is rather costly to punish deviation. Introduction of metanorms changes this by making it costly *not* to punish deviation. This added punishment increases the level of vengefulness—the probability of punishing deviation. Axelrod modifies the norms game accordingly and runs a "metanorms game." The result in all five populations (again, each run for a hundred generations) is that a norm against deviation is established.

As a mechanism of norm building, metanorms can be viewed as procedural norms used to build substantive norms, such as cadre retirement. If a supportive metanorm exists, members of society find it in their interest to enforce the substantive norm.

Yet, the idea of using metanorms manipulatively to build norms leaves a number of important questions unanswered. How does the problem of building a metanorm differ from the problem of building a norm? Specifically, how does raising the cost of social non-enforcement differ from raising the social cost of deviation? Is another mechanism required to transfer the cost of social non-enforcement to society, allowing the state to withdraw from the process? In short, can metanorms operate independently or do they simply add another layer to the problem of norm building?

Axelrod does not provide answers to these questions, but measures taken by Chinese policy makers suggest one interesting answer. Here is the answer in its general form. Metanorms can operate independently as a mechanism of norm building in some situations of latent social conflict. Because people have different preferences, costs of

[48] Axelrod, "An Evolutionary Approach to Norms."

compliance with a policy can be distributed differently in society. (Think, for example, about the costs confronted by smokers and nonsmokers in complying with prohibitions on smoking in public places!) The same is true of costs of enforcement. For some people, preferences dictate that the cost of non-enforcement is greater for them than the cost of enforcement. These people (nonsmokers, for example) are in fact punishing themselves by not punishing others for deviation.[49]

Such situations of latent social conflict present policy makers with a naturally occurring metanorm structure and a set of policy enforcers in society. Policy makers need not build supportive metanorms: they can exploit an existing metanorm situation by manipulating conflicts of interest. In introducing their policy, policy makers make the conflict salient and provide to natural enforcers in society a resource—the information that the state is on their side.

In the case of cadre retirement, policy makers looked to younger cadres as natural enforcers of retirement policy. Retirement and promotion of cadres in the People's Republic of China go hand in hand: without retirement from these positions there cannot be promotion into them. Policy makers linked the two processes together in their various decisions and explanations. Younger cadres enforced the retirement of their senior co-workers in a variety of tacit and indirect ways. Policy makers succeeded in manipulating a conflict of interest between the generations—a conflict that is only partial. Eventually the younger cadres will be pushed into retirement themselves, through a process they had helped to sustain. This metanorm mechanism is perpetual, since there will always be younger cadres to act as unofficial enforcers of retirement.

Association, argument, exemplary rules, exemplary conformers, and metanorms are five theories of how norms emerge spontaneously. They are also mechanisms of manipulative norm building. I found some evidence that policy makers were aware of some of the theoretical logic surveyed above in their tactics to build a norm from their policy of cadre retirement. But I was not particularly searching for such evidence. The case studied here illustrates the mechanisms in operation. Whether Chinese policy makers were conscious of them as theories is an intriguing question, but not central to the issue studied here.

[49] This means that if in enforcing compliance the person also provides a public good, it must also be the case that the benefits to him of providing that good by himself outweigh the costs of the good not being provided. The standard discussion of this problem is Olson, *The Logic of Collective Action*, especially 22–36.

SUMMARY

Norms prescribe certain kinds of conduct as socially correct and socially obligatory. Once a norm is established in a group, it is self-sustaining: people find they do better overall to conform than to deviate, so long as the social group is one that matters to them. This is because groups enforce norms. They reward those who conform and punish those who deviate, usually in tacit and indirect ways. Moral beliefs that correspond to social norms may also develop: a personal feeling of being obliged may accompany a recognition of social obligation. But clearly, norms need not be internalized for conformity to happen. The costs of deviation inhere in the responses of the group, not necessarily in the conscience of the potential deviant.

Building social norms is a way to implement public policies. If policies are enforced by ordinary members of society as norms, then the state is relieved of responsibility for enforcement. We have no reason to expect social norms to emerge spontaneously to support policies introduced by policy makers. But there are a variety of circumstances in which these leaders might intervene to attempt to create conditions for social enforcement of policy. This includes circumstances in which it is difficult to monitor compliance or in which policies present a challenge to existing norms or values (and thus demand an explicit effort to transform beliefs). Further, some effort to build norms makes sense for most policies because the state simply does not possess the coercive and administrative machinery to enforce policies that lack at least the passive support of much of society.

Manipulative interventions to build norms are strategic short-term investments in long-term compliance. They set in motion a process aimed at the eventual superfluousness of state enforcement. What kinds of interventions are likely to work? The perspective in this chapter is that general theories in the literature on how norms come into existence naturally (without interventions) also describe general principles underlying how policy makers can go about getting norms to emerge through manipulative leadership. That is, they suggest what kinds of manipulative interventions are likely to work. We can think of these interventions as mechanisms of norm building.

Policy makers in Beijing used a number of different policy measures in their effort to build a norm of cadre retirement. These measures illustrate five mechanisms of norm building: association, argument, exemplary rules, exemplary conformers, and metanorms.

CHAPTER TWO

Politics and Policy

FIVE MECHANISMS of norm building surveyed in the last chapter—association, argument, exemplary rules, exemplary conformers, and metanorms—describe the principles underlying how policy makers in Beijing went about building a norm to implement their policy of cadre retirement. This chapter gives an account of the mechanisms as specific policy measures adopted in 1978–88. As the account illustrates, policy emphasis changed over time. The two major turning points are 1982 and 1988. Less pronounced changes occurred in 1980 and 1985.

One of the most unusual features of cadre retirement policy is the reflection of Chinese communist political history and the political hierarchy in different retirement statuses. This is due in part to the post–Cultural Revolution political context but also to the conflicting interests of political leaders. By the criterion of age alone, policy makers and other leaders below the top were the most immediate targets of retirement policy. The stratification in cadre retirement permitted policy makers to standardize exceptions for leading cadres, including themselves.

POLITICAL CONTEXT

Veterans of the communist revolution had been criticized, persecuted, demoted, and purged at the peak of Cultural Revolution violence in the mid-1960s. Their liberation, rehabilitation, and eventual reemployment began as early as 1968.[1] Post-Mao policy makers decided to continue with renewed impetus the restoration to power of veteran cadres victimized in the previous decade. Part of the rationale was the general post-Mao "reversal of verdicts" of the Cultural Revolution. Nonetheless, the decision does seem perversely contradictory to a policy to retire cadres—bound to exacerbate problems of old age, low education, lack of expertise, and physical and mental frailty in

[1] See Chang, "Political Rehabilitation of Cadres in China"; Lee, "The Politics of Cadre Rehabilitation since the Cultural Revolution" and "China's 12th Central Committee."

the cadre corps. And in fact, the restoration of veteran cadres did complicate and undermine cadre retirement.

That policy makers were truly serious about restoring veteran cadres to power is evident in an early party document on veteran cadres. Issued by the Central Committee's Organization Department, it affirmed that most veteran cadres were "good or relatively good." Those able to work were to be assigned suitable work as soon as possible. Those with long experience in positions of leadership were to be assigned main positions of leadership. Subordinate organization departments were called on to promote the "backbone" role of veteran cadres in the modernization campaign.[2] As an example of the scope and nature of restoration, the party journal publicized the work of the Hunan party committee's organization department. In Hunan, of the cadres managed by the provincial party committee before the Cultural Revolution, 98 percent had been reassigned work by 1978. Of these, more than 96 percent had been assigned positions ranking at or above their former positions. The rule adopted was: "As long as they are able to work, they are assigned work; those unable to work are permitted to retire upon request."[3]

What explains the coexistence of policies to restore and retire veteran cadres? The answer has to do with the politics of regime transition. Veteran cadres with pre–Cultural Revolution political loyalties were needed to help implement a massive elite transformation. They were supposed to discover and cultivate a new generation of successors. In so doing, they had to sort out one of the Cultural Revolution's thorniest legacies: in the younger generation of cadres that post-Mao policy makers sought overall to promote, there were many who had been recruited under the influence of radical leftist standards thoroughly repudiated by the end of 1978.

The new role of veteran cadres was encapsulated in the following formula: transmit revolutionary traditions, help and lead younger generations of cadres, abbreviated in Chinese to *chuan bang dai*. The official press described the role as a glorious mission, historic duty, and urgent task. The political character of the role was acknowledged openly and early. A *Renmin ribao* article of 1978 called it "a major struggle over the next generation and the future."[4] A 1981 article summarized the role with a question: "In whose hands will leadership

---

[2] Zhonggong zhongyang zuzhi bu, Guanyu jiaqiang lao ganbu gongzuo de ji dian yijian, 29 Dec. 1978.

[3] Zhonggong Hunan sheng wei zuzhi bu, "Zhengque shixing lao zhong qing san jiehe de yuanze."

[4] *Renmin ribao*, 19 Feb. 1978, 1.

of the party and country fall?" The answer affected "whether or not the correct line, guidelines, and policies established at the Third Plenum [of the party's eleventh Central Committee, convened in December 1978] can continue, whether or not unity and stability in politics can be maintained, and whether or not the Four Modernizations can be achieved."[5]

In principle, restoration and *chuan bang dai* were consistent with the policy to retire cadres. Restoration applied only to those physically able to continue work: "Veteran cadres who are in poor health and unable to perform normal duties of office retire and carry out *chuan bang dai* from that position."[6] Moreover, *chuan bang dai* was from the beginning a short-term policy, limited to veteran cadres, and aimed primarily at leading cadres. It was not intended as a rationale for indiscriminately maintaining in power for the rest of their lives all old cadres, all veteran cadres, or all leaders. Apparently, policy makers had rejected such a policy—as they had rejected a policy of indiscriminately retiring all old cadres at one time.[7] Policy makers wanted a proportion of old veteran cadres to be in office provisionally to provide continuity at a time of transition during large-scale replacement with younger cadres.[8] One of the clearest descriptions of the envisaged relationship between the policies of restoration, *chuan bang dai*, and retirement outlined it in the following terms:

> With the exception of veteran cadres who are old, weak, ill, or disabled and cannot continue normal work, the majority of veteran cadres must lead the group and in the leading group train young and middle-aged cadres. Only when young and middle-aged cadres are trained can we have retirement from leading groups—in a planned and gradual way and on the basis of veteran cadres' state of health. Otherwise, veteran cadres will not have played their historical role.[9]

In practice, not surprisingly, restoration and *chuan bang dai* ultimately affected retirement in ways that diverged sharply from the

[5] Huang, "Lao ganbu xuanba zhongqingnian ganbu zhong de lishi zeren," 32.

[6] *Renmin ribao*, 3 June 1981, 2. The author, Song Renqiong, headed the Central Committee's Organization Department in 1979–83.

[7] Chen, "Baozheng dang de shiye jiwang kailai de zhongda juece." The author, Chen Yeping, emerged as a deputy head of the Central Committee's Organization Department when it was reconstituted after the Cultural Revolution and headed the department in 1983–84.

[8] Wang, "Guanyu ganbu 'sihua' he ganbu zhidu gaige de ji ge wenti." The author, Wang Zhaohua, was secretary general of the Central Committee's Organization Department in 1979–80 and later a deputy head of the department.

[9] Huang, "Lao ganbu xuanba zhongqingnian ganbu zhong de lishi zeren," 33.

ideal. Beginning in about 1980, newspapers and journals began to air complaints. Veteran cadres in poor health who were supposed to retire were simply not retiring, and veteran cadres restored to power were not creating the conditions for their own retirement by discovering and cultivating successors.

The responses of veteran cadres restored to power brought out basic disagreements among policy makers about the urgency of replacing old cadres. Apparently, Deng Xiaoping maintained that generational succession was an urgent matter and that younger cadres should be apprenticed while taking on main responsibility for work, with older veterans merely providing guidance as needed. Other top leaders contended that generational succession could be taken slowly, that reinstated veteran cadres could play the role denied them during the Cultural Revolution for several more years at least.[10]

In early 1980 the Central Committee gave a nuanced emphasis to retirement when it passed a resolution to abolish de facto lifelong tenure for cadres.[11] The formal resolution did not end the debate. It probably did precipitate the public airing of complaints and a devastating pseudoscholarly critique of lifelong tenure.

ARGUMENTS AGAINST LIFELONG TENURE

The critique of lifelong tenure appeared in a wide range of newspapers and journals, mostly in 1980.[12] The arguments presented were appeals to reason, largely on the basis of what was functional for society as a whole. Critics of lifelong tenure associated it historically with economic backwardness and political autocracy in the world. They claimed no support for it in the Marxist classics and they found it directly or indirectly responsible for a number of serious defects in the exercise of power since 1949. In fact, they faulted lifelong tenure with a number of problems for which retirement alone could never be an effective solution: abuses of power, nullification of elections, destruction of collective leadership, sabotage of democratic central-

[10] Chen, "Baozheng dang de shiye jiwang kailai de zhongda juece."

[11] Communiqué of the Fifth Plenary Session of the 11th Central Committee of the Communist Party of China, 29 Feb. 1980.

[12] See especially Yan, "Lun feizhi 'zhongshenzhi' "; Gao, "Feichu ganbu zhiwu zhongshenzhi de weida yiyi"; Jia, Cheng, and Wei, "Lue lun zhongshenzhi"; Xiao et al., "Lun feichu ganbu lingdao zhiwu zhongshenzhi"; Peng and Zheng, "Shi tan feizhi ganbu zhiwu zhongshenzhi"; *Renmin ribao*, 28 Oct. 1980, 5; Wu, "Ganbu zhidu shang yi xiang zhongda de gaige"; Bao, "Tantan zhongshenzhi wenti"; Wen, "Ganbu zhidu de yi xiang genben xing gaige." In 1984 Yan Jiaqi elaborated his earlier critique in *Zhongshenzhi yu xianrenzhi*.

ism, stifling of initiative and creativity, creating opportunities for careerists and conspirators, cult of the individual, redundant personnel, bureaucratism, factionalism, elitism, and modern-day superstition!

Critics assailed the problem of an old and aging cadre corps, the inevitable product of lifelong tenure, as one of the system's major defects. They complained that old age and poor health kept many leaders in the hospital for a large part of the year and that many others were so weak or ill that they were "unable to go abroad on visits, unable to go to lower levels to conduct investigations, unable to read through more than a few pages of documents, unable to give reports of more than a few pages, even unable to attend important meetings."[13] Cadres whose age and state of health kept them from close contact with practical work and lower levels were not viewed simply as deadwood. Rather, critics saw them as a dangerous liability: divorced from reality, ossified in their thinking, less able to reason clearly, and more likely to err in judgment and bring about losses to the country.

Critics argued that the lack of regular personnel renewal tended to deprive Chinese officialdom of a vigorous leadership with up-to-date training to cope with modern problems. They argued that the so-called stability represented by old cadres monopolizing top positions for decades concealed a systemic instability of latent succession crisis, an instability heightened by the likelihood that an unfit leader could be in power for a very long time. They pointed out that even with a generational transformation in the 1980s, the problem of old cadres and its attendant consequences were bound to recur in a decade or two unless regular retirement was instituted.

PRINCIPLES OF STRATIFICATION

Anticipating the eventual retirement of about 2.5 million veteran revolutionaries, policy makers had to figure out whether and how to reward retired cadres for their participation in the revolution, revolutionary seniority, and position and rank in the party or government bureaucracy. As in most political systems established through revolutionary struggle, the three were not uncorrelated. Participation in the revolution had generally been a prerequisite for a top or middle-level position in politics or administration. And revolutionary seniority, measured in participation before strategic turning points in the

[13] Xiao et al., "Lun feichu ganbu lingdao zhiwu zhongshenzhi," 21.

history of the revolution, had typically been a fair index of position and rank.[14] Instead of simply rewarding cadres with different pension levels, policy makers chose to distinguish among cadres by assigning them to different retirement statuses. The hierarchy of retirement statuses determined how and how much cadres could be involved in work after retirement and which retired cadres would be treated as special, with unique needs and demands that deserved to be met.

Policy makers used the same criteria that had stratified working cadres to stratify retired cadres: participation in the revolution, revolutionary seniority, and position and rank in the party or government. They made two basic distinctions. Veteran revolutionaries were distinguished from postrevolutionaries, who had joined the communists after their victory in 1949, and, among revolutionaries, leaders were distinguished from ordinary cadres. The result was three strata: revolutionary leaders, ordinary revolutionaries, and ordinary postrevolutionaries. Within each group, smaller differences in status and amount of pension existed. Table 2.1 summarizes the changing eligibility standards for different retirement statuses and the differences in pension and bonus, all discussed more fully below.

In differentiating among retired revolutionaries, policy makers took as a point of departure four strategic junctures in the history of the revolution: 7 July 1937, the end of 1942, 3 September 1945, and 1 October 1949. Because of the complex environment of war in which the communists had struggled to gain national power and the strategic changes in their programs, the periodization broadly demarcates different kinds of incentives for participation in revolutionary work.

The communist program in the first period, dating from the party's founding in 1921 and extending through the Revolutionary Civil Wars (1924–27 and 1927–37), was basically one of broad social revolution. By contrast, the Anti-Japanese War period (1937–45) was characterized by the strategic abandonment of social revolution and the highly successful promotion of the communist party as the leading force of anti-Japanese nationalism. Retirement policy initially distinguished cadres who had joined the communists before the end of 1942 from the much larger numbers who had joined after the most difficult period of the war (1941–42) for the communists. That distinction was dropped in 1980. Most veteran revolutionaries had joined the communists in the War of Liberation period (1945–49),

[14] See especially Barnett, *Cadres, Bureaucracy, and Political Power in Communist China*, 43–47, 188–89, 433; Vogel, "From Revolutionary to Semi-Bureaucrat."

TABLE 2.1

Standards for Cadre Retirement Statuses and Pensions, 1978–88

REVOLUTIONARIES
Revolutionary Service History,

Rank, and Position	*Status, Pension (and Bonus)*		
	1978–79	*1980–81*	*1982–88*
"A few dozen" core leaders			Exempt
Very high prestigious leader with party membership of forty years			Advisory commission member
Revolutionary Civil Wars, 1924–27 and 1927–37			
High, middle leader	Adviser	As in 1978–79	As in 1978–81
High ordinary	Special 100%	As in 1978–79	Special 116.6%
Middle ordinary	Special 100%	As in 1978–79	Special 116.6%
Low	Special 100%	As in 1978–79	Special 116.6%
Early Anti-Japanese War, 1937–42			
High, middle leader	Adviser	As in 1978–79	As in 1978–81
High ordinary	Special 100%	As in 1978–79	Special 112.5%
Middle ordinary	Special 100%	As in 1978–79	Special 112.5%
Low	Regular 90%	As in 1978–79	Special 112.5%
Late Anti-Japanese War, 1942–45			
High leader	Adviser	As in 1978–79	As in 1978–81
Middle leader	Special 100%	Adviser	As in 1980–81
High ordinary	Special 100%	As in 1978–79	Special 108.3%
Middle ordinary	Regular 90%	Special 100%	Special 108.3%
Low	Regular 90%	As in 1978–79	Special 108.3%
War of Liberation, 1945–49			
High leader	Adviser	As in 1978–79	As in 1978–81
High ordinary	Special 100%	As in 1978–79	Special 100%
Middle, low	Regular 80%	As in 1978–79	Special 100%

POSTREVOLUTIONARIES

Work Service History	*Status and Pension*
	1978–88
Post-1949	
20+ years	Regular 75%
15-19 years	Regular 70%
10-14 years	Regular 60%

Rank Key:
Very high = At or above provincial level
High = At or above prefectural level
Middle = At or above county level, but below prefectural level
Low = Below county level

the civil war between the communist and the Guomindang (Nationalist) armies.[15]

While standards for different retirement statuses and pensions changed a few times after 1978, the logic remained the same. Higher status and greater rewards were allotted to those who had participated in revolutionary work earlier rather than later. The vast majority of veteran cadres had joined in the later stages of the struggle for power, when communist victory had seemed very likely if not inevitable. And a large number of cadres had been recruited not long after victory, in the first few years of communist power.

EXEMPTIONS FOR LEADERS

In 1963 the Central Committee's Secretariat had issued a decision calling on leaders of ministries and provinces to retire if old age had affected their ability to lead. In 1965 the Central Committee's Organization Department had drafted a set of regulations based on the decision. The regulations began to be implemented in a few ministries as a pilot project, but were never implemented generally. The whole effort was soon interrupted by the Cultural Revolution.[16] Discounting this effort, the measures issued by the State Council in June 1978 were the first set of general regulations on cadre retirement in twenty years. They established a status of semiretirement to advisory and honorary positions for leading cadres only.[17] Four years later the Central Committee added two new retirement statuses for leaders— full exemptions at the very top and semiretirement to newly created advisory commissions.[18]

Advisory and Honorary Positions

Semi-retirement to advisory or honorary positions, termed retirement to the "second line," was a status created in 1978 for veteran

---

[15] For accounts that shed light on changing incentives for participation in communist activities and organization before the communists won national power, see Bianco, *Origins of the Chinese Revolution, 1915–1949*; Johnson, *Peasant Nationalism and Communist Power*; Kataoka, *Resistance and Revolution in China*; Van Slyke, *Enemies and Friends*.

[16] See Cao, *Zhonghua renmin gongheguo renshi zhidu gaiyao*, 382–83.

[17] Guowuyuan, Guanyu anzhi lao ruo bing can ganbu de zanxing banfa, 2 June 1978.

[18] Zhonggong zhongyang, Guanyu jianli lao ganbu tuixiu [*sic*] zhidu de jueding, 20 Feb. 1982; Constitution of the Communist Party of China, 6 Sept. 1982, chap. 3, art. 22, and chap. 4, art. 28.

cadres in positions of leadership at middle levels and higher, who were physically and mentally well enough to do some work but not well enough to work full time.[19] The introduction of advisory positions for such large numbers of leaders was unprecedented, but the idea of the second line was not new. It dated from 1959, when Mao Zedong had stepped down as head of state in what was intended to be a gradual disengagement from some responsibilities of leadership.[20]

By 1978 standards, county-level advisers had to have joined the communists before the end of 1942 and advisers above that rank had to have joined before communist victory in 1949.[21] In 1980 standards were relaxed. Advisers at the county level had only to have joined the revolution before the end of the Anti-Japanese War in 1945.[22] Leaders could semiretire to advise party committees, governments, party or government departments, or state-owned institutes or factories, all at the county level and higher.[23] They advised their successors and they worked under the leadership of the party organization.[24] Although advisers did not work full time, their positions counted in the authorized positions of the workplace (*bianzhi*), taking up places that could otherwise be occupied by full-time cadres.

Departments of the Central Committee, State Council, provincial party committees, and provincial governments with three or more advisers could set up advisory groups. Advisory groups were to elect a chairman, with the position rotated annually. Party-member advisers in workplaces that did not form advisory groups and advisory group chairmen in departments that did form them could attend party committee meetings.

For years after their introduction in 1978, the actual role of cadres

[19] Eligibility was restricted by bureaucratic rank to those at and above the county level. Those ranks include many ordinary cadres, but advisory and honorary positions were designed for cadres in positions of leadership only.

[20] See MacFarquhar, *The Origins of the Cultural Revolution*, vol. 1, 105–7, 152–56, and vol. 2, 32–33, 173.

[21] Guowuyuan, Guanyu anzhi lao ruo bing can ganbu de zanxing banfa, 2 June 1978.

[22] Zhonggong zhongyang guowuyuan, Guanyu shezhi guwen de jueding, 13 Aug. 1980.

[23] Before 1980, policy did not provide for advisers to party committees or party departments. But even before the policy change, it seems that some party cadres were retiring to advisory positions. For example, a 1980 article in the party newspaper notes a former party committee secretary of a Chongqing district who had been an adviser since 1978. *Renmin ribao*, 26 May 1980, 5.

[24] The initial arrangement introduced in 1978 had advisers advising at a level lower than their pre-retirement position, a problematic relationship given the principle of leadership by the party organization.

on the second line remained unclear, even to those who had designed the system.[25] The role of cadres in honorary positions was never defined. The advisory role was defined in very general terms. Advisers were to engage in investigation and study, develop familiarity with the overall situation, help leaders think up and develop ideas, provide counsel, and transmit to younger generations the party's traditions and style of work as well as their personal experience and knowledge.[26]

The loosely defined advisory positions could provide an opportunity for cadres to transfer their responsibilities only if advisers were permitted to play real roles. This was recognized early. A 1980 *Renmin ribao* article complained that veteran revolutionaries who should have retired to the second line had not done so because in many workplaces advisers were not supplied with documents or other information, were not notified of meetings, were not consulted on important matters, and were ignored when they offered opinions.[27] At a meeting convened by the Central Committee's Organization Department in January 1981, those in charge of veteran cadre work were told to overcome the tendency to treat advisory positions as empty titles set up merely as a show of concern for veteran cadres.[28]

Exemptions at the Very Top

In February 1982 the Central Committee announced that several dozen leaders at the very top would remain in positions at the core of party and government leadership to provide continuity and stability.[29] The exemption of top leaders was made public in the March issue of the party journal *Hongqi*:

> Our party is a big party, our country is a big country. We need a few dozen veteran cadres with international reputation, who are capable of careful and long-term planning, who maintain a comprehensive view of the situation, and who are still in good health. [We need them to remain] in positions at the core of leadership in the party and government, to

[25] See Zhonggong zhongyang zuzhi bu yanjiu shi, *Zuo hao xin shiqi de ganbu gongzuo*, 201–3.

[26] Zhonggong zhongyang guowuyuan, Guanyu shezhi guwen de jueding, 13 Aug. 1980.

[27] *Renmin ribao*, 24 Sept. 1980, 3.

[28] *Renmin ribao*, 29 Jan. 1981, 1.

[29] Zhonggong zhongyang, Guanyu jianli lao ganbu tuixiu [*sic*] zhidu de jueding, 20 Feb. 1982.

help stay the course. Other veteran cadres must gloriously "retire from military service" at the ages specified, in keeping with regulations.[30]

The exemption was clearly a negotiated settlement, the product of compromise among top leaders. We know that top leaders disagreed on the urgency of retiring old cadres.[31] And we know that in 1982 the Central Committee rejected the introduction of objective guidelines that would have speeded up generational succession and made it difficult for old leaders to remain in positions as before. An April 1980 draft of the revised party constitution had set specific average age standards for the Central Committee and party committee standing committees at lower levels.[32] The standards were rejected by 1982, to be replaced with the general statement: "Leading Party cadres at all levels, whether elected through democratic procedure or appointed by a leading body, are not entitled to lifelong tenure and they can be transferred from or relieved of their posts."[33] In short, policy makers exempted leaders at the very top in 1982 and agreed on measures to protect leaders at lower levels from retirement.

Finally, 1982 marks a major shift in cadre retirement policy, detailed in another section below. The policy shift is very probably the rationale for the special exemptions at the top and for weaker language in the party constitution. In 1982 policy makers adopted measures that made retirement less a matter of private choice and more a matter of public obligation. The measures contained unambiguous, objective criteria specifying when cadres must retire. The explicit exemptions at the top established policy makers as exceptions to the general rule, guaranteeing that they would not be included as targets of the new measures.

Advisory Commissions

In addition to exempting some top leaders from retirement altogether, policy makers created a new retirement status for leaders below the top "few dozen" but well above other advisers. The new ad-

---

[30] *Hongqi* bianji bu, "Jigou gaige shi yi chang geming," 5.

[31] Chen, "Baozheng dang de shiye jiwang kailai de zhongda juece." See the discussion of debate over restoration and *chuan bang dai* above.

[32] It set average age ranges as follows: 55 to 65 for the Central Committee, 50 to 60 for provincial party committee standing committees, 50 or below for prefectural party committee standing committees, and 45 or below for county party committee standing committees. Draft of the Revised Constitution of the Communist Party of China, 2 Apr. 1980, chap. 6, art. 32.

[33] Constitution of the Communist Party of China, 6 Sept. 1982, chap. 6, art. 37, 19.

visory status was on specially created commissions to advise the Central Committee and provincial party committees.[34] The advisory commissions were designed to be transitional organs to ease into retirement a generation of aging leaders.

Policy makers did not hide the transitional character of the advisory commissions. In a July 1982 speech Deng Xiaoping stated that the commissions were an expedient measure to facilitate the change to full retirement. He proposed that the transition take ten or fifteen years.[35] Two months later, he suggested a shorter life span for the commissions would be better, although perhaps not feasible: "The earlier we can abolish [the Central Advisory Commission] the better. Probably it will be necessary for the next ten years, the next two terms. One term would probably be too rash."[36]

Eligibility for a position on an advisory commission was restricted to the veteran elite. Advisers on the Central Advisory Commission had to have at least forty years of party membership, be experienced in leadership, and have high prestige in the party and among nonparty members. Eligibility standards for advisers on provincial commissions were to be specified by the provincial party committees, based on the local pool of candidates but also taking into account Central Advisory Commission standards.[37]

Advisory commissions were to set up standing committees, with standing committee members eligible to participate but not vote in plenary sessions of the party committees. Provincial advisory commission chairmen and vice chairmen could participate but not vote in standing committee meetings of the party committees. The Central Advisory Commission chairman was made ipso facto a full member of the Politburo Standing Committee, the most powerful collection of leaders in the country. Vice chairmen could participate but not vote in Politburo meetings.[38]

A NEW ASSIGNMENT FOR REVOLUTIONARIES

The 1978 State Council measures created a special retirement status for cadres, with full salary. Appealing to precedent, policy makers

[34] Ibid., chap. 3, art. 22, and chap. 4, art. 28.

[35] *Daily Report: China*, 22 July 1983, K8–9.

[36] Deng, "Zai zhongyang guwen weiyuanhui di yi ci quanti huiyi shang de jianghua," 66.

[37] Constitution of the Communist Party of China, 6 Sept. 1982, chap. 3, art. 22, and chap. 4, art. 28.

[38] Ibid.

revived the term *lizhi xiuyang*, literally "leave of absence for convalescence" (usually abbreviated to *lixiu*), and substantially redefined it.
Before 1978 the term had referred to the practice, initiated in 1958,
of permitting some veteran cadres in poor health to retire from office
temporarily, receiving full salary while retired.[39] In 1978 policy makers discarded the original notion of *lixiu* as temporary and it became
a special form of permanent retirement. Special retirement status was
considered "unsuitable for workers." For this reason, policy makers
reverted to the pre-1958 practice of separate retirement systems for
cadres and workers.[40]

For nearly four years, rank and revolutionary service history standards defining eligibility for special retirement status were the same
as for advisory status, except that veterans of the Revolutionary Civil
Wars (1924–27 and 1927–37) were eligible for special retirement regardless of rank.[41] Also, advisory positions were created for leaders,
not ordinary cadres, and advisers had to be well enough to do some
work. The vast majority of veteran cadres, more than two million of
approximately 2.5 million surviving veterans, had joined the communists during the War of Liberation (1945–49).[42] Few were eligible
for either retirement status.[43]

Beginning in 1982, policy makers stopped treating advisory status
and special retirement status as two options for the same small population of cadres. They dropped rank standards and relaxed revolutionary history standards for special retirement status so that virtually
all revolutionaries became eligible for special retirement status and
its full pension.[44] The change increased pensions from 80 percent to

[39] Cao, *Zhonghua renmin gongheguo renshi zhidu gaiyao*, 382–83.

[40] Ibid., 381.

[41] Guowuyuan, Guanyu anzhi lao ruo bing can ganbu de zanxing banfa, 2 June 1978,
and Guanyu lao ganbu lizhi xiuyang de zanxing guiding, 7 Oct. 1980.

[42] "Selecting Young Cadres for Leading Posts."

[43] In 1978–81, only cadres of prefectural rank and higher were eligible for special
retirement status if they had joined the communists after 1945. Given the relationship
between revolutionary seniority and bureaucratic rank, not many cadres fit that category.

[44] Guowuyuan, Guanyu fabu lao ganbu lizhi xiuyang zhidu de ji xiang guiding, 10
Apr. 1982. Most, not all, revolutionaries were eligible for special retirement status. The
general formulation was that the following cadres were eligible for special retirement
status once they reached the retirement age specified for their rank and sex: those who
before the communist victory in 1949 had participated in the revolution under the
leadership of the communist party, had not engaged in salaried employment but had
been paid in kind through the communist party supply system, or who had engaged
in underground revolutionary work for the communist party. The most comprehensive regulation on the issue is Zhonggong zhongyang zuzhi bu, Guanyu queding jianguo qian ganbu canjia geming gongzuo shijian de guiding, 27 Sept. 1982. Up through

100 percent of pre-retirement salary for the overwhelming majority of veteran cadres. Pre-1945 participants in the revolution also received annual bonuses, ranging from one to two months' former salary.[45] Special retirement became the retirement arrangement for veteran cadres, excepting those eligible for some kind of exemption for leaders.

The 1982 change was accompanied by an elaboration of the policy to retire cadres. Policy makers reiterated the notion that veteran cadres were "revolutionaries by vocation" (*zhiye gemingjia*) who had, therefore, never considered retirement and who had no psychological preparation for it.[46] Special retirement status for veteran cadres was intended to take that into account. Policy makers presented retirement as a loss of position but not of occupation. In a frequently publicized letter to a retired veteran cadre, the general secretary of the party presented retirement as equivalent to a new work assignment. He reassured the retired veteran that retirement was by no means the end of a revolutionary career, but rather the beginning of a new stage in that career.[47] A number of specific policy measures gave the interpretation concrete meaning.

First, unlike regularly retired postrevolutionaries, specially retired veterans received 100 percent of their salary as pension. Indeed, the term *gongze* (salary) was used to refer to pensions of cadres with special retirement status.[48]

Second, retired veteran cadres were supposed to continue to be involved in some form of work after retirement. Policy makers were serious in their intention to promote the role of retired revolutionaries, in a policy called "exploiting surplus energy" (*fahui yure*).[49] The

---

1988, at least seventeen other regulations, many applicable only to very small groups of cadres, were issued to clarify revolutionary service history standards.

[45] Veterans of the Revolutionary Civil Wars (1924–27 and 1927–37) received a bonus of two months' salary, veterans of the early Anti-Japanese War period (1937–42) received one-and-a half month's salary, and veterans of the late Anti-Japanese War period (1943–45) received one month's salary. Guowuyuan, Guanyu fabu lao ganbu lizhi xiuyang zhidu de ji xiang guiding, 10 Apr. 1982.

[46] Zhao, "Jianli you zhongguo tese de ganbu lixiu tuixiu zhidu." The author, Zhao Shouyi, made the speech in October 1982. He headed the Ministry of Labor and Personnel at the time.

[47] See *Renmin ribao*, 4 Jan. 1983, 1, 10 Jan. 1983, 3, and 28 Jan 1983, 2. The general secretary at the time was Hu Yaobang.

[48] The term *tuixiu fei* (retirement payment) was generally used to refer to the pensions of regularly retired cadres. The term *fei* was occasionally used with regard to specially retired cadres; on the other hand, the term *gongze* was not used with regard to regularly retired cadres. Cao, *Zhonghua renmin gongheguo renshi zhidu gaiyao*, 396.

[49] One indication that the policy was taken seriously appears in an article in the most prominent periodical for the Chinese elderly. The article complains that workplaces are pursuing excessively ambitious goals of combining retirement with work activity,

new assignment generally did not involve them in the regular work of their former workplace and retired veterans were not supposed to receive (further) remuneration for it. Suggested assignments included investigating abuses of power or economic crimes, helping with party rectification, recruiting new party members, checking up on policy implementation at lower levels, writing party histories and revolutionary memoirs, and conducting propaganda work among the masses, especially among young people.[50]

Third, policy makers guaranteed veteran cadres access to documents, reports, meetings, and regular party meetings exactly as before retirement. Because the Chinese communists maintain a system of tightly controlled access (by department and rank) to information, the policy of no change in political access represented an important privilege. It was in keeping with the idea of the new assignment:

> When veteran cadres retire, they leave the workpost and no longer hold administrative or leading positions. Yet, ideologically, politically, and organizationally, they do not retire. No communist party member's revolutionary will and organizational discipline can be retired. They remain communist revolutionaries—serving the people, taking on political responsibility for the people. For this reason, political access for retired [veteran] cadres does not change with their retirement.[51]

In concrete terms, the policy of no change in political access required the workplace to facilitate the participation of retired veteran cadres in the various meetings associated with party membership.[52] And retired veteran cadres were to have access to party and government documents, as before retirement. Party organizations were instructed to establish a system of regular study of documents by retired cadres.[53]

Party and government documents are generally distributed to organizations (not individuals), and so workplaces had to set up reading rooms for retired cadres. While cadres generally had to give up their

---

to the detriment of the health of retired veterans and with little concern for their preferences. "Xian yure bu ke zhuiqiu gao bili."

[50] See, for example, Zhonggong zhongyang zuzhi bu, Guanyu fahui zhongyang guojia jiguan lixiu lao ganbu de zuoyong de yijian, 11 Oct. 1982; Zhonggong zhongyang, Guanyu jin yi bu jiaqiang qingshaonian jiaoyu yu fang qingshaonian weifa fanzui de tongzhi, 4 Oct. 1985.

[51] Zhonggong zhongyang, Guanyu jianli lao ganbu tuixiu [sic] zhidu de jueding, 20 Feb. 1982.

[52] Zhonggong zhongyang zuzhi bu, Guanyu anpai he zuzhi hao lixiu tuixiu tuizhi dangyuan zuzhi shenghuo, 30 July 1981.

[53] Zhonggong zhongyang bangongting zhonggong zhongyang zuzhi bu, Guanyu lixiu tuixiu ganbu yuedu wenjian wenti, 26 Aug. 1981; Zhonggong zhongyang bangongting, Guanyu zhongyang wenjian yinfa yuedu he guanli de banfa, 10 June 1985.

desks or offices upon retirement,[54] they could go to the workplace reading rooms to look at documents and newspapers. Thus the policy of no change in political access also allowed retired cadres to maintain a link with the former workplace.

It is, of course, easy to view the idea of the new assignment cynically, as a transparent effort to mollify veteran cadres. But in the political context of the early post-Mao period, revolutionaries were useful to policy makers. They had years of party membership, networks of contacts, and the prestige of being associated with the party's greatest achievement to date—gaining power. They were also often victims of the Cultural Revolution and so were untainted by the policies of that repudiated period. From the perspective of policy makers, they represented the party's better face.

For the same reasons, policy makers obviously wanted to avoid alienating veterans from politics at a time when some major reforms were being introduced. Political access made veterans more than mere observers. As one retired cadre explained:

> Veteran cadres want the right to read documents just as before they retired. The state has given them this right. This is very strange. Reading documents is to facilitate work. Why are retired cadres reading them? What do these documents have to do with their lives? Documents have two uses: to facilitate work and to share responsibility. If [cadres] are no longer doing the work, why should they read these things? . . . The purpose is to promote the interest [of retired cadres] in affairs of state, to develop their role, and to make them take on some responsibility for policies.[55]

Special retirement was not only a new assignment, but also brought with it privileges to acknowledge that revolutionaries had made particularly important contributions to the communist cause and to reward them accordingly. To commemorate the special contribution of revolutionary veterans, policy makers introduced certificates of honor to be awarded to veteran cadres upon their retirement. Special retirement status signified that revolutionaries deserved better treatment than those who had joined the communists after victory in 1949. One retired veteran summarized the significance as follows:

> We are not the same as those who joined the revolution after Liberation. Our struggle was bitter and dangerous. Many people died. Many people

---

[54] Zhonggong zhongyang bangongting guowuyuan bangongting, Guanyu guanche zhixing lixiu ganbu shenghuo daiyu guiding de tongzhi, 3 June 1984; Guowuyuan, Guanyu zhongyang guojia jiguan cong lingdao gangwei tui xia lai de tongzhi bu zai baoliu yuan bangongshi de tongzhi, 12 Feb. 1988.

[55] Interview subject no. 2.

sacrificed their lives. We are different from the others. We should be treated better. It is right that we get better treatment. After we go, I don't think there will be any more special retirement. It is special (*teshu*), only for us.[56]

In order to make special retirement special, policy makers set up veteran cadre departments to look after the needs of retired revolutionaries. Documents calling for the assignment of personnel to manage veteran cadres and the establishment of specialized structures were issued as early as 1978,[57] although structures were not in place until 1982–83.[58] The importance policy makers attached to proper management of veterans is evident in the status of veteran cadre departments at the provincial, prefectural, and county levels. The departments were not made subordinate to the organization departments at those levels, but equal to them in bureaucratic status. Organization departments were to give professional guidance to the parallel veteran cadre departments but party committees were to exercise direct leadership. Only at the Central Committee level was the veteran cadre department made subordinate to the organization department.

The importance of the issue is also indicated by the party's monopoly of implementation. Until 1987 at the earliest, no specialized departments for cadre retirement existed in the government hierarchy, except at the top level.[59] As late as November 1986, government organizations at the provincial, prefectural, and county levels attended to cadre retirement work by assigning responsibility to the personnel department.[60]

Veteran cadre departments were charged with implementing the policy of no change in political access and a policy of priority to retired veteran cadres in benefits affecting general welfare. This included housing, medical care, and provision of daily necessities. Retired veterans were encouraged to resettle in the countryside, with a

[56] Interview subject no. 21.

[57] Zhonggong zhongyang zuzhi bu, Guanyu jiaqiang lao ganbu gongzuo de ji dian yijian, 29 Dec. 1978. See also Guowuyuan, Guanyu lao ganbu lizhi xiuyang de zanxing guiding, 7 Oct. 1980; Zhonggong zhongyang zuzhi bu, Guanyu tuoshan anpai tuichu xianzhi de lao ganbu de yijian, 2 June 1982; Zhonggong zhongyang zuzhi bu laodong renshi bu, Guanyu zhongyang guojia jiguan lao ganbu ju (chu) zhize fanwei de shixing banfa, 31 Dec. 1982; Zhonggong zhongyang zuzhi bu, Jiu sheng shi lao ganbu gongzuo zuotanhui jiyao de tongzhi, 25 Apr. 1983.

[58] Wang Xingming (Deputy Director of Cadre Retirement Division, Veteran Cadre Bureau, Ministry of Labor and Personnel), interviewed in Beijing, 24 Nov. 1986.

[59] Chen Liang (Deputy Director of Special Retirement Division, Cadre Retirement Bureau, Ministry of Personnel) and Wang Wenbo (Director of Cadre Retirement Bureau General Office, Ministry of Personnel), interviewed in Beijing, 7 Nov. 1988.

[60] Wang, interview, 24 Nov. 1986.

special moving allowance of 150 to 300 *yuan* provided as an incentive. For the majority who (it seems) did not want to resettle, departments were instructed to help resolve housing problems.[61] As to medical care, retired veteran cadres could receive care at a hospital close to their place of residence if it was inconvenient for them to go to the hospital assigned to their former workplace. All retired veterans were to receive priority in getting into hospitals when needed. Public health departments were instructed to build special clinics and rest homes for retired veteran cadres. Retired veterans of the Revolutionary Civil Wars (1924–27 and 1927–37), veterans with special expertise or high professional status, and high-ranking retired veterans received a special medical care card that gave them access to a better quality of medical personnel, better clinics for outpatient services, and special cadre wards for inpatient treatment.[62]

In addition, policy makers instructed veteran cadre departments to do things such as arrange press interviews with retired veterans, convene conferences to solicit their views, organize tea parties for them, and arrange visits of leaders to the homes of retired veterans at holiday times. They were also responsible for promoting an attitude of respect and concern for retired veterans among working cadres and in society generally. Funding for such activities and other needs of retired veteran cadres was guaranteed by the Ministry of Finance, which provided 150 *yuan* annually per specially retired cadre to all workplaces in the public sector and an additional 350 *yuan* annually per specially retired cadre to political and administrative organs, or all public-sector workplaces other than enterprises.[63]

REGULAR RETIREMENT FOR POSTREVOLUTIONARIES

Regular retirement (*tuixiu*) status on less than full salary was for cadres who did not meet the standards for special retirement. Special

[61] Guowuyuan, Guanyu anzhi lao ruo bing can ganbu de zanxing banfa, 2 June 1978, and Guanyu lao ganbu lizhi xiuyang de zanxing guiding, 7 Oct. 1980.

[62] Weisheng bu, Guanyu lizhi xiuyang ganbu yiliao wenti de guiding, 16 Jan. 1981, Guanyu tiaozheng lao zhuanjia yiliao zhaogu de tongzhi, 2 July 1981, and Guanyu zhongyang guojia jiguan zai jing danwei siju zhang yi shang ganbu he zhuanjia yiliao zhaogu de buchong guiding, 13 Dec. 1984; Zhonggong zhongyang zuzhi bu weisheng bu, Zhongyang guojia jiguan zai jing danwei lixiu lao ganbu he zhiming renshi zhuanjia yiliao baojian zanxing banfa, 2 June 1982; Laodong renshi bu, Guanche guowuyuan guanyu lao ganbu lizhi xiuyang guiding zhong juti wenti de chuli yijian, 10 Dec. 1982, and Guanyu lixiu ganbu jiankang xiuyang de ji xiang guiding, 25 May 1983; Weisheng bu baojian ju, Guanyu lao ganbu lao zhuanjia waichu yiliao shouxu deng wenti de tongzhi, 8 May 1986.

[63] Chen and Wang, interview, 7 Nov. 1988.

retirement and regular retirement became retirement to the "third line." The term used for regular retirement had always implied permanent retirement and was the same term used for the retirement of workers. Indeed, the work service standards and pensions for regular retirement were the same as those set for workers. Only age guidelines differed, and those only for women.[64]

In 1978–81 most cadres, veteran revolutionaries and postrevolutionaries, were eligible only for regular retirement status. Standards for regular retirement included age guidelines but no rank guidelines. Amount of pension for revolutionaries was based on revolutionary service history. For postrevolutionaries it was based on work service history, measured in years worked after 1949. Pensions for regularly retired cadres ranged from 60 to 90 percent of pre-retirement salary. Revolutionaries were eligible for 80 or 90 percent of salary, postrevolutionaries for 60 to 75 percent. Policy makers also granted retirement bonuses for regularly retired cadres who were national labor heroes, national labor models, war heroes, or cadres with special contributions to the cause of socialist construction.[65] In most cases, postrevolutionaries received a pension at a level no higher than that set in the 1950s. In some cases, the level was even lower.[66]

The major policy change in 1982 reassigned revolutionaries from regular retirement status to special retirement, with new pensions amounting to 100 percent of pre-retirement salary. For postrevolutionaries, nothing changed. However, by extending special retirement status to all veteran cadres and providing bonuses to some, policy makers exacerbated the gap between revolutionary and postrevolutionary cadres. Whereas in 1978 the smallest difference in pensions for the two groups was 5 percent of former salary, in 1982 it rose to 25 percent. The biggest difference, when bonuses are taken into account, became 57 percent. Although policy makers later introduced small pension increases, mainly to help retired cadres cope with inflation, most applied to all retired cadres and were not aimed at closing the pension gap.[67]

[64] The retirement age for women workers was set five years below that for cadres. See Guowuyuan, Guanyu gongren tuixiu tuizhi de zanxing banfa, 2 June 1978.

[65] Bonuses were set at 5 to 15 percent of salary, added to the pension, with the stipulation that total pension could not exceed pre-retirement salary. Guowuyuan, Guanyu anzhi lao ruo bing can ganbu de zanxing banfa, 2 June 1978.

[66] See Cao, *Zhonghua renmin gongheguo renshi zhidu gaiyao*, 392; Pi and Zhang, *Xiandai gongwuyuan zhidu yanjiu*, 232.

[67] They raised the lowest regular retirement pension by 5 *yuan* per month in 1983 and raised pensions for regularly and specially retired cadres by 12 to 17 *yuan* in 1985 and another 5 *yuan* in 1988. Laodong renshi bu caizheng bu, Guanyu tigao zhigong tuixiu fei tuizhi shenghuo fei de zui di baozheng shu de guiding, 28 June 1983; Guo-

The establishment of veteran cadre departments to ensure that revolutionaries were given special treatment further increased the gap between the two groups. A county personnel administrator observed that people generally considered special retirement as an upper class and regular retirement as a lower class because specially retired cadres were managed under the leadership of the party committees.[68]

Of course, no one noticed the difference between special retirement and regular retirement more than postrevolutionaries. As one remarked: "We are all working together—then this distinction. Of course, to distinguish between specially retired and regularly retired is not unreasonable. These veteran revolutionaries deserve some privileges. But why must it be so much?"[69]

RULES ABOUT WHEN TO RETIRE

The State Council measures issued in June 1978 were similar to previous measures in an important way. As in past decades, they pointed to poor health and inability to continue work, not old age per se, as reasons for cadres to retire. The regulations did set retirement age guidelines for the majority of cadres, but these determined eligibility for pensions and benefits and in no sense mandated retirement at specified ages. More to the point, until 1982 old age was not intrinsically a reason for cadres to consider retirement. Rather, retirement was for cadres whose health prevented them from performing their official duties. The rules acknowledged that old age generally brought with it some decline that could affect ability to work, but the rationales for cadre retirement were two vague intervening variables: poor health and inability to work normally.[70]

The lack of an explicit, direct link between old age and retirement seems to have been a policy choice, not an oversight. This is suggested by a comparison of cadre retirement regulations with regulations on the retirement of workers. The June 1978 Provisional Measures on Arrangements for Aged, Weak, Ill, and Disabled Cadres applied to cadres whose "age and state of health preclude continuing

wuyuan, Guanyu fagei lixiu tuixiu renyuan shenghuo butie fei de tongzhi, 10 Jan. 1985; Laodong bu renshi bu caizheng bu quanguo zong gonghui, Guanyu lituixiu renyuan shenghuo butie fei de tongzhi, 23 May 1988.

[68] Hu, "Lituixiu ganbu ying tongyi guanli."

[69] Interview subject no. 11.

[70] Guowuyuan, Guanyu anzhi lao ruo bing can ganbu de zanxing banfa, 2 June 1978.

normal work." The regulations on retirement of workers, issued at the same time, applied to "old workers and workers who have lost the ability to work due to illness or disability." Cadres meeting the criteria specified above "could retire." Workers meeting the criteria specified "should retire." Even the name of the regulations applying to workers, Provisional Measures on the Retirement of Workers, suggests a different policy orientation.[71]

In 1980 the government did issue regulations stating that cadres who were unable to work normally "should retire." But they applied exclusively to the minority of cadres for whom no retirement age guidelines had been set. Even with the stronger language, the rules cited inability to work normally rather than old age per se as the reason to retire.[72]

Yet another contrast is contained in a government document protesting the pro forma nature of certain retirements. It complained that some workers who had formally retired actually remained employed at their posts.[73] No comparable protest was issued in documents on retirement of cadres in 1978–81. Also, workers who did not retire were, in principle at least, to have their salaries stopped.[74] No comparable arrangement existed for cadres.

In February 1982 the Central Committee passed regulations that finally established age-based retirement from office as a general rule, without reference to health or ability to perform official duties.[75] The government followed up with a more detailed version in April 1982.[76] The rules set retirement ages generally at fifty-five for women and sixty for men. Cadres in specified positions of leadership were to retire later, at sixty (for women and men) or sixty-five, depending on position.[77] Policy makers introduced some flexibility in a supplemen-

[71] Guowuyuan, Guanyu gongren tuixiu tuizhi de zanxing banfa, 2 June 1978.

[72] Guowuyuan, Guanyu lao ganbu lizhi xiuyang de zanxing guiding, 7 Oct. 1980.

[73] Guowuyuan, Guanyu yange zhixing gongren tuixiu tuizhi zanxing banfa de tongzhi, 7 Nov. 1981.

[74] "Guanyu gongren tuixiu tuizhi shi xiang de wenda."

[75] Zhonggong zhongyang, Guanyu jianli lao ganbu tuixiu [sic] zhidu de jueding, 20 Feb. 1982.

[76] Guowuyuan, Guanyu fabu lao ganbu lizhi xiuyang zhidu de ji xiang guiding, 10 Apr. 1982.

[77] The following cadres, men and women, were to retire at sixty-five: government ministers and Central Committee department heads, provincial party committee first secretaries, and provincial governors. The following were to retire at sixty: deputy ministers and Central Committee department deputy heads, provincial party committee secretaries (other than first secretaries), provincial deputy governors, bureau chiefs and their deputies in State Council and Central Committee bureaus, heads and deputy heads in provincial party committee and provincial government departments, prefec-

tary rule: cadres whose poor health prevented them from working normally could retire early and cadres who were needed at work and whose health was good could postpone retirement, with party committee approval.

Clearly, the supplementary rule provided room for discretion. Nonetheless, health and ability to work were no longer first or usual considerations for retirement. Decisions on retirement were usually to be based on the objective standard of age alone. The change had important practical implications. So long as health and ability to work were an integral part of decisions on retirement, as in 1978–81, the decisions had to be made on a case-by-case basis. Necessarily they involved deliberations on how those vague and subjective standards applied to particular cadres at or past specified retirement ages. Retired cadres pointed out that the arrangement had left plenty of room for conflict over interpretation. For example, one noted: "[Without age-based retirement] it was difficult to distinguish who should retire from who should not retire. If it is too flexible, it is the same as not having it at all."[78] And another remarked: "Of course, I realize that [age-based retirement] is simplistic because it lacks concrete analysis of particular situations. . . . But if we do concrete analysis and retire some but not others, those who are retired will ask: 'Why me and not you?' "[79] With an explicit, direct relationship between old age and retirement and retirement at fixed ages as the general rule, the decisions on retirement could be more or less standardized.

In late 1984 and in 1985 policy makers took measures to eliminate erosion of standards and statuses at the top. The supplementary rule that allowed cadres in good health who were needed at work to postpone their retirement had created a loophole. Leaders at middle and lower levels were using the rule to justify remaining at their workposts. Policy makers took steps to ensure that retirement statuses remained as officially established and that a new kind of exemption for leaders at lower levels did not emerge from lax interpretation of the rule.

The first of those steps involved the promotion of two models—the Beijing municipal government and the Anshan Iron and Steel Company. The promotion signaled a policy of strict interpretation of the supplementary rule. The Beijing government had transformed the composition of its leadership corps by requiring that cadres over age sixty be dropped from leading groups, new leaders be under age

tural party committee secretaries and deputy secretaries, and prefectural commissioners and deputy commissioners.

[78] Interview subject no. 21.
[79] Interview subject no. 18.

fifty-five, and 61 percent of leading groups at the various levels under the government be transformed. Anshan Iron and Steel had transformed its leading groups by requiring that cadres over age fifty-five be dropped from leading groups, new leaders be under age fifty, and 80 percent of leading groups in the enterprise be transformed.[80]

At about the same time, the Central Committee issued a notice noting that in the 1982–84 period, many provincial-level leaders who were old and unable to do any real work had retired to advisory commissions, people's congresses, and political consultative conferences. The Central Committee statement reiterated the policy that only cadres who were able actually to work were eligible to postpone retirement. No organization was to be used as a substitute for full retirement for cadres who were too old or unwell actually to do any work—even if these cadres were leaders. The decision also stipulated that cadres aged seventy and above had to retire from the three organizations at the provincial level. The Central Committee decision asserted (without explanation) that the situation at the national level was different and the policy did not apply there.[81]

The effort to close loopholes that had been used by leaders at lower levels was revived again in late 1985, when the Central Committee's Organization Department sent out an urgent telegram on retirement procedures. The regulation contained in the telegram expressed less flexibility on those to be considered under the supplementary rule. Veteran cadres in positions of leadership who had reached the age of retirement, excepting those "who are truly needed at work and whose remaining at work has been approved by the organs responsible" were "urgently requested" to step down and complete retirement procedures.[82]

RULE ENFORCEMENT

Before 1978 cadre retirement was fully self-enforced. Of course, with no norm of cadre retirement or other appeals to private interests, this completely voluntary retirement yielded very little actual retirement.[83] After 1978 policy makers began to adopt measures to involve

[80] The models were promoted in a September 1984 circular issued by the Central Committee's General Office. *Daily Report: China*, 5 Sept. 1984, K3.

[81] Wang, "Guanyu ganbu 'sihua' he ganbu zhidu gaige de jige wenti."

[82] Zhonggong zhongyang zuzhi bu, Guanyu zhuajin banli lixiu shouxu de tongzhi (dianbao), 12 Nov. 1985, 122.

[83] See Yi, Li, and Hu, eds., *Guojia gongwuyuan gailun*, 211.

different groups in enforcing rules on when to retire. Yet for the entire ten-year period, policy makers formally observed the principle of voluntary retirement. At no time in this period did they mandate cadre retirement without the express consent of the cadre. Nor did they ever at any time establish penalties for failure to retire. But as the stipulated monetary incentives to retire were small to nonexistent, cadres at or past retirement age could not be counted on to take the initiative to retire. This was why others had also to be involved in the process to promote the appropriate perspective on retirement.

The principle of retirement with consent was introduced early (in June 1978), as was its corollary—the idea that some form of "ideological work" (*sixiang gongzuo*) was needed to produce a willingness to retire.[84] Middlemen at the workplace were assigned responsibility for this work.[85] Yet policy makers gave them little reason to make a serious effort at enforcing retirement through ideological work or any other means in 1978–81. The disagreement among policy makers on the urgency of retirement was plainly evident, the policy contained no mandated retirement ages or objective measures of performance to constrain middlemen, and the policies of restoration and *chuan bang dai* provided legitimate and probably more popular alternatives to immediate retirement. Moreover, party regulations and government regulations differed in nuance. With the exception of the 1980 Central Committee resolution to abolish lifelong tenure, the party organization failed to issue a document that unambiguously promoted cadre retirement (as government documents did) until February 1982. Instead, party documents focused on the policy of restoration. And because cadre management is a particularly party-dominated issue area, the lack of clear party support for retirement could be expected to blunt any action implications in government regulations. In short, while recognizing that some work was required to get cadres to retire voluntarily, in 1978–81 policy makers effectively defined retirement as an option that eligible cadres were more or less free to choose or reject on an individual basis.

This situation changed in a major way in 1982. Policy makers clarified the rules about when cadres ought to retire by introducing an unambiguous and objective direct link between age and retirement. This meant interpretation of the rules could be fairly straightforward. In addition, policy makers provided more opportunities for middlemen to actively solicit the consent of cadres at or past the stip-

---

[84] Guowuyuan, Guanyu anzhi lao ruo bing can ganbu de zanxing banfa, 2 June 1978.

[85] Zhonggong zhongyang zuzhi bu, Guanyu banli lao ganbu lizhi xiuyang shouxu de tongzhi, 30 Oct. 1982.

ulated ages of retirement. From 1982 through 1984 retirement was implemented as group retirement, in an intensive campaign style, and with the combined involvement of middlemen at the workplace, immediate targets of the retirement policy, and their younger co-workers.

Policy makers linked retirement to structural reform and the transformation of leading groups, two campaigns that were begun at the top in 1982 and conducted at the provincial level and below in 1983–84. Structural reform called for the reduction of staff and departments in party and government. It was aimed at improving policy coordination. Transformation of leading groups was aimed at improving the quality of leadership by changing the composition of the leadership corps in departments and local party committees and governments. New leading groups were to include cadres who were more educated, professionally competent, and younger. Quotas were set for both campaigns.[86]

Retirement was a prerequisite of success in both campaigns. Retirement of older cadres reduced staff generally and retirement of older leaders was necessary to rejuvenate leading groups. The Central Committee's Organization Department instructed communist party members to observe party discipline in the campaigns and to submit to whatever arrangements were made for them.[87] In so doing, it presented retirement as part of the obligation of party members to accept instructions from a higher party organization.

Although policy makers apparently never introduced specific instructions on the matter,[88] it was common practice for cadres to express their willingness to retire in personal written requests, usually addressed to leaders at the workplace. It was a nearly universal informal rule that the administrative procedures that culminated in retirement could not be initiated without a personal written request to retire. That is, without a written request, middlemen had no basis to take action.[89]

Middlemen at the workplace were instructed to conduct ideological work to persuade older cadres of their obligation to retire. Because

[86] On the campaigns see deB. Mills, "Generational Change in China"; Forster, "The Reform of Provincial Party Committees in China" and "Repudiation of the Cultural Revolution in China"; Lee, "Deng Xiaoping's Reform of the Chinese Bureaucracy"; Lieberthal, "China in 1982."

[87] See *Renmin ribao*, 12 Feb. 1983, 1.

[88] Chen and Wang, interview, 7 Nov. 1988.

[89] Su and Lin, *Guojia gongwuyuan zhidu jianghua*, 340. This observation is supported by my own interviews with retired cadres and with officials in the Ministry of Personnel.

few cadres had retired prior to 1982 and the policies of restoration and *chuan bang dai* had been emphasized in 1978–80, in many workplaces there were quite a few cadres at or past retirement age. Rather than carrying out ideological work simply on an individual basis, middlemen responsible for implementing policy called meetings that brought together older cadres with their younger co-workers. At the meetings they explained cadre retirement policy and its rationale—the importance of regularly rejuvenating and transforming the cadre corps and how this related to the campaign for modernization. The explicit, direct link between age and retirement freed middlemen from case-by-case analysis and allowed them to lump older cadres together and retire them in groups.

It is important to point out the participation of younger cadres in the process of achieving the voluntary retirement of their older co-workers. Younger cadres were a natural ally of policy makers and middlemen in getting older cadres to retire and in building a cadre retirement norm. The 1982 Central Committee decision on retirement noted: "At the same time as veteran cadres retire, we must boldly promote young and middle-aged cadres to main positions of leadership. These are two sides to the same question. The Central Committee finds it necessary to remind party comrades that when the party took power, party leaders at all levels were young or relatively young. We must trust young cadres now."[90]

By not enforcing cadre retirement, younger cadres would only be punishing themselves. Since there are a limited number of cadre and leadership positions, there cannot be promotion without retirement. In the words of one younger cadre, remarking on an older co-worker who appeared reluctant to retire: "He wants to hold on to power to get some advantage. His advantage is my disadvantage. The more he gets, the less we get. This is a contradiction between two generations. He is taking [what should be] our place. He knows this, we know this."[91]

By opening up discussion of retirement to all cadres, rather than only older cadres, policy makers provided an opportunity for younger cadres to make the connection between the retirement of the old and the promotion of the young. They gave younger cadres a private reason and a public rationale to take up the task of voluntarily enforcing cadre retirement.

By 1985 policy makers judged that campaign-style retirement had

[90] Zhonggong zhongyang, Guanyu jianli lao ganbu tuixiu [*sic*] zhidu de jueding, 20 Feb. 1982, 10.
[91] Interview subject no. 77.

achieved important gains and that massive readjustments would probably no longer be necessary.[92] As a consequence, middlemen at the workplace were given sole official responsibility for the ideological work to produce retirement with consent. Interpreting and applying rules about when cadres retire was to take place in a dialogue between middlemen and cadres at or near the stipulated ages of retirement. However, written requests to retire were still the common practice.

Finally in August 1988, more than ten years after introducing their first set of regulations on cadre retirement, policy makers officially abolished what had never actually been official. The Central Committee's Organization Department and the Ministry of Personnel jointly stated that there would be no more written requests to retire.[93] They instructed middlemen at the workplace to notify cadres one month in advance and to process the retirement within the month after cadres reached the ages of retirement. From the perspective of policy makers in 1988, retirement had become purely an administrative procedure. All responsibility for persuasion and other enforcement was relinquished to the unofficial enforcers—including, of course, the immediate policy targets themselves. In effect, policy makers assumed a cadre retirement norm was already in place.

EXEMPLARY CONFORMERS

The centralization of political power at the top, typical of communist systems, meant that the scope and severity of defects due to lifelong tenure tended to be greater than at lower levels. And because revolutionary seniority had been rewarded over the years, top leaders tended to be older than cadres at lower levels. Not surprisingly then, critics participating in the 1980 critique of lifelong tenure focused particular attention on cadres in the very highest positions of leadership.

Yet another stated rationale for the focus on the top was that top leaders by their actions provided signals to cadres at lower levels. Critics of lifelong tenure argued that cadres were accustomed to policy changes, often major and sudden and followed by reversals. If top leaders were not prepared to demonstrate a commitment to abolition of lifelong tenure, the consensus on the policy and, consequently, its

[92] See Zhu, "Lun ganbu de xinlao jiaoti."

[93] Chen and Wang, interview, 7 Nov. 1988. See also Shen, "Guojia gongwuyuan de tuixiu tuizhi zhidu."

lastingness would be viewed as questionable at best. In short, there had to be exemplars at the very top. As one group of critics observed:

> Practice has shown that whether or not positions of leadership at the top are lifelong directly influences whether or not leadership positions at the various levels in the localities are lifelong. Only if leading cadres at the top set a personal example, by their actions, to abolish the lifelong tenure system, can leading cadres at the various levels in the localities be impelled to abolish the lifelong tenure system.[94]

However, policy makers ultimately addressed the issue of exemplars at the very top by stratifying the cadre retirement system—in particular, by fully exempting a number of top leaders and creating special advisory commissions to the Central Committee and provincial party committees. This rejected the logic of the argument that retirement conduct at the top served as a model for retirement at lower levels.

There were some prominent displays of retirement at the very top in the 1978–88 period, although the term "retirement" was not used and leaders who "stepped down" (*tui xia lai*) or "resigned" (*cizhi*) from office often turned up in other positions—and not always on advisory commissions. Due to the stratified character of the retirement system, top leaders who took up other important positions were not in fact violating rules or deviating from nascent norms. Even with the exit of office of many at the top, there were many old leaders who remained.

For example, 171 old leaders stepped down from office to form the Central Advisory Commission in September 1982. But at the same time, sixteen other veterans over seventy years old were elected to the Central Committee and all but two of them turned up on the Politburo. This left the Central Committee and the Politburo with at least half of their members over age seventy.[95] Three years later, 131 old veterans handed in their resignations from the Central Committee, Central Advisory Commission, and Central Commission for Discipline Inspection. They included ten Politburo members, Ye Jianying among them. But other old veterans (Chen Yun, Li Xiannian, Peng Zhen, and Yang Shangkun) remained on the Politburo. Deng Xiaoping also remained, in his capacity as chairman of the Central Advisory Commission. Even in 1985 then, half of the Politburo member-

---

[94] Xiao et al., "Lun feichu ganbu lingdao zhiwu zhongshenzhi," 28.
[95] See Ch'en, "Peiping's Current Cadre Policy"; Tseng, "The New Leadership in Mainland China."

ship was over age seventy.[96] And while eight members stepped down in October 1987, most stepped into other positions.[97] Perhaps the least exemplary act was the replacement of seventy-nine-year-old President Li Xiannian with eighty-one-year-old Yang Shangkun in 1988.

In sum, policy makers did not point to exemplary conformers at the very top to serve as models for leaders at lower levels or ordinary cadres. They did make use of the party newspaper to promote exemplary conformers below the top. In 1978 the *Renmin ribao* printed exactly one article specifically on the issue of cadre retirement. By 1982 articles promoting cadre retirement were numerous and important enough to merit their own heading in the index. The number of articles peaked dramatically in 1982 and began to decline after that. Articles in the *Renmin ribao* for the 1978–88 period numbered as follows: one in 1978, four in 1979, seventeen in 1980, twelve in 1981, seventy-eight in 1982, fifty-four in 1983, fifty-nine in 1984, forty-nine each in 1985 and 1986, thirty-eight in 1987, and twenty-two in 1988. About one-fourth of them cite praiseworthy efforts of particular localities or organizations in their veteran cadre work. Most of the rest present model veteran cadres who took the initiative to retire to make way for younger cadres.

From these accounts can be constructed a profile of model retired veteran cadres. Typically, the model retirees do not engage in leisurely activities or self-development. They conduct investigations in the localities and at workplaces (often earning the label "busybody") and present reports and suggestions to leaders and departments. They perform services for the community—rising early, eschewing noontime naps, often neglecting their health. They never accept remuneration. They sometimes donate their lifetime savings of thousands of *yuan* to the community to set up a reading room for delinquent youth or a clinic for a poor rural community—the community to which they have returned, forsaking the comforts of city living. And model retired veterans do not shirk low-status service work or manual labor.

While no model is completely representative, an excellent example

[96] See Fang, "Personnel Changes in the CCP's Central Leadership"; Li, "The Recent Changes in the Peking Leadership."

[97] Moreover, in the case of Deng (as Zhao Ziyang later revealed), party leaders secretly agreed that he would be consulted on all major policy decisions, despite his retirement from all positions except chairman of the Central Military Commission. Of course, most people were ignorant of the deal until Zhao's revelation in May 1989. See the account in *South China Morning Post*, 22 May 1989, 6.

of the kind of activity promoted in the accounts is found in seventy-year-old An Xiujie. He stands out among a large number of humble and generous-spirited retired veterans singled out for praise and emulation in 1982. After his retirement, An wanted to continue to make himself useful. He decided to occupy himself by collecting dung to be used as manure. The *Renmin ribao* describes his extraordinary commitment to this humble task as follows:

> Every day he goes out to collect dung. Winter and spring, year in and year out, An Xiujie's dung basket never leaves his shoulder. People tease him: "You have really become fanatical about collecting dung." He replies: "What's wrong with being fanatical about collecting dung? So long as there is a need, I will go on doing it." [Over the years] An Xiujie has worn out twelve dung baskets; he has shed his sweat in and around Zhengding county seat; a layer of thick calluses covers each shoulder. He has collected 700,000 *jin* of dung.[98]

Retired veterans featured in the *Renmin ribao* also sell breakfast foods at roadside stalls, clean railroad stations, and set potted plants in public places. They devote their time and energies to serving the people, amply earning the title policy makers commonly used for revolutionary veterans—"national treasures."

SUMMARY

From 1978 through 1988, policy makers promoted measures that have created a few "sub-norms" rather than a single norm applicable to all cadres. They instituted different retirement statuses that distinguish leaders from ordinary cadres and veteran revolutionaries from postrevolutionaries. Differences between the groups are represented in more than the variation in pension levels. Policy makers declared leaders at the very top, including themselves, fully exempt from retirement and set up positions of semiretirement to advisory positions for leaders lower down in the political hierarchy. Veteran cadres as a group were treated differently enough from postrevolutionaries to create a general perception of upper and lower classes of retired cadres, respectively.

Policy makers focused on different kinds of measures at different times throughout the decade. At first, they relied nearly exclusively on argument, promoting a critique of lifelong tenure that blamed it for all sorts of defects in the exercise of power. Older cadres were

[98] *Renmin ribao*, 10 June 1982, 4.

left, however, to consider as a private matter the relevance of the appeal to themselves: rules on retirement indicated only that cadres who were in poor health and unable to work could retire and perhaps should do so.

In 1982 policy makers introduced some new measures. For veteran cadres they associated retirement with something familiar and presumably appealing by presenting retirement as a new work assignment. A barrage of newspaper articles provided examples of model retired cadres carrying on the party's revolutionary tradition of serving the people. A campaign environment, lasting through 1984, put pressure on veterans to accept the assignment as part of their duty as communist party members. The campaign also involved younger cadres in the process of applying tacit pressure on older cadres to retire. Younger cadres proved to be natural allies of policy makers because of the explicit link between retirement of older cadres and promotion of younger cadres.

Beginning in about 1985, policy makers relaxed the pace of their efforts to build a retirement norm. Articles in the press dealing with retirement declined significantly. And retirement was no longer carried out in groups. Explicit discussions about retirement became less public. Instead of large meetings at the workplace, middlemen charged with implementing policy sought out older cadres on an individual basis and urged them to write a request to retire.

By 1988, policy makers seem to have concluded cadre retirement no longer required state-sponsored public pressure or individual "ideological work." They abolished the written request to retire, eliminating the heart-to-heart talks between middlemen and cadres at retirement age. For the state, cadre retirement became purely an administrative procedure.

What explains the changes in policy measures? Part of the explanation is endogenous. For years, policy makers did not reach agreement on decisive measures to retire cadres. The discord at the top was reflected partly in the failure of the party organization to issue even a single document unambiguously supporting cadre retirement, as government documents had, until 1982. Instead, party documents issued in 1978–81 contained a message that effectively replaced the policy to retire cadres with a policy to restore veterans to positions of power lost in the Cultural Revolution. With the protection of their own interests by exempting leaders at the top, policy makers could begin to work out measures to retire other cadres.

But part of the explanation for policy change is found not at the top of the policy process but at middle and lower levels. Middlemen charged with implementing policy, older cadres targeted by the policy, and younger cadres eager to get ahead responded to the initiatives of policy makers. Their responses forced policy makers to react in turn with new initiatives. Some of these reactions I have described in this chapter. Others are left out of the account because they are better understood in the context of a discussion of how middlemen and older and younger cadres responded. The next three chapters take up that discussion.

CHAPTER THREE

The Decision to Retire

HAVING DESCRIBED policy measures, I begin to address here the following question: how did cadres targeted for retirement and middlemen charged with implementing the policy respond? Building a norm of cadre retirement comprised three distinct policy objectives for cadres: age-based exit from office, understanding of retirement as a normative standard, and real disengagement from official regular duties after retirement. This chapter takes up the first of these objectives, the act of retirement at specified ages.

I begin with the most obvious issue, aggregate incidence of retirement, and try to sort out the extent to which policy makers succeeded in their efforts to retire cadres who had reached the ages specified in government regulations. Then I shift the level of analysis to the individual to discover the differences among cadres in their response. I look at variation in how cadres responded and describe the process of informal bargaining that was part of many decisions to retire.

AGGREGATE INCIDENCE OF RETIREMENT

An obvious measure of the extent to which policy makers managed to get cadres to retire from office is aggregate incidence of cadre retirement.[1] Table 3.1 presents statistics on the incidence of special and regular retirement of cadres for 1980–88.[2]

More than a decade after the introduction of cadre retirement policy, a total of 1,630,000—about 65 percent of the nearly 2.5 million revolutionary veterans alive in 1978—had retired from office. The

[1] The statistical compilation I used provides only figures on retirement of veteran cadres and only through 1982. See Guojia tongji ju shehui tongji si, *Zhongguo laodong gongze tongji ziliao 1949–1985*, 210. Figures on veteran cadre retirement are printed annually in the *Renmin ribao* from 1982 through 1986 and they are about the same as those I obtained in interviews. I found no published figures on retirement of postrevolutionary cadres. As regularly retired personnel, retired postrevolutionary cadres are lumped together in statistics with the millions of (regularly) retired workers.

[2] Note that incidence of retirement (and cumulative incidence of retirement) does not consider the incidence of death after retirement and is, therefore, not the same as number of cadres in retirement.

TABLE 3.1
Aggregate Incidence of Cadre Retirement, 1980–88

Year	Specially Retired Cadres		Regularly Retired Cadres	
	Yearly	Cumulative	Yearly	Cumulative
1980	—	—	660,000	660,000
1981	—	—	570,000	1,230,000
1982	—	300,000	320,000	1,550,000
1983	420,000	720,000	500,000	2,050,000
1984	220,000	940,000	230,000	2,280,000
1985	180,000	1,120,000	280,000	2,560,000
1986	260,000	1,380,000	370,000	2,930,000
1987	140,000	1,520,000	430,000	3,360,000
1988	110,000	1,630,000	—	3,120,000

Sources: Guojia tongji ju shehui tongji si, ed., *Zhongguo laodong gongze tongji ziliao 1949–1985* (Beijing: Zhongguo tongji chubanshe, 1987), 210; Chen Liang (Deputy Director of Special Retirement Division, Cadre Retirement Bureau, Ministry of Personnel) and Wang Wenbo (Director of Cadre Retirement Bureau General Office, Ministry of Personnel), interviewed in Beijing, 7 Nov. 1988; Wang Wenbo, interviewed in Beijing, 9 Feb. 1990.

Note: Wang Wenbo (Director of Cadre Retirement Bureau General Office, Ministry of Personnel) informed me in early 1990 that the method of computing the number of regularly retired cadres in previous years was not quite accurate but that the cumulative figure of 3,120,000 for 1988 was accurate. My guess is that the discrepancy between the 1987 and 1988 figures reflects the counting of cadres who retired regularly and then had their status changed to specially retired through an investigation of their case or a policy adjustment. Wang Wenbo, interviewed in Beijing, 9 Feb. 1990.

pace of their retirement over the roughly ten-year period was uneven. A government official working on cadre retirement policy informed me that the actual incidence of special retirement before 1982 was practically nil.[3] Therefore the figure of 300,000 retired at the end of 1982 probably reflects almost exclusively retirement in that year alone. This means approximately 44 percent (720,000 cadres in all) of special retirements for the entire period probably took place in two years, 1982 and 1983. After 1983 the incidence of special retirement is lower. It averages 220,000 a year in 1984–86 and drops off to an average of 125,000 a year in 1987–88.

Regular retirement also exhibits a pronounced clumping of retire-

[3] Wang Xingming (Deputy Director of Cadre Retirement Division, Veteran Cadre Bureau, Ministry of Labor and Personnel), interviewed in Beijing, 24 Nov. 1986.

ment in the earlier years. By the end of 1982, for example, more than 1.5 million postrevolutionary cadres had retired—representing 46 percent of all such cadres retired in the 1980–87 period.[4] Interestingly, the numbers decline significantly from year to year in this early period: from 660,000 in 1980, to 570,000 in 1981, down to 320,000 in 1982. And after 1983 the pattern observed in special retirement is reversed. Instead of dropping off in later years, the incidence of regular retirement picks up. It averages 255,000 a year in 1984–85 and jumps to 400,000 a year in 1986–87.

If we consider lifelong tenure as the status quo ante, then the figures indicated in Table 3.1 are evidence of an important change. Policy makers succeeded in getting substantially large numbers of cadres to retire. But because retirement is essentially age-based exit from office, figures on aggregate incidence of retirement are insufficient for assessing *how* successful policy makers were in getting cadres to retire. We need a sense of how many cadres could be expected to reach the government regulated ages of retirement from 1978 through 1988. This is by no means easy.

In the past decade, the Chinese have made available figures on the age structure of the cadre contingent. A careful look at the figures made public to date, however, forces me to conclude that serious gaps, noncomparable categories, and contradictory evidence confound the building of a reliable age profile of cadres. In constructing a profile of expected retirement, we are forced, therefore, to make inferences from other kinds of data.

Regarding veteran cadres alive in 1980, we have the following information: 10,000 joined the communists in the Revolutionary Civil Wars (1924–37), 300,000 joined in the Anti-Japanese War (1937–45), and 2,190,000 joined in the War of Liberation (1945–49).[5] To construct a profile of their expected retirement we must first make an informed guess at a modal age of recruitment to the communists. In 1982, referring to veteran revolutionaries recruited before 1943, Deng Xiaoping estimated that most were recruited at the age of eighteen or twenty.[6] Obviously, the revolutionaries who will most affect the way the profile looks are not the smaller number of survivors who joined before 1943 but the more than two million War of Liberation veterans. From what we know, a good number of these two million had been recruited to other causes or armies in their younger years.[7]

[4] I used the 1987 unadjusted cumulative figure to compute a percentage.

[5] "Selecting Young Cadres for Leading Posts." These figures correspond roughly with figures made available in other official publications.

[6] Deng, "Zai zhongyang guwen weiyuanhui di yi ce quanti huiyi shang de jianghua."

[7] This includes intellectuals and peasants. See Pepper, *Civil War in China*.

They were probably past their teens when they finally joined the communists. It seems reasonable, then, to assume an older rather than younger age of recruitment in constructing a retirement profile. On this basis, I chose to use Deng's higher estimate of twenty years old.[8]

Policy makers set different ages of retirement for women and men. That difference also enters into the construction of a profile of expected retirement. Lacking figures for the relevant periods, I assumed that the proportion of women cadres for each recruitment period did not differ significantly from the 1951 figure of 8 percent.[9] The probable bias of such an assumption is to exaggerate the proportion of women recruits in the early years. However, the consequence of such a bias is not serious, as the number of cadres involved is relatively small. Also, cadres recruited in the early years were presumably old enough to be due for retirement by 1978, whether we assume a retirement age of fifty-five or sixty.

While recruitment figures categorized by war period allow us to identify time spans in which we can expect specifiable numbers of veterans to retire, we really need more precise information. When we are trying to assess the impact of policy within only a decade, it is not very helpful to know, for example, that about two million War of Liberation veterans could be expected to retire forty years later—some time between 1985 and 1989. A breakdown by year of recruitment is, unfortunately, not available. But we do have more or less yearly data on the growth of the communist party. These can be used as a basis for estimation.

I used Franz Schurmann's figures on communist party membership for the Anti-Japanese War and War of Liberation periods,[10] treating the percentage increase in membership for the year or years indicated as a proxy for the percentage of revolutionaries recruited in those years and alive in 1980.[11] For example, 9 percent of the net recruitment to the party from April 1945 to October 1949, roughly the War of Liberation years, occurred in 1948. Applying that proportion to the more than two million War of Liberation veterans alive in 1980 produces an estimate of 200,000 surviving recruits of 1948. If we assume twenty as the modal age of recruitment and 8 percent as the

[8] Below, I discuss the sensitivity of the profile to the assumed modal age of recruitment, what it would look like if we assumed an even older age, and other information that provides perspective on the reliability of the profile.

[9] The figure is from "International Working Women's Day."

[10] The breakdown is not needed for pre-1937 recruits, who could all be expected to retire by 1978.

[11] Schurmann, *Ideology and Organization in Communist China*, 129.

FIGURE 3.1
Expected and Actual Retirement of Veteran Cadres, 1978–88

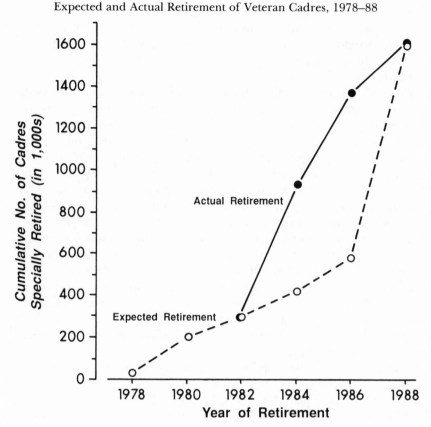

Note: 1982 is the first year for which figures on special retirement are available. The 1982 figure is a cumulative figure for special retirement in 1978–82.

proportion of women in the group, then we can expect about 20,000 of the female recruits of 1948 and 180,000 of the male recruits to retire in 1983 and 1988 respectively. Similar computations yield the profile of expected retirement of veteran cadres shown in Figure 3.1, which also reproduces actual retirement figures for comparison.

By the end of 1982, the first year for which a figure on actual retirement is available for comparison, policy makers had succeeded in retiring from office as many veterans as were due to retire if men retired at sixty and women at fifty-five. After that initial period and through 1986, a comparison of expected retirement with actual retirement produces a surprising result: a large discrepancy between the two, in a direction indicating many cases of early retirement! After 1986 the gap begins to close so that by the end of 1988, expected retirement closely matches actual retirement.

The profile is no more than a reasonable guess, based on very limited information. The most crucial piece of missing information is, of course, the modal age of recruitment for War of Liberation veterans. A difference of even a year or two from the assumed recruitment age of twenty makes a considerable difference in how the profile looks. However, even if we assume a modal recruitment age of twenty-two, for example, a comparison between expected and actual retirement produces similar results up to about 1986. Only by the end of 1986 does the profile begin to diverge significantly from Figure 3.1.

Other kinds of information lend support to the approximation shown in Figure 3.1, as opposed to models assuming an older (or younger) modal age of recruitment. Most importantly, other sources corroborate the surprising finding of early retirement. My own survey in Jilin as well as a survey conducted by the Chinese themselves finds a large proportion of cadres who retired early—that is, before the age of retirement specified in government regulations.[12] Policy makers publicly discussed the phenomenon of early retirement in 1983.[13] And early retirement is not as puzzling as it may seem. Later in the chapter I explain why many cadres had a propensity to retire (and middlemen a propensity to enforce) above and beyond retirement policy prescriptions.

Clearly, it would be helpful to complete the analysis by computing the expected retirement of postrevolutionary cadres recruited in the early 1950s. We know, for example, that 2,353,000 cadres were recruited in the three years after the communist victory.[14] Unfortunately, we lack the most basic data with which to construct a profile of retirement for postrevolutionary cadres. Although we have figures on growth of the cadre contingent in the 1950s, we do not know when those recruited as cadres in that period joined the communists. In particular, there is a risk of double counting: with revolutionary seniority as a basis for recruitment and promotion, it is likely that many veteran revolutionaries became cadres after the founding of

[12] A major survey that randomly sampled specially retired cadres who had retired before September 1983 in Ha'erbin city found 60 percent early retirement. Among the 570 respondents, 56 percent of the men surveyed were below the age of sixty and 41 percent of the women surveyed were below the age of fifty-five at the time the survey was conducted, in 1983 and 1984! Ha'erbin shi shehui kexue yanjiu suo shehuixue yanjiu shi, "Ha'erbin shi lixiu ganbu zhuangkuang diaocha baogao (shang)."

[13] See *Renmin ribao*, 9 Sept. 1983, 3; *Daily Report: China*, 23 Sept. 1983, Q1, and 2 Dec. 1983, Q1.

[14] Emerson, *Administrative and Technical Manpower in the People's Republic of China*, 37.

the People's Republic of China. In this section, then, I leave the discussion of how well policy makers did in getting postrevolutionaries to retire at the purely descriptive level.

Were policy makers successful in getting cadres to retire at specified ages? The description and analysis here indicate that policy had an important impact: large numbers of cadres retired. It also suggests that many of them retired early. This overfulfillment of quotas does not necessarily reflect successful implementation. If the policy objective is age-based exit from office, not simply the creation of a new form of exit, it is by no means clear that early retirement is a good thing from the perspective of policy makers. Early retirement distorts the relationship between age and exit and obscures the generalization that is part of a retirement norm. It also increases the financial burden on the state. In fact, policy makers did not view early retirement as successful implementation. An official at the Ministry of Personnel summarized the perspective of the ministry in unambiguous terms: "There are age guidelines for cadre retirement. These age guidelines are part of state regulations. Violating the guidelines on age of retirement is not considered normal. In particular, early retirement is not normal. Success of the policy is [reflected] only in retirement according to the age guidelines stipulated in state regulations."[15]

That many cadres seem to have responded to policy by retiring early does not mean, of course, that cadres wanted to retire or that many did not also retire late. Aggregate-level analysis cannot address questions about who retired when and why. For a more refined understanding of how cadres responded and variation among cadres in their responses, I shift the level of analysis to the individual.

MATERIAL INDUCEMENTS AND AGE-BASED EXIT

Age-based exit from office means that any variation in when cadres retire can essentially be accounted for by different general standards set for different kinds of cadres—men and women, high-ranking and low-ranking, for example. But although policy makers aimed at these kinds of standardized outcomes, they also distinguished among cadres with different rewards, which may be seen as incentives to retire. If individual cadres themselves had anything to do with the decision to retire, then we might expect these incentives to have had an impact

[15] Chen Liang (Deputy Director of Special Retirement Division, Cadre Retirement Bureau, Ministry of Personnel) and Wang Wenbo (Director of Cadre Retirement Bureau General Office, Ministry of Personnel), interviewed in Beijing, 7 Nov. 1988.

on outcomes. Different appeals might produce different outcomes, such as early (and late) retirement.

One of the distinctions was a monetary inducement reflected in pensions that ranged from 60 to 117 percent of pre-retirement salary. Another distinction, not monetary but nonetheless material, was made in how revolutionaries and postrevolutionaries were treated after retirement. Interestingly, retired cadres interviewed told a story that strongly emphasized differences between revolutionaries and postrevolutionaries and the effect of bureaucratic rank, rather than amount of pension only. As an explanation of why different cadres retired at different times, their story is strongly intuitive in the Chinese context and can be evaluated with inferential statistics.

For pensions to have a significant differential impact on when cadres choose to retire, the difference in amount of pension has itself to be significantly large. It seems reasonable to expect, for example, that cadres eligible for 75 percent of salary as pension will act much the same as those eligible for 80 percent but rather differently than those eligible for 100 percent. Similarly, we might expect to find little impact on the decision to retire when comparing across a set of cadres with pensions of 100, 108, 113, and 116 percent. This partially explains why retired cadres interviewed tended to conflate pension differences with differences between revolutionaries and postrevolutionaries. The pension difference that matters and is most salient is the most typical big difference that emerged in 1982—between most postrevolutionaries at or near the age of retirement (who, having worked for twenty years, were eligible for 75 percent of salary) and most revolutionaries (who, as veterans of the 1945–49 War of Liberation, were eligible for 100 percent).

But material inducements were not restricted to money alone. Policy makers also distinguished among cadres by singling out revolutionaries as deserving of special treatment. Certainly revolutionaries, as a generally older group of cadres, were by definition more immediate targets of retirement policy. That by itself seems sufficient cause for the policy's initial focus on them. Whatever the rationale, the result was a cadre retirement system that treated revolutionaries as special from the very first but even more so beginning in 1982, when revolutionary service alone qualified a cadre for special retirement status. As the account in chapter 2 observed, policy makers set up veteran cadre departments to look after the needs of retired veterans and implement a policy of preferential treatment in matters affecting their general welfare, such as housing, medical care, and the provision of daily necessities.

The special treatment for revolutionaries compared to postrevolutionaries was bound to have an impact beyond that produced by the pension gap. Because cadre retirement policy was oriented to meet the needs of veterans, postrevolutionaries considering retirement confronted much greater uncertainty about the future than did revolutionaries. Policy toward retired postrevolutionaries was far less developed. Further, veteran cadre departments provided retired revolutionaries with an institutional channel particularly for them, a channel through which they could voice grievances and gain access to goods and opportunities. Retired postrevolutionaries had no such organization. And finally, retirement policy gave assurances to veterans of priority in access to material benefits, assurances that were not extended to retired postrevolutionaries.

Such differences were emphasized by a top government official in a review of problems encountered in getting postrevolutionaries to retire. Wang Xingming noted that all regulations on regular retirement for cadres were officially "provisional" measures, creating tremendous uncertainty among postrevolutionaries and a mentality of waiting for changes and final revisions. He called attention to an overall lack of clarity about regular retirement for cadres, in contrast to the well-articulated system of special retirement for veterans. He pointed out that retirement policy stipulated pension amounts, but made no mention of benefits for retired postrevolutionaries or of who was to manage them and look after their needs.[16]

Nonmonetary material inducements such as those provided for retired veteran cadres can usually be expected to affect actions, but in the Chinese context they are likely to have an even more powerful effect. The appeal of monetary inducements presupposes the usefulness of money in obtaining goods and opportunities. In an economy where goods and opportunities are scarce and the market mechanism greatly restricted and highly inefficient in distributing them, as in the People's Republic of China, the power to obtain goods is not so strongly linked to money. Access, rather than money, is typically the critical determinant of who gets how much of what. In the words of a retired postrevolutionary: "The main difference between special retirement and regular retirement is one of benefits. Benefits are better for specially retired cadres. But also, the veteran cadre departments do a better job of taking care of specially retired cadres. They have the conditions to do a good job."[17] Probably more than the pension gap, then, it is the differential access to goods and opportunities that distinguishes retired revolutionaries from postrevolutionaries. These

[16] Wang, interview, 24 Nov. 1986, and "Chuyi ganbu tuixiu zhidu de gaige."
[17] Interview subject no. 5.

goods and opportunities include things as basic as housing and medical care, as well as perks such as annual holiday trips and transportation in cars supplied by the workplace.

But if access is so important, then we must look beyond the officially assured differences in access for retired cadres. Having a position in the bureaucracy can also offer leverage to obtain things. As Thomas Gold notes, the Chinese bureaucracy is such "a major locus and target for instrumental relations" that it "frequently assumes the form of outright corruption."[18] Retired cadres interviewed pointed out that access is often a function of bureaucratic rank. Higher-ranking positions tend to provide greater leverage, while low positions offer little. Indeed, for veteran cadres in high office, official assurances of access after retirement were usually no match for the certain leverage that derived from being in a position of power. A veteran cadre of ministerial rank provided this view from the top: "There is a problem of material goods. When people retire, they have no position to use to get things done. When they have a position, they have a lot of power. Without a position they can do nothing. They want things, for themselves and also for their children."[19] The view from the bottom, by an ordinary cadre reflecting on the issue, corroborates that of the minister:

> If a cadre is high ranking, he does not want to leave his position because then he has no power. If he has no position, no one listens to him. Power is important. Those with power do not want to retire. In China you need a broad network of social relationships. You do not want to retire and lose these relationships. Ordinary cadres . . . have no power whether they retire or not. They have no power in their position and they have no bonus [while employed] as workers do. So they want to retire. Of course, if they do not meet the standards for special retirement but only for regular retirement, they do not necessarily want to retire, particularly if their salary is low.[20]

Summing up the discussion above, material inducements can be expected to influence cadres in their decision to retire. In simple monetary terms and also when we include nonmonetary material inducements such as access and special privileges, postrevolutionaries confront a retirement future that is less appealing than that faced by veteran cadres. But the appeal of any kind of material inducement

[18] Gold, "After Comradeship," 661. For an excellent analysis of the relationship between instrumental relations and the structure of authority, see Walder, *Communist Neo-Traditionalism*, especially 162–89.

[19] Interview subject no. 3.

[20] Interview subject no. 6.

depends too on how much leverage cadres have in office. Higher-ranking cadres are less likely to find material inducements appealing because their positions provide greater access to scarce goods and opportunities than can be officially assured them after retirement.

How did differences in material inducements affect the effort to realize standardized policy outcomes—age-based exit from office? To isolate and assess the effects of pensions, nonmonetary material inducements, and bureaucratic rank on the decision to retire, I used multivariate regression analysis on a data set that combined retired cadres interviewed with respondents to the self-administered questionnaire. All cases are cadres who retired from mid-1978 through 1987.[21]

Dependent Variable. My dependent variable is not age of retirement, for that would tell us little in the analysis that follows. Rather, the dependent variable captures the idea of deviation from on-time retirement. It measures the amount and direction of difference between actual age of retirement and that prescribed in government regulations (with necessary adjustments, discussed below). It is a continuous variable and is measured in years. It takes on negative, zero, and positive values to reflect early, on-time, and late retirement, respectively.

By measuring the difference in terms of deviation from on-time retirement (rather than retirement age, for example), I take account of how standards differ by rank and sex. For example, an ordinary cadre who retires at age sixty is assigned a deviation value of +5 if female and zero if male, because prescribed ages of retirement for ordinary cadres are fifty-five for women and sixty for men. If the cadre were of bureau rank, the value would be zero regardless of sex; if a minister, the value would be −5, again regardless of sex—because prescribed ages of retirement are sixty and sixty-five respectively for these ranks and do not distinguish between men and women.

I make one adjustment to the dependent variable. Some cadres in my sample and in the population of interest were already past the age for on-time retirement when the policy was introduced in mid-1978. As constructed above, the dependent variable does not capture any element of their choice about whether to retire on time or late, in a way comparable to other cadres. For example, an ordinary male cadre who retired at age sixty-two in 1978 did not in fact choose to

---

[21] I combined the two in order to increase variance in rank. Retired cadres interviewed were typically higher in rank than questionnaire respondents and the latter included few cadres above section rank.

retire two years late. Indeed, he retired as close to on time as possible considering when retirement policy intersected with his life. In order better to reflect choices of older cadres, I adjusted the value of on-time retirement for them by adding to it the number of years past on-time retirement age in 1978. With that adjustment, the case just described, for example, is assigned a value of zero for deviation from on-time retirement.[22]

Let me give some more examples to clarify how I coded deviation from on-time retirement. A seventy-year-old division-level male cadre who retired in 1978 retired ten years later than regulations stipulate. He should have retired at age sixty. But in my coding, the dependent variable for this cadre is not seventy (his age) or ten (ten years older than sixty). Rather, it is zero because once again this cadre retired as close to on time as he could, given when the introduction of the retirement system intersected with his life. If this same cadre had retired in 1980, the dependent variable would not be seventy-two or twelve but rather +2—that is, he would be coded as two years late, given his age relationship to when the system was introduced. Similarly, then, the dependent variable for a fifty-five-year-old division-level female cadre who retired in 1980 would not be fifty-five (age) but zero, because female cadres at the division level are supposed to retire at age fifty-five. In these examples, then, the seventy-two-year-old male and the fifty-five-year-old female differ by only two on the dependent variable, despite a seventeen-year difference in the ages at which they retired. This age difference is not of primary analytical interest. We are interested in how and why these and other cadres responded differently to a policy stipulating that they should retire. Here, one retired two years late, the other on time. What explains this?

Adjusting for Sample Selection Bias. Included in my sample are some cadres who in 1987, when the data were collected, were too young to have retired late. This problem of younger cadres in the sample reflects a sample selection bias. It is fundamentally different from the problem of older cadres described above and impossible to resolve with adjustments of the dependent variable. The sample selection bias confounds the analysis of choices made by the population of interest, essentially because we lack information about the appropriate group of younger cadres for comparison. The "choices" reflected in early retirement of younger cadres in my sample are an artifact of

---

[22] Obviously, the dependent variable in such cases can never take on negative values. I treat as on-time retirement what may, in terms of the decision calculus, be more comparable to early retirement. But that is a problem without solution, as far as I can tell.

how I collected my data. If the young cadres are in my sample, then they could only have retired early; by 1987 sufficient time had not yet elapsed to select cadres in the same age cohort who had retired on time or late! Think of how my conclusions about the choices of younger cadres might be different if the sample included both retired and working cadres.[23]

To illustrate, consider the implications for examining the difference between revolutionaries and postrevolutionaries. Although the measure is one of revolutionary seniority, it is clearly correlated strongly with age. Young cadres could not have joined the revolution before 1949 because they were not old enough then to have done so. When the regression is run using the entire sample, I find a significant difference between revolutionaries and postrevolutionaries: postrevolutionaries retire nearly two years *earlier* than revolutionaries, other things equal. This makes no theoretical sense, but it makes good mathematical sense. Postrevolutionaries who got into my sample are there precisely because they retired relatively earlier than prescribed.

Unlike the older group of cadres in the sample and in the population, all early retirees can in principle choose among all options— early, on-time, and late retirement. But we can only analyze them comparatively as decision makers from a time perspective that places them in a group that has more than one option to choose. Cadres in my sample who are so young that they could only have retired early reflect a selection bias that cannot be corrected without more information than is available to me.[24] For that reason, I adjust for the bias by deleting from the sample all cadres who in 1987 were too young to have had late retirement as an option in 1978–87.

Independent Variables. The predicted effect of all but one of the independent variables can be expressed in terms of a direction. Here, the term "later" refers of course to deviation from on-time retirement in a positive direction and thus means later relative to the prescribed ages of retirement. I include in the equation three variables that in some sense capture the impact of material inducements on the decision to retire: pensions, bureaucratic rank, and whether a cadre is a revolutionary veteran or a postrevolutionary. The first isolates the simple monetary inducement to retire, and we expect that cadres eligible for lower pensions would choose to retire later than those eligible for higher ones. The second reflects the importance of having

[23] A research design including employed cadres in the sample is far better for a number of other reasons too, but unfortunately in my case not feasible.

[24] See the discussion of censored data in Achen, *The Statistical Analysis of Quasi-Experiments*, 73–137.

a position in order to gain access to goods and opportunities. We expect cadres of higher rank to retire later than cadres of lower rank
because their positions offer relatively more leverage. The third explanatory variable represents the nonmonetary material inducements
available to retired cadres. We expect postrevolutionaries to retire
later than revolutionaries, because they lack equivalent institutional
channels and official assurances of preferential access to basic goods
and services as well as perks.

I also include in the equation a number of control variables: state
of health at the time of retirement, attitude toward retirement, level
of education, sex, and period in which retirement took place. Other
things equal, we expect later retirement for cadres in good health
(compared to cadres in poor health) and for cadres who did not want
to retire (compared to those who did). Level of education may affect
when cadres retire in the sense that highly educated cadres are more
likely to be encouraged to postpone retirement and to fit into the
category of those needed at work, compared to cadres with little or
average education. Sex may also have a significant impact, because
women seem more likely to retire to take care of grandchildren, a
function that is traditionally performed less often by men. Finally, I
include policy stage as a control variable: it seems reasonable to suppose that with the routinization of retirement in later years, there was
less opportunity and toleration of significant deviation from prescribed ages of retirement.

Analysis.   Results of the regression analysis are presented in Table
3.2. Three variables have a statistically significant (and substantively
important) impact on deviation from on-time retirement: rank,
whether the cadre is a veteran or a postrevolutionary, and health.
The effect of each is in the predicted direction.

Consider first the impact of rank, a four-level ordinal variable. As
expected, rank makes a difference to a cadre when he considers
whether or not to retire at the prescribed age. Other things equal,
cadres at the ministerial level retire about 1.5 years later than those
at the bureau level, cadres at the bureau level retire about 1.5 years
later than those at the division level, and cadres at the division level
retire about 1.5 years later than those at the section level and below.
Other things equal, then, the difference between a position at the
bureau rank (which roughly marks the lower end of what is considered high rank) and that of an ordinary section-level cadre is three
years; the difference between a very high-ranking (ministerial-level)
cadre and an ordinary (section-level) cadre is nearly five years. In
short, higher ranks are worth quite a lot more than lower ranks and

TABLE 3.2
Impact of Material Inducements
on Deviation from On-Time Retirement

Explanatory Variables	Coefficients	Standard Errors	t-Ratios
Intercept	0.35	3.46	0.10
Pension	2.63	2.73	0.97
Rank	1.48	0.37	**4.03
Status	2.06	0.88	*2.35
Health	1.40	0.49	*2.84
Attitude	−0.03	0.46	−0.07
Education	0.11	0.68	0.16
Sex	−0.33	0.62	−0.53
Policy stage	1.14	0.66	1.74

Note: The dependent variable, deviation from on-time retirement, is the difference in years between observed and prescribed age of retirement and the direction of this difference. Pension is the fraction of salary received as pension at retirement. Rank is a four-level ordinal, with values from 4 to 1 for cadres of ministerial, bureau, division, and section (or below) ranks, respectively. Status has a value of 1 for postrevolutionaries, 0 for revolutionaries; health has a value of 1 for cadres reporting good health at retirement, 0 for those reporting poor health; attitude has a value of 1 for cadres reporting they wanted to retire, 0 for those reporting they did not want to retire; education has a value of 1 for cadres with education beyond senior middle school, 0 otherwise; sex has a value of 1 for males, 0 for females; policy stage has a value of 1 for cadres who retired in 1985–87, 0 for those who retired in 1978–84.

No. of cases: 128
R^2: .38
Standard error of estimate: 2.45
*$p < .01$, one-tailed test
**$p < .001$, one-tailed test

cadres are more interested in holding on to them—regardless of what they are assured of receiving after retirement.[25]

The variable directly representing the impact of nonmonetary material inducements is also significant. As expected, the officially assured differential access to goods and opportunities after retirement makes a great deal of difference to cadres. Controlling for other ef-

[25] Cadres with higher rank are also likely to have more clout to use when they bargain with middlemen about their retirement. See the discussion of bargaining, below.

fects, postrevolutionary cadres retire about two years later than veteran revolutionaries.

One control variable, health, also turns out to have a significant effect. Other things equal, cadres who reported good health at the time of retirement retired 1.4 years later (relative to when they should retire) than those who reported poor health.[26] Other control variables are not statistically significant. In the case of attitude toward retirement, the self-reports may be an unreliable measure. Cadres who indicated they wanted to retire may have been rationalizing the inevitable. If their true attitude was similar to the majority in the sample who reported they did not want to retire, then the measured variation in attitude does not capture the construct of interest here.[27] In the case of policy stage, we cannot predict a direction of effect. We expect that as retirement becomes more routinized there will be less deviation from on-time retirement overall, but the relevant model is not in fact the one specified here. The predicted effect is one of decrease in *absolute* deviation from on-time retirement, i.e., both less early and less late retirement. I discuss this model and its implications about the growth of a norm in chapter 4.

One of the most surprising (but not entirely counterintuitive) results of the regression is the lack of significant impact of pensions, the simple monetary inducement to retire. One problem may be that nonmonetary differences between revolutionaries and postrevolutionaries, as reflected in the status variable, dwarf the effect of pension differences. I ran the regression with status dropped; pensions should then capture the very typical big difference between postrevolutionaries and revolutionaries in fraction of salary received as pension (75 percent and 100 percent, respectively). The sign of the pension variable in the new equation was in the predicted direction, but the effect remained statistically insignificant.[28] We cannot reject the hypothesis that money, reflected in fraction of salary received as pension, has no effect on a cadre's decision about when to retire relative to when he is supposed to retire.

To sum up, the multivariate regression reveals variation among cadres in their response to policy, variation that could not be explored in the aggregate-level analysis of the preceding section. Different inducements produced different outcomes and the attractiveness of material inducements varied among cadres in a systematic

[26] But see the discussion of employment substitution, below.

[27] In the discussion of work for the former workplace in chapter 5 I propose and test an alternative explanation, which turns out to be supported by the evidence.

[28] The coefficient was -1.70, with a standard error of 2.05 and a t-ratio of $-.83$. Other coefficients remained fairly stable.

and predictable way. The data indicate that the really important material inducements to retire have little to do with money per se and a lot to do with access to goods and opportunities. In addition to favoring revolutionaries with higher pension levels, policy makers treated revolutionaries and postrevolutionaries differently. This difference, which represents a nonmonetary but nonetheless material inducement, had a major effect on when cadres retired. Existing differences among cadres in terms of access due to rank also significantly affected when cadres chose to retire.

The regression analysis and the analysis at the aggregate level both focus on outcomes. Yet they suggest something about process— namely, that preferences of individual cadres figured somehow into the retirement calculus. I now turn to a discussion of this process, supplying the rationale for using "choice" and "decision" to refer to an act essentially driven by a policy of the state.

BARGAINING FOR A BETTER DEAL

Part of our interest in how successful policy makers were in getting cadres to retire from office is based on an implicit assumption that cadres did not want to retire. My surveys, as well as articles and surveys reported in Chinese periodicals, corroborate this view: most cadres preferred not to retire.[29] I also found, however, that most cadres had a price at which their acquiescence, indeed active cooperation, in the decision to retire could be purchased. Cadres interviewed described the act of retirement as a process of bargaining (*shangliang*) between middlemen and older cadres targeted for retirement. Cadres bargained for a better retirement deal than that explicitly offered in party and government regulations:

> Retirement decisions come from the organization department at the workplace. It has records of how old cadres are and who should retire.

[29] In my data set, 39 percent of cadres reported they wanted to retire and 61 percent reported they did not want to retire. The most conscientious and extensive Chinese survey of retired cadres I found shows 32 percent of veterans reporting they wanted to retire, another 24 percent reporting they succumbed to the general trend, and 44 reporting outright they did not want to retire. See Ha'erbin shi shehui kexue yanjiu suo shehuixue yanjiu shi, "Ha'erbin shi lixiu ganbu zhuangkuang diaocha baogao (shang)." I note that in Wang Jisheng's sample of fifty-three retired veteran cadres, 66 percent reported they wanted to retire. But his surveys of retired cadres (listed in Works Cited) as he reports them are not obviously conscientious, his analysis is quite clearly faulty in places, and he and his interview subjects are consistently and unusually upbeat about nearly everything. See his "Tuixiu, lixiu ganbu xinli fanying de tantao."

> To get people to retire, the organization department cadres come to talk
> to you. Cadres bargain with them. They may say: "First you resolve my
> housing problem or my son's employment problem, and then I will re-
> tire." Before the Cultural Revolution, people did whatever the [party]
> organization told them to do. They went wherever the [party] organiza-
> tion decided they should go. Now, people do not listen. People are not
> so obedient. The organization has to bargain with them.[30]

Better housing, a position for a son or daughter, the postponement
of retirement during the 1985 salary reform, and a pre-retirement
promotion or salary raise were common items over which cadres and
middlemen bargained.

In other cases, of course, agreement to retire could not be purchased at such prices. Typically, high-ranking cadres were not only
less willing to relinquish positions in the bureaucracy, but also pos-
sessed more resources (such as old age, prestige, and contacts) to use
when they bargained with middlemen. According to retired cadres
interviewed, middlemen were less likely to succeed in attempts to enforce the retirement of higher-ranking cadres. One reported that a
common stalling technique of leaders was simply to refuse to leave
until the party organization found people they got along with to replace them. A bureau chief interviewed delayed his retirement by arranging a transfer to an elective position.

Responses to my questionnaire sustain this image of retirement as
a two-way process in which cadres bargained with middlemen to obtain a better retirement deal. Eighty-five percent of questionnaire respondents asked middlemen to resolve some kind of problem for
them before their retirement. Of the requests made, finding employment for a son or daughter is by far the most common. If we include
cadres who made more than one request, then over half of all questionnaire respondents asked middlemen at the workplace to find a
position for their son or daughter. This finding most likely reflects
the practice of employment substitution (*dingti*), which seems to have
bought the willingness of many cadres to retire early, until the mid-
1980s.

EMPLOYMENT SUBSTITUTION AND EARLY RETIREMENT

Employment substitution and its association with early retirement
dates back to 1953, when the government issued regulations to give
priority in hiring a son or daughter of workers who had retired due

[30] Interview subject no. 6.

to a disability and whose family was experiencing financial difficulties. From 1953 through 1978, government regulations on employment substitution were frequently revised, changing from flexibility to strictness and back again, sometimes in the span of a few years.[31] The State Council regulations on the retirement of workers issued in 1978 stated that workplaces could hire a son or daughter of a retired worker if the family was experiencing financial difficulties or had several children who had been sent to the countryside and few children working.[32]

Regulations on cadre retirement neither provided for nor specifically disallowed employment substitution. There is no doubt, however, that many localities extended the employment substitution option to cadres and that it was appealing enough to a large number of lower-ranking cadres to produce early retirement.

In Guizhou province, for example, authorities found more than eight thousand cases of inappropriate early retirement of cadres from August to December 1983. More than half involved employment substitution.[33] A major survey that randomly sampled specially retired cadres who had retired before September 1983 in Ha'erbin city found 60 percent early retirement, of which 65 percent involved employment substitution.[34]

Younger cadres interviewed volunteered that employment substitution and associated early retirement had been widespread in their localities in the late 1970s and early 1980s. A few used almost interchangeably the terms "employment substitution" and "retirement for reasons of poor health" (*bingtui*). Conflation of the two terms is easily understood. As they explained, state of health is one variable that lends itself to flexible interpretation: "Everyone has something wrong with him at that age."[35] Regulations on cadre retirement explicitly called for early retirement only for cadres in poor health. Cadres who retired early to give a position to their son or daughter typically requested retirement for reasons of poor health.

The appeal of employment substitution to lower-ranking cadres, whose positions offered little leverage to obtain scarce goods and opportunities (including employment opportunities for their sons and

---

[31] See the discussion in Cao, *Zhonghua renmin gongheguo renshi zhidu gaiyao*, 406–9. Deborah Davis discusses employment substitution for workers in "Unequal Chances, Unequal Outcomes."

[32] Guowuyuan, Guanyu gongren tuixiu tuizhi de zanxing banfa, 2 June 1978.

[33] *Daily Report: China*, 23 Sept. 1983, Q1, and 2 Dec. 1983, Q1.

[34] Ha'erbin shi shehui kexue yanjiu suo shehuixue yanjiu shi, "Ha'erbin shi lixiu ganbu zhuangkuang diaocha baogao (shang)."

[35] Interview subject no. 81.

daughters) is hardly surprising. The Employment substitution provided an immediate financial guarantee for the family, a certainty that could transform retirement from a cost to a net benefit, even for cadres who received pensions amounting to less than full salary. Indeed, employment substitution may account for the remarkable early success of policy makers in getting cadres to retire. In particular, it may explain the retirement of large numbers of postrevolutionaries up to the end of 1983, when the State Council issued its first major clarification of policy. Employment substitution can therefore be viewed as a price at which postrevolutionaries chose to retire, indeed to retire early.

The association of employment substitution with early retirement also reflected an effort to hedge against future changes in policy:

> [Sometime between 1982 and 1984] there was a rumor, not a formal announcement, that in a few years this policy of employment substitution would be stopped. This is probably because the policy was being discussed or a regulation had been agreed on but not issued. So all the basic-level cadres rushed to retire early [to provide] employment for their children. . . . It was similar to panic buying during inflation.[36]

According to younger cadres interviewed, cadres were aided in the effort to hedge against policy changes: middlemen at the workplace warned cadres of impending government restrictions on employment substitution and quickly processed early retirements before restrictions came into effect.

By all accounts, then, the association between employment substitution and early retirement was significant. In the words of one younger cadre: "As long as there is employment substitution, early retirement is unavoidable. Employment substitution is an incentive for early retirement."[37]

Policy makers reacted strongly to early retirement and to the extension of employment substitution to cadres, clearly indicating that the practices were deviations from policy. In September 1983 the State Council issued a regulation criticizing abuses of employment substitution, noting that the extension of employment substitution to cadres was something the localities had initiated on their own. The regulation called for an immediate end to employment substitution among cadres, a thorough investigation of past practices, and a rectification of errors made in implementation. It also introduced new stricter standards for employment substitution among workers, vir-

---

[36] Interview subject no. 73.
[37] Interview subject no. 49.

tually eliminating it for those who retired early.[38] A similar regulation was issued in February 1984.[39] The response of workplaces could not have been satisfactory from the perspective of policy makers. In 1986 the State Council announced the abolition of employment substitution, citing too many abuses of it over the years.[40]

POSTREVOLUTIONARIES AND LOCAL GOVERNMENTS

In the mid-1980s policy makers acknowledged publicly that middlemen were encountering serious difficulties in getting postrevolutionaries to retire. In late 1984 Deputy Minister of Labor and Personnel Jiao Shanmin diagnosed the problem as low pensions:

> At present there are several hundreds of thousands of cadres who have reached the age of regular retirement, but will not retire. . . . The main reason is the great gap in pensions between revolutionaries and postrevolutionaries. By current pension standards, regular retirement affects the standard of living. This issue should be considered an urgent matter to be studied and resolved.[41]

The problem was almost certainly, in part at least, a consequence of the new strictness on employment substitution. It may also have been a reflection of the age structure, although we lack the data to examine the possibility that greater numbers of postrevolutionary cadres were reaching the ages of retirement.

In any case, it is clear that postrevolutionaries rejected as inadequate the pensions and benefits fixed by policy makers in regulations on cadre retirement, especially as compared to those granted veteran cadres. Retired postrevolutionaries interviewed were virtually unanimous in expressing their dissatisfaction with low pensions and their resentment of the gap in pensions and benefits between the two groups. For example, one suggested a redistribution was appropriate, as postrevolutionaries tended to be lower ranking and earn lower salaries than veterans: "Specially retired cadres get better benefits than

[38] Guowuyuan, Guanyu renzhen zhengdun zhaoshou tuixiu tuizhi zhigong zinu gongzuo de tongzhi, 3 Sept. 1983.

[39] Laodong renshi bu, Guanyu guanche zhixing "guowuyuan guanyu renzhen zhengdun zhaoshou tuixiu tuizhi zhigong zinu gongzuo de tongzhi" zhong ruogan wenti de yijian, 10 Feb. 1984.

[40] Guowuyuan, Guanyu fabu gaige laodong zhidu si ge guiding de tongzhi, July 1986. This is a preamble to four new regulations on the labor system. The abolition of employment substitution was effective 1 Oct. 1986.

[41] Jiao, "You guan renshi zhidu gaige de jige wenti," 285–86.

we do. Their pensions should not be so high. Part of these [funds] should be used to help support regularly retired cadres. Our financial situation is not as good as theirs to begin with!"[42]

Questionnaire respondents also viewed the gap as unreasonable. Seventy-one percent of postrevolutionary respondents called the difference in pensions and benefits between retired revolutionaries and postrevolutionaries unreasonable (*bu heli*). Not surprisingly, only 18 percent of revolutionaries shared that perception.

Local governments handled the problem in a simple but costly way: they gave retired postrevolutionaries more money. The provincial measures governments adopted did not explicitly challenge central party and government standards. Rather, they granted additional monthly "maintenance subsidies" to regularly retired personnel. Henan province, for example, granted subsidies amounting to 5 to 15 percent of pre-retirement salary.[43] Sichuan province granted subsidies that increased total monetary income of regularly retired personnel generally to 85 or 95 percent of pre-retirement salary and to more than 100 percent in some cases.[44] By the end of 1986 twenty-five provincial governments had passed regulations to adjust upward the monetary income provided to retired postrevolutionaries.[45] Such increases may help account for the increased incidence of regular retirement in 1986–87.[46]

Obviously, not all provincial governments increased pensions for regularly retired cadres. As late as 1987, Beijing (a municipality ranked at the provincial level) was marching in step with the State Council. Retired cadres interviewed offered as an explanation the view that deviations from policy were more difficult to implement in a locality so close to the center of policy making. However, middlemen at the workplaces in Beijing had their own way of handling the problem. A retired cadre interviewed described the situation at the end of 1986:

[42] Interview subject no. 11.

[43] "Guanyu gei tuixiu zhigong jiafa buzhu fei de tongzhi"; "Guanyu fagei lixiu tuixiu tuizhi renyuan linshi shenghuo butie de tongzhi."

[44] Liu, "Zhigong tuixiu fei de zhifu biaozhun jidai yanjiu"; Yang, "Gongxian yu shanyang."

[45] Wang, interview, 24 Nov. 1986.

[46] It is tempting to see the provincial increases in income to retired postrevolutionaries as an explanation of the statistically insignificant effect of pension levels in the multivariate regression analysis presented above. That is, pension levels may not make a difference because they do not represent the full money income actually granted to retired cadres. However, this does not seem to be the case. When I deleted from the sample postrevolutionaries who had retired after 1985 (when the subsidies began to take effect), pensions remained insignificant.

There is no question or complaint about veteran cadres deserving the label of "veteran revolutionaries" and some honorary status. But there is grumbling about their extra material benefits. So the workplace is putting off processing cadre [regular] retirement, because there is a sense that the policy will probably change soon. The workplace wants to show consideration for the cadres who do not meet special retirement standards but are at the age of retirement.[47]

In short, some middlemen simply postponed processing the retirement of postrevolutionary cadres, in the expectation that policy makers would ultimately ratify the increases made by provincial governments.[48]

The local government initiatives put policy makers in an awkward position. An official at the Ministry of Personnel explained that policy makers had no choice in the matter: if they refused to allow the subsidies, then there would be no regular retirement. In his words, policy makers were forced "tacitly to recognize (*mo ren*) the changes."[49] While the subsidies were not exactly a revision of State Council pension standards, they were clearly viewed as a violation and an irregularity: "We think this is a matter for an overall State Council decision, not local decisions. We cannot have each locality handling the situation on its own. Pensions are part of a policy. This situation is bad for the establishment of a regular retirement system."[50]

In the end, however, policy makers took the local government measures as "a signal to review the policy."[51] The State Council issued a report in early 1987, pointing out that the subsidies had created a heavy financial burden on the state and that departments were studying the matter to recommend policy revisions. It asked the localities to take into account the financial burden and the adverse effect of the increases on building a cadre retirement system. However, policy makers did not explicitly demand a repeal of the increases.[52]

In 1988 policy makers took a step toward shrinking the gap between retired postrevolutionary and revolutionary cadres, by combining management of the two groups—although they kept in place their policy of lower pensions for postrevolutionaries.[53] They also

[47] Interview subject no. 6.

[48] According to Wang Xingming, this method of handling the problem was not unique to Beijing. Interview, 24 Nov. 1986.

[49] Chen, interview, 7 Nov. 1988.

[50] Ibid.

[51] Ibid.

[52] Caizheng bu laodong renshi bu, Guanyu yange kongzhi fafang ge zhong butie jintie he kongzhi zixing tigao tuixiu daiyu wenti baogao, 10 Jan. 1987.

[53] Shen, "Guojia gongwuyuan de tuixiu tuizhi zhidu."

took the very significant step of eliminating the request to retire. This curtailed the costly interactions between middlemen and cadres due to retire. In eliminating the request to retire, which reduced the opportunities for bargaining between middlemen and older cadres, policy makers were in fact following the initiative of local governments. The elimination of requests to retire was almost certainly welcomed by middlemen at the workplace.

MIDDLEMEN AND THEIR INCENTIVE STRUCTURE

That cadres bargained for a better retirement deal is not surprising. That they were successful requires some explanation. An article in a journal published by a provincial department of personnel reminded workplaces "not to consider issues only from the perspective of benefits and costs to [older] cadres."[54] Why were the interests of cadres such important considerations for middlemen charged with implementing the policy of retirement?

Middlemen responsible for implementing cadre retirement policy were at the same time responsible for implementing other policies. As discussed in chapter 2, after 1980 those other policies included rejuvenating the cadre ranks and leading groups and reducing staff size. For some policy objectives, policy makers had set rough quotas—specifying average ages of cadres and authorized staff size, for example. Moreover, in 1982–84 policy makers called for quick results, promoting campaign-style implementation. Party organization departments and government personnel departments had multiple goals to meet. The retirement of cadres helped them meet several. It lowered the average age of the cadre corps, opened up positions of leadership to younger cadres, and reduced staff size. In short, middlemen were constrained by several policies to retire older cadres.

Most cadres preferred not to retire and, in what were essentially end-game tactics with the authorities who control career chances, had little to lose by trying to get a better deal. Further, both targets of retirement policy and middlemen charged with implementing it were well aware of a number of possibilities to be exploited. To review those briefly, first, policy makers had made it clear that middlemen were to help older veterans resolve practical problems and to guarantee them preferential treatment in matters affecting general welfare. Requests such as better housing or a pre-retirement salary raise were not unreasonable in that context. Second, employment substi-

[54] Gong, "Zhaogu xing tiba bu zu qu," 39.

tution was not, after all, something cadres and middlemen had thought up on their own. Policy makers had introduced it widely as an option for workers in 1978. Extending it to cadres was bending the rules, but not exactly the same as making up new ones. Third, the deputy minister of labor and personnel himself had called public attention to the low pensions of retired postrevolutionaries, calling for urgent study and resolution of the problem. All in all, then, what cadres bargained for and middlemen granted appeared to be at least vaguely authorized by policy makers.

Even early retirement was not without a foothold in official policy. From the perspective of enforcement, early retirement resolved a problem arising from the policy of rejuvenating the ranks by promoting younger cadres (in their forties), skipping over cadres in their fifties. Policy makers did not advocate the blanket exclusion from promotion of all cadres in their fifties. Yet in 1983–84 especially, policy guidelines did suggest that even healthy cadres in their fifties could be asked to step down during structural reform if younger, better qualified candidates for office were available.[55] This view could easily be seized upon to validate early retirement. From the perspective of propensity to retire, cadres in their fifties who faced no chances of promotion were likely to find early retirement appealing—especially if promised a position at the workplace for a son or daughter.

Policy makers had set up a situation in 1982 where middlemen could not ignore the requests of older cadres. By official policy, the retirement process was supposed to include a dialogue between middlemen and immediate targets of the policy. A 1983 party document issued by Liaoning province, for example, explicitly required workplace leaders or party committee members responsible for cadre work to have "heart-to-heart talks" with veteran cadres due to retire, to give the cadres an opportunity to raise their opinions and make requests. The document also recommended visits to the homes of older cadres, to persuade family members if necessary.[56]

The pre-retirement heart-to-heart talks were situations loaded with opportunity for older cadres to get what they wanted. One provincial journal noted: "Cadres make use of their retirement as an opportu-

---

[55] See, for example, *Laodong renshi bao*, 27 May 1987, 3; "Kefou tiqian banli lixiu?"; Zhonggong zhongyang zuzhi bu yanjiu shi, *Zuo hao xin shiqi de ganbu gongzuo*, 209–14; Li, "Xin xingshi yu ganbu gongzuo." The rigid exclusion of cadres in their fifties is criticized in Qian and Lu, "Wushi duo sui jiguan ganbu guanli de duice"; Zhu, "Lun ganbu de xinlao jiaoti."

[56] Lao ganbu shouce bianxie zu, *Lao ganbu shouce*, 42–43. Liaoning was promoted often in the *Renmin ribao* as a model in cadre retirement work.

nity to make high, even unreasonable demands. The comrades in charge of concrete implementation find it difficult to respond to comrades who have such seniority. This makes it difficult to get the work done."[57]

The dialogue provided a structure within which older cadres could ask for more than was explicitly promised in government regulations. Middlemen could imaginatively interpret policy guidelines to grant at least some requests, thereby also satisfying the demands on them from the top to implement cadre retirement policy as well as other policies. Obviously, such a dialogue drove the costs of policy implementation up above those reflected in retirement regulations. It also held no guarantee that middlemen and older cadres would reach agreement on prices for retirement. The result was often inaction. As one older cadre observed: "The leaders cannot easily make us retire if we do not really agree to do so."[58]

In 1986–88 some local governments began to experiment with putting the initiative fully in the hands of middlemen. They abolished what had previously been an integral part of retirement procedures: the individual request to retire.[59] Once cadres reached the ages specified in government regulations, middlemen simply processed retirements, whether or not they had received a request to do so. No longer did middlemen have to persuade cadres to agree to retire or work out agreeable prices with them for retirement.

Accounts in journals of the provincial departments of labor and personnel suggest that older cadres adapted to the new rule where it was practiced. Recognizing that retirement at the ages specified in government regulations was unavoidable, cadres tried to generate goodwill from the authorities by "looking at things from a broader perspective (*da ju*)" and taking the (unnecessary) initiative to request retirement at those ages—rather than waiting for middlemen to call on them.[60] Thus in 1988 when policy makers in Beijing eliminated the request to retire, as a general practice to be implemented

[57] Wang and Li, "Wei xian gaige ganbu lixiu tuixiu zhidu chujian chengxiao," 13.

[58] Interview subject no. 6.

[59] I do not know how widespread were the local government initiatives. I have found accounts of them in six provinces (Guangdong, Guangxi, Hebei, Henan, Shanxi, and Zhejiang) and Shanghai. See *Laodong renshi bao*, 8 July 1987, 1; *Daily Report: China*, 15 Sept. 1986, P1; "Dadao lituixiu nianling ganbu yao ruqi banli lituixiu shouxu"; Wang and Li, "Wei xian gaige ganbu lixiu tuixiu zhidu chujian chengxiao"; "Xinyang xian dui lituixiu renyuan xianqi banli shouxu"; "Shi wei pizhuan shi wei zuzhi bu 'guanche zhixing zhongyang zuzhi bu guanyu ganbu lixiu shouxu tongzhi de yijian' "; "Guanyu tuixiu ganbu guanli gongzuo de zanxing guiding."

[60] See, for example, "Xinyang xian dui lituixiu renyuan xianqi banli shouxu."

throughout the country, they were taking their cue from the experience of the localities.

SUMMARY

Beyond a doubt, cadre retirement policy had a substantial impact. By the end of 1988 the situation of de facto lifelong tenure for cadres had been transformed. Millions of cadres had retired. Yet policy makers had as their objective age-based exit from office, not simply a new form of exit. By that standard, policy makers were not fully successful. An estimate of expected retirement of the veterans who had survived to become the policy's most immediate targets suggests many cases of early retirement up to 1986. Conversely, while postrevolutionaries were retiring in large numbers in the early 1980s, by 1984 policy makers were encountering much resistance and postponement of retirement. In sum, both early and late retirement figured significantly among targets of the policy. Why?

Analysis at the individual level as well as descriptions of the retirement process point to an important part of the answer. Whether and when cadres retired and what they got in the process were in no small way determined, not at the top by policy makers but at lower levels, to take into account the preferences of policy targets. Cadres seized on retirement as an opportunity to bargain for a better deal. Bargaining affected when cadres retired. Some arrangements, such as employment substitution, were appealing enough for cadres to want to retire early. Some were necessary to coax whole groups into retirement: postrevolutionaries simply held out for more money and got it. Other cadres, those in high ranks, for example, could find virtually no arrangement as appealing as holding onto their positions.

Policy makers reacted to the adjustments in policy that emerged in the course of implementation. They specifically ruled out some arrangements such as employment substitution, which worked against age-based exit from office. And they eliminated the request to retire. That measure was borrowed from the localities to curtail the bargaining that had increased the costs of policy and distorted the relationship between age and exit. In eliminating both the employment substitution typically associated with early retirement and the request to retire that structured the retirement process as a bargaining environment, policy makers took actions that seem bound to promote less early retirement and less late retirement in the future.

Considering only the behavioral part of a norm, a decade of cadre retirement presents a mixed record: much cadre retirement, but much of it not on time. But by restructuring the retirement process as a purely administrative procedure, policy makers seem to have taken for granted an orientation to retirement that makes it sufficiently unproblematic for the state to wind down its effort at building a norm. Whether or not this kind of normative perspective on retirement in fact exists is an empirical question—much thornier than the one considered above. Chapter 4 takes up this question.

CHAPTER FOUR

A Normative View of Retirement

IN BUILDING a norm, policy makers aim to create conditions that allow the state eventually to hand over responsibility for policy enforcement to ordinary members of society. This chapter asks how successful policy makers in Beijing have been in creating these conditions. It examines orientations to cadre retirement that indicate how and how much cadres view age-based exit from office as an "ought," a normative standard that binds them.

Again, private interests figure prominently in the analysis. But while the interests of older cadres targeted for retirement can obstruct the emergence of a norm of cadre retirement, the interests of younger cadres can promote it. Younger cadres play a key role in making older cadres believe they may do "less well" (to use the language of chapter 1) by not retiring on time.

I begin by describing the arguments retired cadres use to explain why they retired, arguments that reflect an understanding of the official version of the rationale for cadre retirement. I follow this discussion of public language with an attempt to sort out private views on age-based exit. Comparing views of retired cadres and younger, employed cadres, I find a relationship exists between private views and private interests. Further, younger cadres act on their views, playing the role of unofficial enforcers of retirement policy. I conclude by examining change over time and find evidence of the growth of a norm of cadre retirement.

CORRECT THINKING ABOUT RETIREMENT

Chinese cadres summarize their situation of career security before 1978 in the phrase, "entry without exit, promotion without demotion."[1] Of course, lifelong tenure as a general rule for cadres did not bring full career security. Many cadres lost their positions because of changes in the political standards used to evaluate their past and current performance. For almost three decades of communist rule, the dominant form of exit from office for cadres was purge for political

[1] *Neng jin bu neng chu, neng shang bu neng xia.*

error.[2] These parallel traditions of lifelong tenure and political purge had predictable effects on views about cadre retirement. A 1984 handbook on cadre work observed that the first wave of retired cadres encountered widespread misunderstanding among other cadres, in the party, and in society generally. They were often viewed as "guilty of some [political] error."[3] A deputy head of the Central Committee's Organization Department summarized initial views: "Everyone is in office, why are you out? You must have committed a [political] error."[4]

Policy makers anticipated and attempted to counter this view by manipulating beliefs about retirement. Through a variety of channels—documents, newspapers and periodicals, speeches, and meetings at the workplace—beginning in 1980 and especially after 1981, they used the mechanisms of argument and association to define retirement as socially functional and progressive, and part of norms and practices already familiar to Chinese cadres.[5] In so doing, policy makers attempted to free cadre retirement from the stigma of the tradition of political purge and develop a view of retirement as a regular practice.

Among the most common arguments aired officially were the following three. First, official channels promoted an argument for regular personnel renewal per se: younger cadres cannot rise if elderly co-workers continue to dominate cadre positions, especially leading positions. Second, it was argued that physical and mental ability naturally decline in old age and work suffers as a result. If older cadres continued to work, the management of many important projects would be harmed. Finally, policy makers argued that modernization continually requires cadres with new kinds of expertise and higher education. Older cadres must step down on a regular basis if the country is to progress. In addition to arguments, policy makers associated cadre retirement with already established and legitimated traditions of public service, regular career assignments, and submission to communist party discipline.

Obviously, if these mechanisms of norm building are to work, then individuals immediately targeted by the policy (or in a group that matters to them) must be familiar with its contents. Knowing "correct thinking" reflected in policy is a minimal prerequisite for implementation of a policy as a norm.

We expect Chinese cadres to be adept at divining and paraphrasing

---

[2] Oksenberg, "The Exit Pattern in Chinese Politics and Its Implications." See the discussion of the policy to retire cadres in the Introduction.

[3] Zhonggong zhongyang zuzhi bu yanjiu shi, *Zuo hao xin shiqi de ganbu gongzuo*, 213.

[4] Wang, "Guanyu ganbu 'sihua' he ganbu zhidu gaige de ji ge wenti," 108.

[5] See the discussions of argument and association in chapter 1.

the prevailing views of those at the top. Cadre careers depend on this kind of correct thinking and have depended on comprehending far more subtle signals than the appeals policy makers made for cadre retirement. It is not surprising, then, that retired cadres interviewed demonstrated they know how to generalize about cadre retirement in ways that clearly indicate their familiarity with the official arguments. Here is a small, representative sample of this kind of generalization:

> We should let younger people rise. If we do not step down at a certain age, then younger people have to wait. Then, by the time we step down, these people are not so young anymore.[6]

> [Before,] young people had to wait until the old died. In this respect we do not even compare favorably with the capitalist countries.[7]

> If we all stay in office, then others cannot take up these positions. Many people occupy positions but don't do any work: they don't shit and don't get off the pot (*zhan zhe maokeng bu lashi*). They are taking up positions that others should have.[8]

> Before, the country was young (only thirty years old) and cadres were young too. Also, we were so involved in class struggle we had no time for cadre retirement. Now we need to modernize. The Four Modernizations need young people, we old people cannot do it.[9]

Retired cadres described retirement as "natural" and pointed out the need for "a generational transfer" of responsibilities. They acknowledged that "the country now has this system" and "things are becoming more regularized." They admitted that old cadres are quite often "conservative," "set in their ways," "slow at work," "lacking in energy," "muddle-headed," and "incapable of managing modernization."

More than this, however, cadres also know how to make shrewd use of official arguments as a resource when they bargain with middlemen. When cadres discussed with me their pursuit of private interests, they usually buttressed explanations of their motives with justifications saturated in the language of official policy. Nowhere was this more evident than with cadres who reported they really wanted to retire. One explained to me:

> I understood that the country was trying to achieve the Four Modernizations. And also that the state now has this system [of cadre retirement]. I am a party member. Therefore, I ought to step down. I did not want

[6] Interview subject no. 10.
[7] Interview subject no. 27.
[8] Interview subject no. 21.
[9] Interview subject no. 17.

to take up a position and hold back the country's projects. . . . If there is no cadre retirement, there is no way to resolve the problem of the young replacing the old. So I support the system. Also, I want my freedom. I want to do whatever I please. Of course, I would like to make a contribution to society, but now I really want my freedom. [Interjection from another cadre: We asked him to work with us on the university for the elderly, but he refused.] Yes, some people want me tied up in a lot of work. I don't want it.[10]

Another cadre elaborated with obvious delight the tactics he had used in his request to retire:

"What the top tells you to do, you do." I had lived by this rule for forty-eight years. I wanted to do things I found interesting. I wanted more freedom in my life. Of course, I did not put this in my request. . . . My request stressed the following reasons. First, there is this state system [of cadre retirement]. I ought to submit to the call. Second, I am past the age of retirement. (Forty-eight years of revolutionary service is enough!) Third, I want to devote myself to social work. . . . Finally, my health is poor. [A few years ago] I had to spend time in the hospital because of nervous exhaustion. (Actually, my health was fine. I used this as an excuse so I would be allowed to retire.)[11]

Other cadres responded to the appeal to submit to the discipline of the communist party hierarchy and retire as instructed, although they did so quite unwillingly, using the term *fucong* (to submit) frequently in reviewing their own retirement. Many described official arguments and association with other norms and practices as flawed. While they may not have communicated their views to middlemen or others at the workplace, many questioned the notion of their retirement as a net social benefit. Moreover, they did so without abandoning public language, because other official arguments were available to counter the logic of official appeals to retire.

For example, the appeal to retire to make way for younger cadres better qualified to lead the country's modernization was seen as problematic. As an expression of public service, it was quite as easy for older cadres to rationalize staying in office as retiring from it. Many older cadres seem to value their own rich experience above the skills and education of unseasoned younger cadres. This is particularly so for recently reinstated cadres who were not allowed to work during the Cultural Revolution years. In their view, cadre retirement policy

[10] Interview subject no. 4. This cadre was interviewed with others at a veteran cadre center.

[11] Interview subject no. 27.

deprived them of a last chance to make a contribution before their health gave out.

Attempts to resolve this inconsistency were not always successful, as the following view of retirement illustrates:

> At the time I could not get used to the idea of retiring. Even from an ideological perspective, I could not accept it. . . . My thoughts on the matter were very confused and I was filled with ambivalence. . . . I was just sixty years old. I was in good health. Why should I be retired? . . . Of course, from a broader perspective, I knew I should retire and let young people take my place. . . . Yet, from my own point of view, I felt I had not yet played my role. In particular, I had been prevented from working during the Anti-Rightist Campaign [in 1957] and again during the Cultural Revolution. For those years I could play no role. Now that the Cultural Revolution had ended, I should be able to play a role. So when the [party] organization asked me to retire, I thought: "Why is the [party] organization doing this to me?"[12]

Others found ways to express their views on the inconsistency of official arguments, even as they submitted to party discipline. One retired veteran told me:

> It was hard to get used to the idea of not working. Also, we had been persecuted during the Cultural Revolution and had not been able to work during those years. We wanted to do our work now. We did not raise a fuss, but we found the idea hard to get used to. They asked us to complete a form. On the form we were supposed to write "voluntary." Not one of us completed that part of the form. How could we write that we voluntarily gave up our work?[13]

Policy makers also actively promoted the idea of retirement as a "new assignment" for veteran revolutionaries, subsuming the new policy under an already established career practice. A veteran of the Anti-Japanese War, who retired in 1982, explained his response to the appeal as follows:

> I was in the first group of cadres to retire. We had no psychological preparation for retirement. . . . At that time there was a movement to streamline administration. The authorized number of positions (*bianzhi*) was to be cut. We knew this. But we did not know they would begin by asking veteran comrades to step down. They called meetings, bureau by bureau. We had to obey. We all had to obey in actions, the psychological adaptation would have to come gradually (*sixiang man man sheying*).

[12] Interview subject no. 25.
[13] Interview subject no. 22.

Of course, we are used to being transferred, to being given new work assignments, so in a way the ideological work was not difficult for them. . . . We are all veteran comrades. We could submit to the party's call. We are used to being transferred to other assignments. It has been like this since Liberation.[14]

To sum up, interviews with retired cadres suggest that policy makers have been successful in communicating to cadres a version of retirement as a regular and functional practice. Some cadres have used their understanding of official arguments as a resource when bargaining with middlemen. Others have found official arguments inconsistent and unpersuasive, even according to the logic of public service. These cadres have submitted to retirement not as a matter of social obligation, but as part of their obligation as party members to observe party discipline.

The different orientations have in common one thing: an acknowledgment of correct thinking about retirement. The examples presented in this section and numerous other observations by retired cadres lead to a modest conclusion: Chinese cadres know what they ought to think about retirement, even if they do not necessarily think this way.

PRIVATE VIEWS AND PRIVATE INTERESTS

Through argument and association, policy makers attempted to manipulate beliefs about exit from office in order to destigmatize retirement and build an orientation to it as a usual and correct practice—that is, a practice which is expected of cadres once they reach specified ages. Cadres seem to know the reasons why retirement is a correct way to act. This by no means implies, however, that they have assimilated those reasons. They understand age-based exit as public policy, but their private views may or may not be supportive of it.

What difference does it make? Norms need not be internalized to sustain themselves. It is required only that individuals recognize that certain actions are evaluated by others according to a normative standard.[15] Strictly speaking, cadres need not accept and support age-based exit on a personal basis in order for it to become a norm. They need only believe others do. But if there is widespread personal rejection of age-based exit among cadres, then chances are that cadres know about it. Certainly, such a situation is not conducive to the

[14] Ibid.
[15] See the discussion of moral beliefs and internalized norms in chapter 1.

emergence of a norm. This is one reason to examine private views on age-based exit. The analysis in the last chapter suggests another reason. Material interests explain a great deal about behavioral outcomes in the retirement process. Do interests similarly provide information about how cadres view age-based exit from office? As it turns out, they do.

Before turning to the question of support for age-based exit from office, it is useful to reinforce a widespread view on age guidelines that surfaced often in interviews. In discussing the 1982 retirement policy change, described in chapter 2, retired cadres and younger cadres alike noted the importance of introducing age guidelines as the basic criterion by which to make decisions on cadre retirement. Before 1982, state of health and ability to work normally were the criteria established to decide who should stay on and who should retire. Decisions on retirement had to be made on a case-by-case basis because they necessarily involved deliberations on how the vague and subjective standards applied to particular cadres. But beginning in 1982, cadre retirement became essentially age-based retirement.

Cadres interviewed pointed to the objective criterion of age as vitally important to reducing conflict at the workplace and facilitating the task of retiring those who did not want to retire. One noted, for example: "We need to implement age-based exit. If not, then how could we decide who should retire and who should not? . . . Without age-based exit, everyone is dissatisfied."[16] And another concluded: "The most effective way to get cadres to retire is strictly to observe the age guidelines. Some cadres will say that their health is still good and that they are still able to play a role at work. We should answer them that they are at the age of retirement and must retire."[17] Others reiterated these views. There seems to be little disagreement that given a policy to retire cadres, the effective way to implement it is to adopt age-based exit as a decision rule.[18]

What did cadres think about age-based exit as a decision rule per se? It makes no sense simply to examine responses from retired cadres surveyed: without some basis of comparison, we can have no idea of how to interpret the data. We can, however, compare responses of retired cadres to those of another group—the younger, employed cadres interviewed. Of course, neither group has reason to be neutral on the question and so neither is in any sense a control group when we analyze the impact of private interests on private views.

[16] Interview subject no. 22.

[17] Interview subject no. 6.

[18] For further discussion and similar opinions, see chapter 2 on rules about when to retire.

Younger and retired cadres differ in two important ways that are likely to affect views on age-based exit. First, they have different perspectives on old age. One elderly veteran commented on the difference through a recollection: "When I was younger, I thought people who were sixty or seventy years old were really old. [I thought] they were inefficient and walked bent over, with the aid of a cane. But now that I am seventy years old I don't think I am inefficient. I am in good health, I do not need a cane."[19] Another noted: "It is not really accurate to say we step down from office because we are old. In China, sixty years old is not old."[20] One simple but powerful indicator that the younger generation does not see it this way is my finding that 83 percent of younger cadres interviewed cited the age of 60 or younger as the age at which Chinese are generally considered old (*lao le*).

Second, in addition to different perspectives on old age, younger and retired cadres have different interests regarding the question of age-based exit. Younger cadres share an immediate interest in the retirement of older co-workers to liberate positions to which the younger generation can be promoted. The interest of already retired cadres as it concerns age-based exit is more complex. On the one hand, they have lost their positions because of age-based exit. However, already retired cadres also have a stake in age-based exit. To the extent that retirement decisions are believed to be based on age guidelines, already retired cadres are not by definition ill, feeble-minded, or lacking in the appropriate skills and education to help the country modernize. They are simply cadres who have reached a certain age.

In sum, we can expect younger cadres to view age-based exit without much ambivalence and to accept and support it more strongly than retired cadres do. Yet it is by no means predictable on the basis of interests that retired cadres will be on the whole unsupportive.

Table 4.1 compares opinions of retired and younger cadres on how decisions on cadre retirement ought to be made for cadres other than national leaders. The two groups differ significantly and in the predicted direction. Proportions choosing age as the strict-decision rule differ, but not by all that much. The real differences are about whether retirement decisions ought to be made on a case-by-case basis and whether cadres ought to have to retire at all. Forty-two percent of retired cadres hold views that, in essence, oppose a policy of age-based exit, compared to 19 percent of younger cadres. Support for a practice of age-based exit is considerable and considerably greater among younger cadres.

[19] Interview subject no. 7.
[20] Interview subject no. 30.

TABLE 4.1
Appropriate Decision Rules for Cadre Retirement

Decision Rule	Younger Cadres (%)	Retired Cadres (%)
Age	38	32
Mainly age	44	27
Mainly situation	16	28
Entirely situation	3	12
No retirement	0	2
Total	100% (71)	100% (227)

Question: My view on cadre retirement is that, with the exception of national leaders: all cadres should retire at stipulated ages; as a general rule, cadres should retire at stipulated ages; as a general rule, the decision should be handled according to the particular situation; the decision should be handled entirely according to the particular situation; as a general rule, cadres should be allowed to continue to work without retirement.

Note: Percentages may not add up due to rounding.

No. of cases: 298
Pearson chi-square: 14.691
Probability: .005

Hierarchy and special exceptions for those at the top are integral features of the Chinese cadre system, and the official decision rules for cadre retirement are not uniform. The system is in fact a stratified one. In building a norm of retirement, policy makers created "sub-norms" for leaders. Leaders at the very top are fully exempt from retirement, leaders below the very top can semiretire to advisory commissions and positions. The communist party newspaper made much of lower-level exemplars who volunteered to retire. At the same time, standard exceptions for leaders have excused them from a personal obligation to provide cadres with similar models.[21] Such exceptions blur generalization about retirement and challenge a view of cadre retirement as a usual or correct practice.

Do cadres accept the policy of a stratified system? Or do they privately reject the different decision rules for leaders at the top and other cadres below? Cadres interviewed presented me with a great variety of views about retirement for leaders. The crucial datum, however, is the extent to which they accept different standards for

[21] See the discussions of exemptions for leaders and exemplary conformers in chapter 2.

TABLE 4.2
Appropriate Decision Rules for
Retirement of Leaders and Other Cadres

National Leaders		Other Cadres		Total
	Age	Situation	No retirement	
Age	141	20	0	161
Situation	44	77	1	122
No retirement	2	1	3	6
Total	187	98	4	289

Questions: (1) My view on retirement of national leaders is that: all should retire at stipulated ages; with the exception of certain individuals, all should retire at stipulated ages; as a general rule, the decision should be handled according to the particular situation; the decision should be handled entirely according to the particular situation; as a general rule, they should be allowed to continue to work without retirement. (2) My view on cadre retirement is that, with the exception of national leaders: all cadres should retire at stipulated ages; as a general rule, cadres should retire at stipulated ages; as a general rule, the decision should be handled according to the particular situation; the decision should be handled entirely according to the particular situation; as a general rule, cadres should be allowed to continue to work without retirement.

Note: Both age and situation decision rule categories are created by combining two response options (see questions above).

leaders compared to other cadres. This is easily seen by cross-tabulating responses to two questions on how decisions on cadre retirement ought to be made—one for cadres in general and another for leaders in particular.

Table 4.2 presents raw frequencies that combine responses of retired and younger cadres to these questions. The five decision rules on retirement (shown in Table 4.1) have been collapsed into three categories, for ease of presentation. Table 4.3 presents the same information but separates out responses of retired cadres from those of younger cadres and uses percentages to facilitate comparison between the two groups.

Consider first Table 4.2. An examination of frequencies along the diagonal from top left to bottom right suggests a lack of support for stratification. Seventy-seven percent of all combinations are on this diagonal and these are the preferred combinations for each of the three decision rules. That is, most cadres who believe retirement decisions should be based on age believe this rule should hold for national leaders and other cadres alike. Most cadres who believe retirement decisions should be based on a case-by-case analysis of the situation believe this rule should hold for both cadre groups. The

TABLE 4.3
Appropriate Decision Rules for Retirement of Leaders and
Other Cadres: Comparing Views of Retired and Younger Cadres

National Leaders	Other Cadres			
	Age (%)	Situation (%)	No retirement (%)	Total (%)
Age	R:45	R: 6	R: 0	R:51
	Y:61	Y:10	Y: 0	Y:71
Situation	R:13	R:33	R: 1	R:47
	Y:21	Y: 9	Y: 0	Y:30
No retirement	R: 1	R: 1	R: 1	R: 3
	Y: 0	Y: 0	Y: 0	Y: 0
Total	R:59	R:40	R: 2	100
	Y:82	Y:19	Y: 0	100

R: Percentage of retired cadres choosing this combination
Y: Percentage of younger cadres choosing this combination
No. of cases, retired cadres: 218
No. of cases, younger cadres: 71

Questions: (1) My view on retirement of national leaders is that: all should retire at stipulated ages; with the exception of certain individuals, all should retire at stipulated ages; as a general rule, the decision should be handled according to the particular situation; the decision should be handled entirely according to the particular situation; as a general rule, they should be allowed to continue to work without retirement. (2) My view on cadre retirement is that, with the exception of national leaders: all cadres should retire at stipulated ages; as a general rule, cadres should retire at stipulated ages; as a general rule, the decision should be handled according to the particular situation; the decision should be handled entirely according to the particular situation; as a general rule, cadres should be allowed to continue to work without retirement.

Notes: Both age and situation decision rule categories are created by combining two response options (see questions above). Percentages may not add up due to rounding.

same is (weakly) true of the small number of cadres who reject retirement policy altogether.[22]

Table 4.3 allows us to compare the opinions of retired and younger cadres. The preference for combinations along the diagonal from top left to bottom right holds roughly for retired cadres.[23] It does not hold for younger cadres. Moreover, there are big differences between younger and retired cadres in some categories. The differ-

[22] A statistical test is inappropriate for this table, as there is little guidance for a hypothesis that posits causality in one direction rather than the other.

[23] Retired cadres who reject retirement altogether either prefer or are indifferent to this choice for both leaders and other cadres, compared to choices that include rejection of retirement for one group only.

ences along the diagonal are similar to those presented above in Table 4.1, which compares views of retired and younger cadres on the retirement of cadres other than national leaders. Compared to retired cadres, younger cadres are more supportive of age-based retirement for all (61 percent, compared to 45 percent), less supportive of case-by-case decisions on retirement for all (9 percent, compared to 33 percent), and less supportive of no retirement for all (0 percent, compared to 1 percent).

The more interesting comparison lies in the off-diagonal combination of flexibility (situation-based decisions) for leaders and age-based retirement for other cadres, a combination that most closely resembles actual retirement policy. Differences between retired and younger cadres are large: 13 percent of retired cadres chose this combination, 21 percent of younger cadres chose it. The direction of the difference seems surprising, until we take into account the different interests of the two groups. Younger cadres, as noted above, have an immediate interest in the exit of their senior co-workers because they occupy the limited number of cadre positions at the workplace, blocking advancement of the younger generation. Already retired cadres have an interest in standardized decisions on retirement, so that their own exit from office is not viewed as unusual. Exceptions for leaders that are formalized in policy draw attention to the fact that cadre retirement decisions are not fully standardized, that exceptions are in fact the rule for cadres who are considered too important to step down. The same logic that leads some already retired cadres to support an age-based decision rule leads some to reject exceptions for leaders. By contrast, the logic that leads younger cadres to support an age-based decision rule for cadres in general does not have implications for the retirement of national leaders, who are not blocking their path to promotion at the workplace.

Private views supportive of public policy can help promote its growth as a norm and private rejection of policy can hinder it. This is particularly the case when supporters and detractors take action on their views. Having introduced the differences in private views and private interests of retired and younger cadres, I explore the action implications of these differences at the workplace.

VOLUNTARY ENFORCEMENT BY YOUNGER CADRES

The best sign that a policy is being implemented as a social norm is its enforcement by ordinary members of society. Chinese cadres work at workplaces with other cadres. An obvious arena for social enforcement is the workplace, the focal point for action in cadre retirement. If cadre retirement is indeed becoming a social norm, then it must be the case that cadres at the workplace are supplementing and will eventually replace the enforcement of retirement by middlemen.

My survey work turned up no evidence that retired cadres or older cadres still at work take action to exert pressure on targets of retirement policy to retire. To the contrary, retired cadres interviewed and questionnaire respondents reported that cadres at or near the age of retirement do not generally discuss retirement with co-workers—a surprising finding, in my view. Only 22 percent of questionnaire respondents reported discussing their retirement with co-workers before they retired. In interviews, retired cadres described to me two reasons why open discussion of retirement among co-workers is uncommon.

First, because the policy is a relatively new one, cadres at or near the age of retirement observe one another for signals on appropriate responses: "People influence each other. People look around and say: 'If he is not raising the issue, why should I?' "[24] Open discussion of retirement risks being construed as pressure to respond by taking the initiative to retire. A retired cadre explained it as follows: "I did not talk to my co-workers about my retirement. There was nothing to discuss. And if I had talked to them, they would have seen it as an attempt to influence them. They would have thought: 'You are talking about retirement, so we must also retire because we are also at that age.' "[25]

Second, such pressure can create awkward personal relations at the workplace, particularly if the other cadre does not in fact retire. It is also considered an unnecessary appropriation of the official responsibility of middlemen, one without advantage and probably with disadvantage: "In applying pressure to get cadres to retire, the most important people are the organization department cadres. Co-workers do not want to stick their necks out, because it will spoil relations at work. What good will that do them?"[26]

Obviously, the informal taboo among older co-workers on open discussion of their retirement means that older cadres do not help enforce retirement, but also that they do not openly foster a belief that retirement is widely rejected. It does not mean that retirement happens only as the product of private negotiations between middlemen and immediate targets of the policy. I asked retired cadres sur-

[24] Interview subject no. 8.
[25] Interview subject no. 36.
[26] Interview subject no. 6.

veyed whether or not a cadre who stayed on past the age of retirement would sense resentment on the part of co-workers. Responses were mostly positive among both retired cadres interviewed and questionnaire respondents. Among questionnaire respondents, 64 percent reported that at least some co-workers would make their resentment (*you yijian*) known to the cadre who stayed on, and 34 percent of respondents reported that a majority of co-workers would make their resentment known.[27] In sum, most retired cadres reported from experience that retirement is not socially enforced at the workplace through vocal or direct pressure on cadres who violate standards on age of retirement. Most observed, however, that co-workers do enforce it tacitly.

According to retired cadres interviewed, tacit pressure from co-workers can create an unproductive and uncomfortable working situation for cadres who stay on past the age of retirement. One retired veteran described the pressure which led him ultimately to disregard party committee instructions to continue working, even though he was officially retired, until a replacement for him could be found:

> Eventually I felt I had to leave. I could stay on no longer. The situation was really awkward. I was officially retired, but I had been told by the [party] organization to continue working. When I read documents or examined projects and had certain opinions on how things should be done, I wondered: "Should I raise my opinions about the work?" People at my workplace had their own views about my staying on. They didn't like it. How could I do my work? Finally, I simply stopped going to the office. I did not even notify the [party] organization or explain. I simply stopped going to work.[28]

Who are the voluntary enforcers of age-based exit at the workplace? Questionnaire respondents pointed to an obvious source of the perceived resentment—their young and middle-aged co-workers, those who stood most to gain from the retirement of their seniors. Sixty-eight percent reported young and middle-aged cadres as the main source of resentment, compared to 10 percent for retired cadres and only 4 percent for other cadres at the workplace.[29]

Before turning to a discussion of enforcement from the perspec-

---

[27] That this issue is viewed as taboo among older cadres is suggested also by the large number of questionnaire respondents who did not respond to this item. There are sixty-four missing observations for this item!

[28] Interview subject no. 1.

[29] Again, missing observations are many, sixty-two in all, on this item. See note 27 above.

tive of younger cadres, it is useful to draw attention to the political and historical context that has affected relations between older and younger cadres. In discussing retirement, several retired cadres spontaneously commented on past political events and current reforms. Generational cleavage was at the heart of their discussions.

Veteran cadres were the primary victims and young people the immediate beneficiaries and main activists of the Cultural Revolution. We know little about how the experience affected the values and beliefs of participants.[30] Generational tensions that do remain appear to be reinforced by different views about post-Mao reforms. Many retired cadres expressed skepticism about economic liberalization policies and revulsion against the culture of materialism it has unleashed:

> I am more conservative than my son regarding the reforms. I think the reforms are the same as capitalism. I really do not see the difference. So I am too conservative for the reforms. My views are different because of my revolutionary experience. . . . Now, with the standard of living raised in China, there are so many more things that need to be done—buying good food, cooking tasty dishes, getting nice clothes. It keeps you so busy you don't know whether you are coming or going (*mang le yi ta hutu*). Before, we would eat in the dining hall, wear whatever clothes were allocated, and not care about having nice furniture. Now everyone is thinking only about money.[31]

> Work was always the top priority for us veteran comrades. Even my children I gave to others to raise. I did not want to hold back the work by raising children and doing housework. Now, people are always thinking about money—bonuses, salary reform, promotions. We do not think in this way. In those days we were not afraid of sacrifice. I did not get married until after victory in the Anti-Japanese War. In those days there were people dying around us every day. . . . Young people today do not understand the situation then. During the Cultural Revolution they persecuted me. A young miss in a People's Liberation Army uniform! She did not understand a single thing about those days.[32]

Whether or not this sense of political generation gap and distrust is widespread remains speculative. Objectively, however, both the Cul-

---

[30] To my knowledge, a systematic study of this question has yet to be done. Many excellent biographical and autobiographical accounts are available in English, but most are written from the perspective of youths who were Red Guards at the time or from the persective of persecuted intellectuals. We know comparatively little about the effects of the Cultural Revolution on the beliefs of cadres.

[31] Interview subject no. 6.

[32] Interview subject no. 22.

tural Revolution and post-Mao economic modernization have pitted the generations against each other. The policies of cadre retirement and rejuvenation of the cadre corps also split the generations.

Policy makers let all cadres know that retirement of the old and promotion of the young and middle-aged were "two sides to the same question."[33] From the opening sections of this chapter, we know that retired cadres are familiar with this argument, although they may not support its implications. Of course, younger cadres also got the point. Younger cadres interviewed demonstrated amply that they perceived the relationship as zero-sum. Here is a small sample of their comments on the issue:

> People really resent it. If the old ones don't move, we young people can't move up.[34]

> This affects young people's promotion. And these old cadres are no good themselves, but they look down on young cadres.[35]

> This affects the promotion of young cadres. There are not many positions.[36]

> Each workplace has an authorized number of positions (*bianzhi*). If a cadre does not retire, he occupies a place on the *bianzhi*. Also, if he is a leader he takes up a leading position. So young cadres can't rise. It affects their immediate interests.[37]

> You might want these [old cadres] to stay on to be resources. But it is in your interest to want them to step down, this [latter] perspective is the most common.[38]

> Young people want retirement because they are being held back.[39]

> The young want cadres to retire. If they don't retire there is a conflict between the two generations.[40]

> If a cadre does not retire, maybe he thinks he can still do a good job. But young people think they can do as good a job. So they resent it.[41]

[33] See the discussion of rule enforcement in chapter 2.
[34] Interview subject no. 100.
[35] Interview subject no. 76.
[36] Interview subject no. 68.
[37] Interview subject no. 94.
[38] Interview subject no. 85.
[39] Interview subject no. 46.
[40] Interview subject no. 52.
[41] Interview subject no. 67.

TABLE 4.4
Reactions to Late Retirement of Co-Workers

Reaction	Respondents Indicating Reactions Specified (%)
Resentment	91
Talk among themselves	80
Directly communicate views to co-worker [violating age standards]	2
Indirectly communicate views to co-worker [violating age standards]	69
Communicate views to workplace leaders or those responsible for cadre work	47

No. of cases: 65, 58, 58, 54, 55 in above order.
Percentages are based on these numbers.

Question: Suppose that at your workplace a cadre past the age of retirement continues to work and does not retire. What would be the reactions of most young and middle-aged cadres? Reactions were presented sequentially in above order with response options: agree/disagree. If subjects indicated there would be no resentment, other reactions were not probed.

I asked younger cadres about the reactions of young and middle-aged cadres at their workplaces to senior co-workers who work past the ages of retirement.[42] Responses are summarized in Table 4.4.

The first thing to note about Table 4.4 is the overwhelming majority of younger cadres reporting that young and middle-aged co-workers do indeed resent (again, *you yijian*) older cadres who stay on to work past the stipulated age of retirement. Thus the perception of retired cadres surveyed is not inaccurate: 91 percent of younger cadres interviewed corroborated their view that younger co-workers resent violations of retirement age standards. And 80 percent reported that young and middle-aged cadres talk among themselves about older cadres who violate these standards. In sum, younger cadres resent late retirement and older cadres know it. How is the resentment communicated to them?

Apparently, it is not communicated directly. Nearly all who were

[42] I phrased the question as a hypothetical situation. Despite usual problems with the hypothethical line of questioning with Chinese respondents, I had little difficulty in obtaining responses. This was probably because most interviewed had in fact encountered the situation.

asked (all but 2 percent) responded with a vigorous negative when presented with this alternative. One cadre summed up their inhibitions with a categorical (and normative) statement: "This is not permitted (*bu yunxu*) in China."[43]

Even without direct communication, however, older cadres know what their younger co-workers think of late retirement. A large majority of younger cadres (69 percent of those asked) choose to communicate their resentment indirectly. Indirect communication takes on many forms. Younger cadres pretend to express concern over the older cadre's health, suggesting to him he ought to take a rest. They joke casually with him, reminding him he is no longer young. They suggest that others resent his postponement of retirement. They talk to his friends or relatives about it. They discuss their disapproval of late retirement in general terms at group meetings organized at the workplace, perhaps using an example from the newspaper. They can also be passive or even uncooperative in work situations, creating obstacles for the older cadre. Merely discussing the problem with other young and middle-aged cadres can be enough to get the message across. One younger cadre remarked: "If I talk to co-workers, it will very quickly get relayed to him."[44] Others reiterated this view: "When we talk about him, he may or may not hear it. But he will sense the feeling about it."[45]

Younger cadres interviewed were about evenly divided on the question of confiding their views to leaders or officials in charge of implementing the policy at the workplace. Clearly, the views of younger cadres are fully consistent with official policy. However, those responsible for cadre retirement are in the powerful party organization department—the department that keeps personnel files, investigates and vets cadres, and recommends for or against promotions.[46] Because of this, younger cadres are cautious in their dealings with leaders and the department. Here is a sample of their views:

> If you raise your views the leaders will think: "This person is a careerist (*you yexin*)." So people are pretty correct with leaders, they don't tell them what they are really thinking. If you reveal your views, especially to the organization department, then you will never rise.[47]

[43] Interview subject no. 87.
[44] Interview subject no. 56.
[45] Interview subject no. 60.
[46] See Burns, "China's *Nomenklatura* System"; Manion, "The Cadre Management System, Post-Mao"; Lee, *From Revolutionary Cadres to Party Technocrats in Socialist China*, 329–84.
[47] Interview subject no. 85.

If he doesn't retire, he must have his reasons. And in this society he must also have backing (*kaoshan*). Saying something is no use, [you] might as well say nothing.[48]

It's no use. There's nothing in it for you. You have to keep your own interests in mind. It can only work against you, it can't work to your advantage.[49]

If I raise my opinion it might hurt me. Personal relations are very complex. I can get "punished" for raising opinions. You have to be careful who you talk to among leaders.[50]

In transferring from state to society the responsibility for enforcing cadre retirement policy, policy makers can rely on the tacit and indirect (but nonetheless widespread and widely sensed) enforcement of retirement by younger cadres. As noted, younger cadres have a vested interest in enforcing the retirement of their senior co-workers because moving up into positions depends largely on older cadres moving out of them. In this sense, policy makers have succeeded in manipulating an objective conflict of interest between the two generations.

Of course, cadre retirement in the form policy makers have presented it, as a process to be institutionalized, will one day be the fate of younger cadres too. Though they may perceive the situation as zero-sum, the conflict of interest is in fact only partial. Younger cadres are beginning a process of social enforcement that will eventually force them to retire. The mechanism at work here, described in chapter 1 as a "metanorm," exploits the immediate self-interest of one group to perform what would otherwise be a costly state function. And it is self-sustaining, since there will always be younger cadres willing to act as unofficial enforcers of retirement.

Does it make sense for younger cadres to cooperate in enforcing retirement? The answer is yes, for two reasons. First, younger cadres will reap the benefits of enforcement before they incur the costs. For them, the prospect of promotion is immediate, the prospect of retirement is distant. In fact, for younger cadres interviewed, their own retirement seems so distant as to be beyond consideration. Most had simply not given it a thought. The potential reward of promotion in the near future carries far more weight for younger cadres than the eventual cost of retirement in the remote future. Second, uncertainty undoubtedly plays a role in the conscious or unconscious calculations

[48] Interview subject no. 88.
[49] Interview subject no. 91.
[50] Interview subject no. 80.

of younger cadres. Policy in the People's Republic of China shifts frequently and dramatically. While both the reward of promotion and the cost of retirement lie somewhere in the future for younger cadres, the degree of uncertainty about the latter is clearly greater.

GROWTH OF A NORM

Up to this point, the examination of variation has focused mainly on differences across individuals and groups. This section looks at variation across time. In the course of a decade, from 1978 to 1988, there were important changes in how cadres responded to policy. These changes suggest the growth of a norm of cadre retirement.

Retired cadres interviewed were easily able to review for me official arguments supporting the policy of cadre retirement, which led me above to the modest conclusion that cadres know at least what they ought to think about retirement. Of course, their review of policy arguments reflects the situation in 1986–87, when the interviews were conducted. I was also interested to know the extent to which the understanding of policy had developed over the years since it was first introduced. How much did it reflect the efforts of policy makers to promote it, its simple persistence in time, and an increasing population of already retired cadres?

My research was conducted essentially at one point in time and, therefore, I lack the observations for a proper longitudinal study. However, cadres surveyed had retired at different points in time. Rather than abandon completely the question of change, I decided to rely on their recall. I asked retired cadres to recall their initial understanding of how cadre retirement policy applied to them personally. I reasoned that if an understanding of policy had in fact developed over the years, then the more recently retired cadres would report a better understanding of it—in the sense that they would have grasped better than cadres who had retired in the policy's earlier years that retirement policy applied to them. I found (with a few notable exceptions) that retired cadres did indeed describe their sense of understanding and surprise or expectations about their retirement in ways that form such a trend.

Cadres who had retired soon after the policy was introduced seemed not to recognize their retirement as part of an official policy, set in Beijing, to establish a cadre retirement system. A veteran who had retired in late 1978 noted: "In 1978 when I retired, there was no cadre retirement system."[51] And one who had retired some years later remarked: "Before 1982 I did not think about retirement, because there was no such system."[52]

Indeed, as late as mid-1982 when the first big wave of retirements took place and a cadre retirement system clearly existed, it seems that cadres could still be caught by surprise to discover that the policy applied to them. One observed: "For the first group, my group, the ideological work was inadequate. It was too sudden. We heard about the policy of cadre retirement. Then, only a few months later, we learned *we* would be the ones to step down."[53]

This is surprising, considering the attention the press gave to the issues of lifelong tenure and cadre retirement in 1980. The year 1982, however, marks the peak of official attention to cadre retirement. Top party and government organizations issued nearly as many documents in that year as in 1978–81 altogether. And the party newspaper *Renmin ribao* printed more than twice as many articles on cadre retirement in 1982 as had been printed on the subject in 1978–81. Cadres who retired at the end of 1982 and in 1983 seem to have been well prepared for it, as they indicated in their comments, which also suggest the key role of official documents in communicating policy intentions:

> In 1982 the Central Committee issued the decision on cadre retirement. There were documents. I heeded the party's call. I requested retirement. It was approved quickly.[54]

> I did not feel any real lack of psychological preparation (*sixiang zhunbei*) for my retirement. I had read the documents about cadre retirement. Even before this, I had heard rumors about the retirement system being established.[55]

> I had studied the documents and I responded to the party's call: I took the initiative to raise the issue of my retirement, I requested retirement on my own initiative. The leaders consented. I understood the rationale of cadre retirement policy.[56]

By 1986 most cadres seemed to know exactly what to expect and when to expect it:

[51] Interview subject no. 35.
[52] Interview subject no. 17.
[53] Interview subject no. 22.
[54] Interview subject no. 33.
[55] Interview subject no. 9.
[56] Interview subject no. 17.

FIGURE 4.1

Understanding Retirement Policy

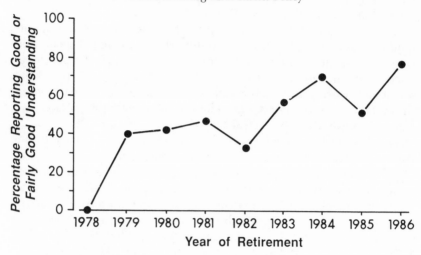

No. of cases: 237

Question: At the time of my retirement, my understanding of cadre retirement policy is best characterized as: essentially, I did not understand it; I did not understand it too well; I had a fairly good understanding of it; I had a very good understanding of it.

Before I retired, the rationale for cadre retirement policy was clear to me. This is because a lot of people had already retired.[57]

There is now no problem of cadres being psychologically unprepared for retirement. Everyone has read the documents, everyone knows he will probably have to retire at the age specified. (But there are those who do not want to retire.)[58]

On the whole, the understanding of official policy that retired cadres demonstrated in interviews in 1986–87 seems to have been accumulated over time. I also explored this question in the questionnaire distributed to retired cadres, asking them to recall and report on their understanding of retirement policy at the time of their own retirement. Results are summarized in Figure 4.1, which sorts respondents by year of retirement and shows the percentage that reported a good or fairly good understanding of policy for each year.

There are two interesting things about Figure 4.1, which tend to support and indeed refine the conclusion drawn from interviews with retired cadres. First, the general trend is clearly one of increasing

[57] Interview subject no. 30.
[58] Interview subject no. 12.

understanding of policy over time. Second, there are two marked dips in the trend line, in 1982 and 1985, and these low points in understanding of policy make good sense. Policy on cadre retirement changed significantly three times since its introduction in 1978: in 1982, 1985, and 1988.[59] It is quite reasonable to suppose that the targets of these changes did not understand immediately the new policy or its relevance to them personally. A process of learning is at work here. This makes particular sense for the most important set of policy changes, introduced in February 1982. That was when age finally became the standard decision rule for retirement, when retirement was linked to campaigns to streamline the bureaucracies and rejuvenate leading groups, and when cadres began to be retired in groups. It is also reasonable for the policy changes in 1985, when campaign-style retirement was ended and replaced by routine processing of retirement after talks with middlemen at the workplace.

Not only do the 1982 and 1985 dips make sense when we take changes in policy into account, they also add credibility to all the data points. We can easily imagine that reports of understanding of policy at the time of retirement, based entirely on recall, can be unreliable for a number of reasons. Cadres may confound their current understanding with that at the time of retirement, revealing no systematic pattern at all. Less recent retirees may have greater difficulty with recall and thus report less reliably than more recent retirees, producing a trend line only for the later years of policy. Most relevant for the case here, a near-perfect trend line (such as that suggested by aggregating comments of retired cadres interviewed) can also be an artifact of recall: the greater the difficulty with recall, the more likely it may be for cadres simply to respond negatively, that is, to report that they did not understand the policy. The pattern in Figure 4.1, which looks generally as posited, also rules out this last alternative hypothesis because the low points coincide with policy changes in 1982 and 1985 and this association makes sense.

There is good reason to conclude, then, that as the policy of cadre retirement persisted over the years and more and more cadres retired, understanding of the policy grew and was accompanied by expectations of retirement at the ages specified.

Analysis at the aggregate level in chapter 3 suggested age-based exit from office was probably not the norm, in the simple behavioral sense, in 1978–88. Analysis at the individual level and an examination of the retirement process provided some notion of why. Obviously, because we are interested here in assessing change over time, it is

---

[59] See chapter 2, passim.

important to ask whether or not there are signs of increasing proportions of on-time retirement over the years. As best I can tell, the answer is yes.

First of all, interviews strongly indicated cadres were retiring closer
to prescribed ages by the late 1980s. Younger cadres interviewed responded almost unanimously that they no longer observed the aber-
rations in retirement characteristic of the late 1970s and early 1980s.
On-time retirement, by their accounts, has become a "hard and fast
rule" (*ying gang*). Retired cadres interviewed also commented on the
change in discussing the current situation at their former workplace.
Some noted a trend in adaptive self-enforcement of retirement:

> They have records of how old cadres are. Now, as soon as people reach
> that age, they seek them out and these people retire. People know this
> now and so they take the initiative to request retirement when it is time.[60]

> Now, the implementation of retirement is stricter. Now, you must retire
> at retirement age. For example, now at my former workplace, every
> cadre retires at retirement age. Even if you do not want to retire, you
> must retire.[61]

Second, recall that the regression analysis presented in chapter 3
included policy stage as an explanatory variable. My purpose was to
test for change in deviation from on-time retirement beginning in
1985, when policy makers began to routinize implementation of retirement policy. I found policy stage statistically insignificant, but
pointed out that the dependent variable in the regression was in fact
inappropriate to the hypothesis. The predicted effect we really want
to explore is both less early and less late retirement, that is, decrease
in *absolute* deviation from on-time retirement. This is a way of measuring the growth of age-based exit from office as a behavioral norm.

To this end, I ran the same regression again but with the dependent variable transformed to absolute values. With this model, policy
stage is indeed significant: the variable coefficient is -1.10, with a
probability of .02.[62] Other things equal, in 1985–87 there was less
deviation from on-time retirement than in previous years. In sum,
cadres were indeed retiring closer to the ages prescribed by government standards.

Finally, it is not unreasonable to speculate about the impact of two
policy adjustments, in 1986 and 1988, that seem highly relevant to

---

[60] Interview subject no. 1.

[61] Interview subject no. 7.

[62] The standard error is .53, the t-ratio is -2.08, and the test for statistical significance is one-tailed.

increases in on-time retirement. The comparison of expected and actual retirement of veterans suggested many cases of early retirement in 1982–86. We also know that early retirement was typically associated with employment substitution.[63] In abolishing employment substitution, which policy makers eventually did in 1986, it seems probable that policy makers greatly reduced the appeal of early retirement. A younger cadre interviewed made precisely this point in describing the situation in his locality: "At the end of the 1970s there was a lot of early retirement. It was linked to employment substitution. Now there is almost no early retirement. There is also no employment substitution."[64]

A second policy adjustment that seems relevant here has to do with the request to retire. According to reports in provincial journals, eliminating the request to retire had a major impact on whether and when cadres retired. With the retirement decision entirely in the hands of middlemen, the process of retirement became an administrative routine in which cadres were retired within a month or so of when they reached the age stipulated for their retirement.[65] Policy makers in Beijing eliminated the request to retire on a countrywide basis in 1988. There is no reason to expect that the impact of the change in localities where it was initiated is not similar to that being experienced across the country.

Another factor, having to do with demography rather than policy, may also help to promote the growth of age-based exit from office as a behavioral norm. In 1978, especially after the reinstatement of veterans purged during the Cultural Revolution, workplaces had larger proportions of cadres at or past the age of retirement. The retirement of millions of cadres has changed this situation and left the workplaces with higher proportions of young and middle-aged cadres. Given what we know about the role of younger cadres as voluntary enforcers of retirement policy, there is good reason to believe that the workplace atmosphere is more conducive to cadre retirement than it was previously—and that, barring major changes in policy, this will continue to be true.

SUMMARY

Chinese cadres are adept at discovering and paraphrasing the views prevailing at the top. They clearly know what they ought to think

[63] See chapter 3 on aggregate retirement and employment substitution.
[64] Interview subject no. 64.
[65] See chapter 3 on middlemen and their incentive structure.

about retirement, whether or not they actually think this way. Actual private views of cadres tend to reflect their private interests. Younger cadres have an interest in the retirement of their senior co-workers: moving up into positions depends largely on older cadres moving out of them. Not surprisingly, then, the younger generations of cadres support age-based exit from office in greater proportions than do older cadres.

These private views have action implications. Older cadres do not enforce retirement among themselves. Indeed, they observe an informal taboo on discussing retirement. This taboo is not conducive to promoting the growth of a norm of retirement, but it also implies that older cadres do not foster a belief that retirement is widely rejected. Further, while older cadres do not actively promote the emergence of a norm of retirement, younger cadres do. Younger cadres resent violations of the age standards for retirement and they find ways to communicate this resentment at work. Older cadres sense the resentment.

Policy makers have succeeded in manipulating a conflict of interest between the two generations. In transferring from state to society the responsibility for enforcing policy, policy makers can rely on the tacit and indirect enforcement of retirement by younger cadres. Most important, regardless of a perception of the situation as zero-sum, the conflict is only partial. Younger cadres are setting in motion a machinery of social enforcement that in time will put them too out of office. This machinery is self-sustaining, given younger cadres who will always be present to act as natural enforcers of retirement.

CHAPTER FIVE

After Retirement

POLICY MAKERS in Beijing aimed to achieve more than the formality of age-based exit from office. Their effort to build a retirement norm to replace the tradition of lifelong tenure was designed to change substantially the relationship between older cadres and regular work. Their policy measures proposed some sort of role for retired cadres, particularly veteran cadres, but formal retirement procedures were supposed nonetheless to bring about actual severance from regular work at the workplace.

This chapter asks whether and how formal retirement has made any real difference in the relationship between retired cadres and work. The key issue is the extent to which retirement has brought about severance from regular work. I begin by elaborating briefly the policy principles that provide a rationale for retired cadres to persist in some sort of work role. I then examine the evidence that suggests cadre retirement has in fact been accompanied by a change that amounts to severance from regular work. I follow this with a closer look at two kinds of activities that seem so closely to resemble the pre-retirement work experience and are so widespread among retired cadres as to challenge the argument that retirement has made a substantial difference.

As in the previous two chapters, I rely a good deal here on information from retired cadres I surveyed. But, where relevant, I supplement this material with findings from surveys conducted and reported by Chinese social scientists in a wide range of scholarly journals. To be sure, some of these reports neglect to provide basic information about how the survey was conducted and how the sample was selected. Many are descriptive listings of univariate distributions, only some examine bivariate relationships, and none attempt any multivariate analysis. Most provide no rationale for tests of relationships between particular variables. All the same, by drawing on surveys conducted in other localities where relevant and focusing on relationships between variables where possible, I broaden the empirical perspective on questions in my own surveys and supplement my work with other information.

POLICY PRINCIPLES ON WORK AFTER RETIREMENT

The best articulated principles on work after retirement are those designed for retired veteran cadres. By contrast and as in other aspects of cadre retirement policy, the principles governing work for regularly retired cadres are less developed. As a result of this, two different ethos of work after retirement seem to have developed: one for retired veteran cadres, another for retired postrevolutionary cadres. It may be that the latter is only a set of common practices that have evolved and to which policy makers have yet to turn their attention.[1] The former is more clearly a product of policy, implemented by the veteran cadre departments charged with managing retired revolutionary cadres.

In early 1983, policy makers began to publicize the notion of retirement as simply a new work assignment in a career devoted to making revolution. Retirement was introduced not as the end of a revolutionary career but as the beginning of a new stage in that career. The term "exploiting surplus energy" (*fahui yure*) was aired at about the same time.[2] The principle of exploiting surplus energy was designed to promote post-retirement activities, that is, the new assignment, for veteran cadres. Both ideas have been consistently applied to veteran cadres only.[3] Policy makers have assured veteran cadres that they will continue to play an active work role after retirement. Indeed, as described in chapter 2, through the promotion of exemplars in the Chinese press this role has been elevated almost to the level of duty.

The idea of the new assignment is by no means intended to nullify cadre retirement policy. It generally does not involve cadres in the regular work of their former workplace; it is supposed to be purely voluntary and unpaid; it does not usually require going into the workplace regularly or often; and retired cadres are usually free to work at their own pace. Typically, the work is political work or specially created projects. Examples I noted in chapter 2 include investigating abuses of power or economic crimes, helping with party rec-

---

[1] This was suggested by Wang Xingming (Deputy Director of Cadre Retirement Division, Veteran Cadre Bureau, Ministry of Labor and Personnel), interviewed in Beijing, 24 Nov. 1986, and in his "Chuyi ganbu tuixiu zhidu de gaige."

[2] The expression comes originally from the use of residual thermal energy of an industrial furnace. This residual energy is used for purposes such as providing hot water—thus continuing to supply an economic and social benefit. Apparently, some veteran cadres resent the implications of the term because the raging flames of the furnace have become faint and dying embers. See Shi, "Hai shi bu ti 'yure' hao."

[3] See the discussion in chapter 3 about a new assignment for revolutionaries.

tification, recruiting new party members, checking up on policy implementation at lower levels, writing party histories and revolutionary memoirs, and conducting propaganda work among the masses, especially among youth.

The Ministry of Labor and Personnel newspaper has summarized the unique dual character of the veteran cadre retirement system as follows:

> The absolutely strict feature [of the system] is the implementation of [retirement] procedures according to regulations that cadres must leave the workpost. The relative feature is [the fact] that after [veteran] cadres retire, their status ... does not change. They continue to realize the spirit of involvement in the socialist cause and party members continue to participate in party building. They do their best to contribute their surplus energy.[4]

In short, severance from regular work is not considered in the least inconsistent with taking part in work activities, even activities arranged by leaders and veteran cadre departments at the former workplace. Certainly, each of the activities listed as examples above are properly subsumed under the category of work. But policy makers as well as retired cadres distinguish clearly between these activities and the regular work in which cadres engage before retirement.

The continued work role after retirement is supposed to make the transition easier for veteran cadres who had expected to be in office for the rest of their lives. And it is also the case that, even for a relatively elite group such as Chinese communist cadres, there was no established culture of leisure in 1978, when retirement policy was introduced. When veteran cadre departments were only starting to be organized, a leisurely retirement meant, at best, nothing to do. At worst, it could be construed as a form of parasitic behavior.

For this reason, at the same time policy makers promoted a post-retirement work role, they promoted schools and recreation centers for retired cadres. The first university for the elderly was founded in September 1983. Only five years later, nearly 500 universities and schools for the elderly were operating, spanning practically the entire country. And over thirty newspapers and popular magazines for the elderly were in circulation.[5] In cities all across the country, veteran cadre departments established veteran cadre centers for retired revolutionaries. In these centers, retired veterans come together regu-

---

[4] *Laodong renshi bao*, 29 July 1987, 2.
[5] "Proportion of Elderly is Increasing."

larly to read newspapers and magazines, catch up on important documents, play cards and other games, or simply chat.

Since funding and organizations for retired postrevolutionary cadres are not well established, the veteran cadre centers reflect again the differences between veterans and postrevolutionaries. Leisure activities are not typically organized for retired postrevolutionary cadres. For them, activities after retirement are more often new jobs they find for themselves and with which they supplement their pension income. I take a closer look at their post-retirement experience in the final section of this chapter.

SEVERANCE FROM REGULAR WORK

What interests us most about the post-retirement experience of Chinese cadres in the past decade is a simple question: "So what?" That is, to what extent has formal retirement made a real difference in the relationship between retired cadres and work? Judging from my own surveys, it seems that for those cadres who were not exempted by policy from full retirement, retirement has brought about an actual and perceived severance from regular work. On the whole, other information from survey work conducted by the Chinese supports this conclusion.

Retired cadres interviewed described a workplace with a continually changing work agenda. They expressed the opinion that without routine association with work at the workplace, they were practically disqualified from participating in work as before. The link between work role and physical presence at the former workplace is hardly surprising. The post-retirement dislocation experienced by the first wave of retired cadres was further exacerbated by the reduction and merger of departments in the structural reform begun in 1982. For them, to return to the workplace after retirement is to find a different workplace.

If, in fact, it is the case that retirement has not produced a substantial change in the relationship between older cadres and work, then this is surely bound to be reflected in frequent visits to the former workplace. On the other hand, because of the multifunctional character of the Chinese workplace and because retirement is not necessarily supposed to be accompanied by termination of the relation with the workplace, frequent visits after retirement are not a sufficient indicator of no change.

With this in mind, I asked questionnaire respondents about how frequently they returned to the former workplace and for what pur-

TABLE 5.1
Visits to the Former Workplace

PURPOSE OF VISIT	FREQUENCY OF VISIT			
	Frequent (%)	Moderate (%)	Infrequent (%)	Total (%)
Work	9	3	1	14
Collect pension	2	29	13	45
Political	4	14	3	20
Social	2	2	2	7
Other	0	3	2	5
No basis for response	0	0	9	9
Total	18	52	31	100

No. of cases: 208

Questions: (1) I return to my former workplace: a few times each week; a few times every two weeks; a few times each month; a few times each half-year; I basically do not return. (2) The main reason I return to my former workplace is: the requirements of work; to visit with co-workers; to familiarize myself with major national events or participate in [party] organizational activities; to collect my pension; other; because I basically do not return, I am unable to respond.

Notes: "Frequent" refers to visits of several times per week or two weeks, "moderate" refers to visits of several times per month, and "infrequent" refers to visits less frequent than this. Percentages may not add up due to rounding.

pose. Their responses are summarized in Table 5.1. In my opinion, they strongly suggest a severance from regular work and, more generally, perhaps an attenuated relation with the former workplace.

There are a few kinds of information we can extract from Table 5.1 that lead to this conclusion. Erring first on the side of underestimating the significance of retirement, we can consider frequency of visits to the office as the critical indicator of involvement in regular work. We can view, again conservatively, visits of at least a few times every two weeks as frequent enough for cadres to maintain familiarity with work. By this standard, we find 18 percent of retired cadres reporting a frequent enough presence at the former workplace to allow them to continue regular work. Alternatively, if we focus instead on why cadres return to the former workplace, we find a slightly smaller proportion, 14 percent, who reported they return mainly for reasons having anything to do with work. Probably the most sensible standard combines frequency and purpose of visits, which cuts the original estimate in half. Nine percent of cadres reported they return to the workplace frequently and do so primarily to work.[6] The remaining 91 percent of respondents return no more often than a few times a month, return mainly for reasons other than work, or both. For them, the workplace has essentially ceased to be a work center. It has become instead a center for political involvement, socializing, or simply the administrative unit that manages practical matters such as pension and housing.

Even as regards the activities that make up organized political life (attending political meetings, hearing speeches and reports on policy, going to party member activities, and reading important policy documents, for example), the relationship with the workplace appears weak.[7] An extensive and methodologically conscientious 1984 survey of 576 retired veteran cadres in Ha'erbin found 39 percent of cadres reporting irregular (*bu zhengchang*) participation in political life and another 23 percent reporting no one pays attention (*wu ren guan*) to their political life at all.[8] Retired cadres I interviewed offered similar reports, some expressing the view that retirement from political life, while not in keeping with official policy, was welcome. One noted: "I can still read the same documents as when I was on the job. Actually, there are too many documents. Some of them are not worth reading. The important ones I can read in the newspapers anyway."[9] Others were more emphatic in their views:

> At first I went back to the workplace to read newspapers and documents, to catch up on current events of state. Now I don't know and I don't care. If you are working every day at the workplace, you will lose face if you don't know what is going on nationally. Now, who cares? . . . Now I think that even reading documents is too much work. All those tiny, tiny characters give me a headache and make me feel sick (*exin*).[10]

Consistent with this picture of a weak relationship with the workplace is evidence about the socializing that cadres engage in after retirement. The 1984 Ha'erbin study found the highest proportion of retired veteran cadres, 37 percent, have most of their social interaction with relatives, while another 28 percent have the most social interaction with neighbors or friends.[11] A 1982 study that sampled 237

---

[6] The entire 9 percent report they return to the workplace several times per week.

[7] This may have nothing to do with retirement. It does, however, clearly contradict retirement policy for veteran cadres.

[8] Ha'erbin shi shehui kexue yanjiu suo shehuixue yanjiu shi, "Ha'erbin shi lixiu ganbu zhuangkuang diaocha baogao (shang)."

[9] Interview subject no. 32.

[10] Interview subject no. 6.

[11] Ha'erbin shi shehui kexue yanjiu suo shehuixue yanjiu shi, "Ha'erbin shi lixiu ganbu zhuangkuang diaocha baogao (shang)."

retired personnel in Beijing found that retired cadres have most of their social interaction with family members. Friends and neighbors (who are not former co-workers) rank second and third. Before retirement, cadres in the sample interacted socially most often with co-workers. Excluding family members and relatives, this same study found 67 percent of retired cadres interact socially with no more than five people.[12] A study sampling 207 retired veteran cadres in Guangzhou found 45 percent interact most with old comrades they met during the revolutionary wars. Another 31 percent interact most often with relatives, friends, and neighbors. Before retirement, 70 percent of cadres interacted socially most often with co-workers.[13] An excellent 1985 survey of nearly three thousand Tianjin residents in different age groups found only 42 percent of respondents over age sixty claim to have any friends among co-workers. The comparable figures for young and middle-aged respondents are 86 and 83 percent, respectively.[14] In sum, the Chinese surveys find that as retired cadres decrease the time spent at the workplace they also "retire" from regular social interaction with co-workers and enter instead a more private world of social interaction with family, friends, and neighbors. This too is bound to weaken the relationship with the former workplace.

The above suggests an actual attenuation of the relationship with the workplace—especially as work center. The severance from regular work at the former workplace is also a perceived one. Retired cadres interviewed acknowledged that with retirement and the lack of familiarity with the changing work agenda, they no longer felt they belonged at the workplace:

> I don't return to the workplace. I don't know what's going on there. The work is always changing and I can't get a word in edgewise. I don't want to disrupt the work. . . . If they ask for our opinions we give them, otherwise we don't give them. In any case, after the merger of ministries we have no idea about what's going on anymore. We can't play a role.[15]

> I don't like to return to the workplace unless I have some real business. Everyone there is busy, they have their own things to do. I am interrupting the work.[16]

[12] Lin and Geng, "Tuixiu zhigong kaocha."
[13] Li, "Lixiu lao ganbu manyi chengdu fenxi." Retired cadres who interact most often with co-workers are fewer in number in both this survey (20 percent) and the Ha'erbin survey (23 percent). The Beijing survey does not provide this information.
[14] Wang, "Laonianren shehui jiaowang de zhuyao tezheng ji bianhua quxiang."
[15] Interview subject no. 22.
[16] Interview subject no. 17.

I don't return often. I am retired and they are working. I don't really know what is going on, so I can't really raise useful opinions about work. I just bother them if I go in.[17]

Most questionnaire respondents also indicated they felt they had no useful role to play in work at the workplace. Asked about their former workplace, only 19 percent responded that they could still play a role and raise useful opinions about work.[18] More to the point, only a small proportion (9 percent) indicated they could play no role because those at the workplace were unwilling to listen to their views. Most respondents did not attribute their lack of a useful role to particular individuals at the workplace but to the retirement situation per se: 34 percent responded they were unable to raise useful opinions because of unfamiliarity with ongoing work, and 19 percent responded that those without a position ipso facto have no role to play. This suggests that cadres accept severance from regular work as an integral part of the implicit retirement contract, as opposed to violation of the terms of that contract by cadres at their former workplace.

Additional evidence supporting this inference is provided by perspectives on a problem discussed in the Chinese press as a cold reception after retirement (*ren zou cha liang*), especially at the former workplace. Specific manifestations are a lack of respect for retired cadres, unwillingness to listen to their views, inattention to their right to unchanged access to political information, lack of personal warmth toward them, and reluctance to be the administrative channel to resolve their mundane concrete problems.

Among retired veteran cadres sampled in the 1984 Ha'erbin study, 37 percent noted that leaders at the former workplace have a markedly less warm attitude toward them compared to that experienced before they retired. But only about half of these cadres reported that this change made them feel at all resentful or dissatisfied.[19] Retired cadres I interviewed also complained about a cold reception after retirement, although several insisted they were relating problems of friends rather than their own problems. Their complaints focused overwhelmingly on difficulties in getting simple things done for them

[17] Interview subject no. 1.

[18] The question was worded as follows. When I return to my former workplace I feel: I can still play a role, I am able to provide useful opinions about work; I am not very familiar with the work situation and so am unable to provide useful opinions; when you hold no office, you play no role in matters of office (*bu zai qi wei bu mou qi zheng*); people at work do not want to listen to my opinions; because I basically do not return, I am unable to respond.

[19] Ha'erbin shi shehui kexue yanjiu suo shehuixue yanjiu shi, "Ha'erbin shi lixiu ganbu zhuangkuang diaocha baogao (shang)."

and on concern for their material welfare. The following is a typical observation:

> Many of my friends who have retired tell me they have experienced this problem [of a cold reception]. People simply do not help them get anything done. Young people are promoted to positions of leadership and sometimes they don't care about retired cadres. This is especially a problem if the newly promoted cadres have been transferred from another workplace. Then you don't have any connection with them. The truth is: we old revolutionaries have done a lot for the country. And these young people are taking our positions. They should give us more attention. As for me, I can get a car when I need it. But some of my friends cannot get a car from the workplace when they need it. Cars are available but the workplace simply won't let them have a car to use.[20]

By the content of their complaints, which focus on the mundane rather than on participation in work, retired cadres implicitly seem to acknowledge retirement as severance from regular work. This is even more evident in responses to questions specifically exploring the problem of a cold reception for their opinions about work:

> Of course I feel a cold reception after retirement. My retired friends complain about this a lot. They feel it more than I do. But we cannot be too demanding. We are not on the job. We are not doing the work anymore. We don't know what is going on at work. I could raise my views but I don't really understand what is going on. So it is natural that some people don't pay attention to my views.[21]

> Of course it is not the same as when you are working. After all, you are not working. And so your demands should not be the same as when you were working. You are not doing the work anymore. You should not demand the same attention as those doing the work.[22]

Questionnaire respondents were also asked about a cold reception after retirement. Because of the presumed sensitivity of the issue, I did not phrase the question in terms of their own experience. Rather, I asked them to identify what they considered as the core problem area of a cold reception after retirement. Here too, dissatisfaction with the post-retirement relation with the workplace does not seem to be centered on work-related issues. A large proportion of responses (61 percent) reported concern for material welfare as the core problem area, while only a small proportion (13 percent) re-

[20] Interview subject no. 26.
[21] Interview subject no. 21.
[22] Interview subject no. 32.

ported respect for opinions as the core problem area.[23] These findings seem further to support the proposition that retired cadres generally acknowledge retirement as severance from regular work.

Practical and material matters also emerge as the main concern of
retired cadres in surveys conducted by the Chinese. The 1984
Ha'erbin survey finds over half their sample reporting some unre-
solved practical problem (*shiji wenti*, not including financial problems)
as the most important concern after retirement. Only 19 percent of
cadres in this survey report practical problems as a problem before
retirement.[24] Two other surveys that ask about problems encountered after retirement find similar results. A 1982 survey of 150 retired personnel in Jilin city finds housing to be the most common
problem after retirement.[25] A Guangzhou survey of 452 retired personnel also finds housing to be the problem most want resolved.[26]

While severance from regular work is not an easy concept to measure, the evidence suggests at least that retirement matters: formal
retirement produces a substantial change in the relation between cadres and work. Evidence from my own surveys and from surveys conducted by the Chinese in other localities suggests more than this. The
notion of severance from regular work seems to accurately capture
what is going on. Retired cadres go to the office much less frequently
and they are unfamiliar with the work being done there. They asso-
ciate far less with former co-workers and far more with people having no connection with work. They do not seem to perceive a useful

[23] The question was worded as follows. The most important sense of a cold reception
(*ren zou cha liang*) is: a lack of concern for you as regards political matters; a lack of
concern for your material welfare; people no longer help you get things done; people
no longer listen to your opinions; in society generally, people do not respect you.

[24] Ha'erbin shi shehui kexue yanjiu suo shehuixue yanjiu shi, "Ha'erbin shi lixiu
ganbu zhuangkuang diaocha baogao (xia)."

[25] Jilin shi di si renmin yiyuan Jilin sheng meikuang gongren wenquan yiyuan, "150
ming chengshi tuixiu gongren, ganbu de xinli diaocha."

[26] Zhu, "Guangzhou shi lixiu tuixiu laonianren de shehui, xinli ji jiankang zhuangkuang de diaocha baogao." It is not surprising that many retired cadres find housing
a serious problem after retirement. A large proportion of the elderly share housing
with a married son or daughter and many of the stories and letters in magazines for
the elderly are about conflicts between the generations living together. Further, several
surveys indicate that the living arrangements are not necessarily desirable from the
perspective of the elderly. For example, a 1984 Tianjin survey found 58 percent of the
elderly in the sample agreeing with a statement that after sons and daughters marry,
they should move out. See Jia, "Lue tan wo guo xianxing yanglao zhidu." And the 1982
survey of 237 retired personnel in Beijing found that of the respondents living with
three generations, about half would prefer a different arrangement; of respondents
living with a married son or daughter, about one-fourth would like to live alone with
their spouse; but all respondents living with their spouse only preferred this arrangement to any other. See Lin and Geng, "Tuixiu zhigong kaocha."

role for themselves in ongoing work at the workplace, but this is by no means a source of great resentment. Rather, what they seem to expect from the workplace after retirement is help managing the mundane problems of daily life.

AN OVERVIEW OF WORK AFTER RETIREMENT

If, as it seems, cadre retirement typically entails severance from regular work, this by no means necessarily implies retirement to a life of leisure. Nor, according to cadres I interviewed, do retired cadres necessarily want such a life. Many subjects described to me a difficult period of adjustment after retirement, characterized by very intense feelings of loneliness, emptiness, and uselessness. Cadre retirement policy was supposed to mitigate those feelings with its explicit assurance that retired cadres could and should continue to play an active role in society. By this policy, severance from regular work was not inconsistent with taking part in various sorts of work activities, even activities arranged by the former workplace.

This policy explains an important and otherwise curious finding: when asked about their main activity after retirement, one-fourth of respondents to my questionnaire identified it as helping the former workplace with work. The size of this group is much larger than the proportion discussed above, the 9 percent of cadres who go to the workplace frequently and do so for the purpose of work. The smaller group is virtually a subset of the larger.[27]

Focusing on post-retirement activity sheds additional light on what cadre retirement means, beyond severance from regular work at the former workplace. Table 5.2 summarizes my survey findings on what sorts of activities cadres engage in after retirement. Note that at least half the veteran cadres participate in some form of work after retirement. For postrevolutionaries, the figure is more than 60 percent. In two separate sections below, I explore in greater detail the categories of work for the former workplace and work for pay. Here, I present a brief overview of work after retirement, supplementing the information provided in Table 5.2 with findings from surveys conducted by the Chinese. These all suggest that continued work activity is common among retired cadres.

Two 1984 surveys of retired veteran cadres in Beijing found large proportions of cadres participate in political or social work after re-

[27] Of the 9 percent, all but one cadre indicates work for the former workplace as the main activity. The exception indicates social work as the main activity.

TABLE 5.2
Work after Retirement

Activity	Veteran Cadres (%)	Postrevolutionary Cadres (%)
Helping my former workplace	25	24
Paid work in a new job	14	26
Social work	12	11
Leisure activities	45	33
Other	5	6
Total	100% (165)	100% (70)

No. of cases: 235

Question: My activities after retirement mainly consist of: helping out my former workplace with some work; adding something to my income in a newly found job; doing social work; resting and spending my later years peaceably; other.

Note: Percentages may not add up due to rounding.

tirement. Liu Yongchuan conducted a survey of 106 veteran cadres retired from workplaces under Beijing municipality, over 60 percent of whom were in their sixties at the time the survey was conducted. He found 39 percent of cadres surveyed continue to do some kind of work. Almost all such work is political or social work—such as helping with party rectification, working in neighborhood committees, working for the elderly, and lecturing on party history to youth groups.[28] Wu Fang conducted a survey of 849 retired veteran cadres in Beijing, including cadres retired from central organizations of the state. Over 60 percent of cadres in his sample were under age sixty-five at the time the survey was conducted. Wu found 36 percent of cadres surveyed participate in social work (of the sort noted above) and 21 percent of cadres surveyed continue to do some form of work at the former workplace or elsewhere. (The latter figure double counts some cadres who participate in social work.)[29]

Zhu Gaozhang surveyed a slightly different and also older sample of retirees: 452 retired personnel, including but not restricted to cadres, in the city of Guangzhou. About half the cadres in Zhu's sample were in their sixties and half in their seventies at the time the survey was conducted. He found 27 percent of personnel surveyed continue

[28] Liu, "Dui Beijing shi 106 ming lixiu ganbu xiankuang de diaocha baogao."
[29] Wu, "Lixiu ganbu 'lao you suo wei' de tedian, fangshi he fazhan qushi."

to do some form of community work or social work after retirement.[30] Li Juemin conducted a survey of 207 retirees, all retired veteran cadres, also in Guangzhou. Li found a significantly smaller proportion, only 19 percent, engaging in some sort of (unspecified) work after retirement.[31]

These studies provide some perspective but their findings are difficult to evaluate and compare for a number of reasons. For example, some provide no information on the age structure or other background characteristics of the sample. Others fail to indicate when the sample was conducted. More generally, the samples are not probability samples of the populations of interest in either Beijing or Guangzhou, and it is therefore very unfortunate that most findings are reported simply as univariate descriptions. Far more useful to us in cases of nonprobability sampling are surveys that explore the relationship between work after retirement and other variables. The best of these is the 1984 survey done in the city of Ha'erbin.[32]

The 1984 Ha'erbin survey is a stratified probability sample of cadres in Ha'erbin who had specially retired as of September 1983. Sampling 10 percent from a sampling frame of 5,845 yielded 570 usable questionnaires for analysis. At the purely descriptive level, the Ha'erbin survey finds 23 percent of specially retired cadres continue to do some work at the former workplace and 12 percent work at another workplace.[33]

The survey goes on to evaluate the relationship between work at the former workplace after retirement and each of the following variables: age, rank, health, schooling, and sex. The survey finds retired cadres under age sixty work at the former workplace in significantly greater proportions than cadres age sixty and older. It finds retired cadres who report good health work at the former workplace in significantly greater proportions than cadres who report poor health. Retired male cadres work for the former workplace in significantly greater proportions than their female counterparts. And work for the former workplace is weakly related to level of schooling: cadres with higher levels of schooling work for the former workplace in larger proportions than cadres with less schooling.[34] Each of these

[30] Zhu, "Guangzhou shi lixiu tuixiu laonianren de shehui, xinli ji jiankang zhuangkuang de diaocha baogao."

[31] Li, "Lixiu lao ganbu manyi chengdu fenxi."

[32] Ha'erbin shi shehui kexue yanjiu suo shehuixue yanjiu shi, "Ha'erbin shi lixiu ganbu zhuangkuang diaocha baogao (shang)," and "Ha'erbin shi lixiu ganbu zhuangkuang diaocha baogao (xia)."

[33] Ha'erbin shi shehui kexue yanjiu suo shehuixue yanjiu shi, "Ha'erbin shi lixiu ganbu zhuangkuang diaocha baogao (xia)."

[34] Ibid.

relationships supports a commonsense understanding of the issue. None is particularly surprising.

But the Ha'erbin survey does turn up a surprising finding in its evaluation of the relationship between work for the former workplace and rank. It is not the case that higher-ranking cadres are more likely to stay on to work at the former workplace compared to their junior co-workers. In fact, the opposite is true. The proportion of cadres below section level who stay on to work is 23 percent, the proportion of cadres at section level is 24 percent, the proportion of cadres at division level is 16 percent, and the proportion of cadres at bureau level is 17 percent.[35]

Unfortunately, even the Ha'erbin study reports findings as bivariate relationships only. The bivariate analysis and presentation leaves important questions unanswered. We know, for example, that cadres in higher ranks tend generally to be older than cadres in lower ranks. Is the reported relationship between work after retirement and rank simply another way of reporting the relationship between work and age? Controlling for age, would we still find lower-ranking cadres staying on to work after retirement in significantly greater proportions than their senior co-workers? This and similar sorts of questions can easily be answered using the Ha'erbin survey raw data. To my knowledge, they are not addressed in any reports available to us. However, I can evaluate these relationships with data from my own survey and use multivariate analysis to isolate the separate effects of variables.

WORK FOR THE FORMER WORKPLACE

To evaluate the relationship between work for the former workplace and variables such as those explored in the Ha'erbin survey, I used logit analysis on the data set of responses to my self-administered questionnaire. Logit analysis shares some important characteristics with regression analysis: it allows us to isolate the separate effects of more than one independent variable and test those effects for statistical significance. However, the dependent variable in logit analysis is categorical, not continuous, and this difference affects the interpretation of logit coefficients. Logit analysis answers the following sort of question: what is the isolated effect of variation in independent variables on the probability of individual cases turning up in one or another category of the dependent variable? For example, logit analysis can answer the question posed at the end of the previous section:

[35] Ibid.

are higher-ranking cadres more or less likely to continue work after retirement than their junior co-workers, holding other specified variables (such as age) constant?

My main concern in this chapter is the extent to which formal retirement from office matters. I have argued that it does matter, that retirement has typically brought about an actual and perceived severance from regular work at the former workplace for most cadres. Yet fully one-fourth of my questionnaire respondents report work for the former workplace as their main activity after retirement. Surveys conducted by the Chinese also suggest that some sort of work after retirement is common among cadres. This activity need not be inconsistent with severance from regular work, but it clearly merits our attention as an activity that resembles (more closely than social work or leisure, for example) pre-retirement circumstances. Which sorts of cadres are we likely to find working at the former workplace after their retirement? And does this tell us anything more about whether retirement matters?

Dependent Variable. My dependent variable is main activity after retirement, constructed here as a dichotomous variable. Work for the former workplace is the category of interest and all other main postretirement activities are lumped together as a residual category. This variable is the same as that for which I reviewed the findings of the Ha'erbin study above.

Independent Variables. I included as independent variables in the model all the same variables used in the Ha'erbin bivariate analysis: age, rank, health, education, and sex—although some were measured somewhat differently. I added three variables not considered in the Ha'erbin analysis: status (whether a cadre is a veteran or postrevolutionary) and recentness of retirement. The Ha'erbin analysis did not consider the impact of status because the survey sampled retired veterans only. As to recentness of retirement, some cadres I interviewed reported that work for the former workplace was often a transitional arrangement to help cadres adjust to retirement. Other things equal, if this is indeed the case, cadres whose retirement is recent are more likely than retirees of earlier years to spend their time mainly working for the former workplace.

I added another variable of considerable interest to me: attitude toward retirement. Recall that the regression analysis of chapter 3 concluded that individual preferences, in the sense of whether or not cadres wanted to retire, made no difference in when cadres actually retired (relative to when they were obliged to retire). Here, I consider the possibility that preferences have a significant impact on the work relationship with the former workplace after retirement. Other things equal, cadres who want to retire are less likely to want to continue to work for the former workplace, compared to cadres who do not want to retire. Cadres who do not want to retire are more likely to pursue a post-retirement life that to some degree resembles the situation before retirement. We expect preferences to have an impact on whether or not cadres maintain a work relationship with the former workplace after retirement because middlemen at the workplace are instructed to take into account these preferences when arranging activities for them.

We also expect the commonsense reasoning behind the Ha'erbin findings on the impact of age, sex, and education to hold here. And other things equal, we expect cadres who report good health at the time of retirement to be more likely to stay on to help the former workplace after retirement, compared to cadres who report poor health. This is most likely to be the case if self-reports are accurate, but it is also probable if reports reflect false information provided to obtain employment substitution for a son or daughter. The latter case is usually associated with early retirement.[36] A cadre who succeeds in processing a (false) early retirement due to poor health (regardless of whether or not the workplace knowingly cooperates in the process) is not likely to be encouraged by the former workplace to contradict the rationale for early retirement by returning to continue work, compared to cadres who report good health.

A central question of interest here is: does the impact of any variables pose a serious challenge to the argument above that work for the former workplace is consistent with severance from regular work? The key variable, in my view, is rank. We suspect retirement is meaningful for high-ranking cadres: the regression analysis in chapter 3 indicated that higher-ranking cadres hold on to their positions longer than their junior co-workers, relative to when they should retire and holding other variables constant. But if retirement is not very meaningful, then cadres who have power and authority before they retire do not, in fact, relinquish it upon retirement. This statement is consistent with only one kind of prediction in the logit analysis here: that higher-ranking cadres are significantly more likely to spend most of their time after retirement working for the former workplace, compared to their junior co-workers and holding other variables constant. The Ha'erbin bivariate finding of a relationship in the opposite direction or any finding that rank makes no difference at all both tend to support the view that retirement makes a difference.

Analysis. Results of the analysis are presented in Table 5.3. Three variables—health, attitude, and sex—are statistically significant.

---

[36] See chapter 3 on employment substitution.

TABLE 5.3
Work for the Former Workplace

Explanatory Variables	Coefficients	Standard Errors	t-Ratios
Constant	−1.39	3.02	−0.46
Age	−0.05	0.05	1.06
Rank	−0.33	0.58	−0.57
Status	−0.09	0.47	−0.20
Health	0.68	0.38	*1.80
Attitude	−0.89	0.39	**2.28
Education	0.11	0.09	1.23
Sex	2.06	0.85	**2.43
Recentness	0.11	0.53	0.21

Note: The dependent variable, work for the former workplace, has a value of 1 for cadres who report this as their main activity and 0 otherwise. Age is age in 1987. Rank is a four-level ordinal, with values from 4 to 1 for cadres of ministerial, bureau, division, and section (or below) ranks, respectively. Status has a value of 1 for postrevolutionaries, 0 for revolutionaries; health has a value of 1 for cadres reporting good health at retirement, 0 for those reporting poor health; attitude has a value of 1 for cadres reporting they wanted to retire, 0 for those reporting they did not want to retire; education is years of schooling; sex has a value of 1 for males, 0 for females; recentness has a value of 1 for cadres who retired in 1985–87, 0 for those who retired in 1978–84.

No. of cases: 199
Full model chi-square: 18.29
Statistical significance of model: .0192
*p < .05, one-tailed test
**p < .01, one-tailed test

The impact of health and attitude are as predicted. Other things equal, cadres who report good health are more likely to work for the former workplace after retirement, compared to those who report poor health. Cadres who do not want to retire are more likely to work for the former workplace than those who do want to retire, holding other variables constant. And other things equal, men are more likely than women to work for the former workplace after retirement.

Other variables are not statistically significant. This suggests that the Ha'erbin finding on the relationship between age and work for the former workplace may be explained by a direct relationship between age and health or age and attitude toward retirement.

The logit analysis does not corroborate the Ha'erbin bivariate finding on the impact of rank. Higher-ranking cadres are neither more nor less likely than lower-ranking cadres to work for the former workplace, once we control for the effect of other potentially confounding variables. This finding leaves unchallenged the argument that retirement matters, although a replication of the Ha'erbin bivariate finding would have been more compelling on this point.

Both the Ha'erbin bivariate finding on rank and my own seem to contradict anecdotal evidence about the continued influence of high-ranking retired cadres. In fact, they are not as inconsistent with that view as they might seem. First of all, only high-ranking cadres are eligible for advisory positions of semiretirement and there are plenty of good examples of cadres in advisory positions who continue to exercise influence.[37] This issue is not addressed here or in the Ha'erbin analysis, as both use samples of fully retired cadres only. It may be that high-ranking cadres with clout to throw around succeed in using that clout to avoid full retirement. Second, the dependent variable of both the Ha'erbin analysis and my own is not work after retirement generally but work for the former workplace. If cadres who achieve high rank typically have better personal connections and more influence (as I suspect they do), then they will surely be attractive resources for many workplaces. In the relatively permissive economic environment of the mid-1980s, retired cadres with these assets did indeed transform them into material reward by working for enterprises or setting up their own commercial ventures. I discuss this issue in the following section.

WORK FOR PAY

Policy makers encouraged retired cadres with scarce skills and scientific or technical expertise to continue to work. This kind of contri-

[37] A good example is Zeng Zhi, a former deputy head of the Central Committee's Organization Department and wife of Tao Zhu, a top party leader. Zeng conducted an investigation in several localities in Fujian province, where she had connections dating back to 1927. She discovered a number of problems and made an oral report to the Fujian provincial party committee, offering suggestions for improvements. Upon returning to Beijing, Zeng submitted a written report of her investigation to party General Secretary Hu Yaobang, who requested provincial authorities to resolve the problems. Zeng's case exemplifies the use of influence, derived from personal connections and prestige rather than position, to get information, bring problems to the attention of relevant authorities, and bypass regular channels to ensure that problems get resolved. The case was cited as a model in the journal *Liaowang*. See Hu and Tang, "Yi xin de fangshi luxing zeren."

bution was not penalized with adjustments in pension or restrictions on new income, although at high income levels they were obliged to pay personal income tax. A similarly permissive policy applied to retired cadres engaged in small-scale household occupations, which were common in the countryside.[38] The policy applied to both veterans and postrevolutionaries. Policy makers distinguished these contributions from work in enterprises or involvement in business or commerce after retirement, which they began to regulate in the mid-1980s.

In December 1984, the Central Committee and State Council set guidelines governing the involvement of retired party and government cadres (veterans and postrevolutionaries) in setting up businesses or engaging in commercial activity. The guidelines did not prohibit the cadres from such activities but did limit the amount of pension they were entitled to receive. Retired cadres receiving a new income from business or commercial activities were to have their pensions reduced. If new income exceeded the amount of pension, pension payments were to cease altogether; if new income was less than the amount of pension, pension payments were to be reduced by the amount of new income. This guaranteed working retired cadres no loss of income overall, but gave them the possibility of increasing their income only in circumstances where new income from work exceeded former pension payments. In other circumstances, new income simply substituted for pension payments. For most cadres, the guidelines eliminated any monetary incentive to engage in business or commercial activities. The guidelines concluded with an explicit prohibition against the use of personal ties and influence to engage in illicit activities for private gain.[39]

In February 1986, the Central Committee issued a new set of guidelines, tightening up restrictions on retired cadres working for pay in enterprises. Cadres, veterans and postrevolutionaries, who had retired from party and government organizations, would have their pension and other retirement benefits cut altogether if they worked for pay in any enterprise. They were flatly prohibited from holding any position in a state-owned enterprise. They were permitted to work in enterprises not owned by the state, but only after two years had elapsed since retirement. And even then, they were not

---

[38] Zhonggong zhongyang guowuyuan, Guanyu yanjin dangzheng jiguan he dangzheng ganbu jingshang ban qiye de jueding, 3 Dec. 1984. See also Zhonggong zhongyang bangongting guowuyuan bangongting, Guanyu fahui lixiu tuixiu zhuanye jishu renyuan zuoyong de zanxing guiding, 6 Oct. 1986.

[39] Zhonggong zhongyang guowuyuan, Guanyu yanjin dangzheng jiguan he dangzheng ganbu jingshang ban qiye de jueding, 3 Dec. 1984.

permitted to hold a position in any enterprise in the line of work administered by their former workplace.[40] These regulations also applied to cadres with specialized skills or technical expertise, retired from party or government workplaces, and working at an enterprise or engaging in commerce.[41]

The December 1984 guidelines had discouraged most retired cadres from working for pay in business or commerce. Only cadres with wide networks of personal connections could expect to earn significant material reward from working for pay after their retirement. The February 1986 regulations aimed to curtail this exploitation of connections. In October 1988, new regulations were introduced to further restrict influence peddling by retired cadres.

The 1988 guidelines, issued by the State Council General Office, pointed out that some retired cadres had continued to use contacts and influence from their former positions to engage in speculation. The 1988 guidelines reiterated the restrictions introduced in February 1986. Retired party and government cadres at and above the county level were specifically prohibited from setting up enterprises, holding any position in a commercial enterprise, deriving any income from buying or selling commodities, speculating in raw materials or scarce commodities, soliciting funds from state organs, and engaging in any financial activities for pay. Further, cadres who worked for pay at those workplaces permitted by regulations could receive a new income no higher than their former salary plus the average bonus of cadres in their former workplace.[42] For all specially retired cadres, high-ranking and low, these restrictions effectively eliminated any legitimate monetary incentive to work for pay. However, for postrevolutionaries the situation was different.

The regulations limited new income to roughly the difference between pension and pre-retirement salary. For specially retired veterans, who retired on full salary, the difference was, by definition, zero. But postrevolutionaries, with pensions ranging from 60 to 75 percent of pre-retirement salary, were eligible to receive new income amounting to 25 to 40 percent of that salary. This new income was informally called the "differential supplement" (*bucha*). According to regularly retired cadres I interviewed, even before the 1988 regulations were issued, retired postrevolutionaries who worked for pay typically re-

[40] Zhonggong zhongyang guowuyuan, Guanyu jin yi bu zhizhi dangzheng jiguan he dangzheng ganbu jingshang ban qiye de guiding, 4 Feb. 1986.

[41] Zhonggong zhongyang bangongting guowuyuan bangongting, Guanyu fahui lixiu tuixiu zhuanye jishu renyuan zuoyong de zanxing guiding, 6 Oct. 1986.

[42] Guowuyuan bangongting, Guanyu xian yi shang dang he guojia jiguan tui(li)xiu ganbu jingshang ban qiye wenti de ruogan guiding, 3 Oct. 1988.

ceived the differential supplement or a little more than the supplement as new income. Apparently, this practice was one that had evolved rather than been promoted or suggested as policy.[43] Years before the October 1988 regulations, then, retired postrevolutionaries had a monetary incentive to work for pay that was typically denied to retired veterans. This may explain why work for pay has been far more common among retired postrevolutionaries than among retired veterans. In my own survey, for example, the proportion of postrevolutionaries who work for pay is about twice that of veteran cadres. Retired postrevolutionaries interviewed explained that they were usually able to bargain for more than the supplement:

> When a regularly retired cadre finds a job, the workplace guarantees the supplement. The salary is not high, of course. In addition to the supplement, the cadre bargains for other benefits—such as transportation stipend, extra pay, et cetera. The supplement is guaranteed, the rest is [the result of] bargaining.[44]

According to retired cadres interviewed, most jobs were found through friends, family, or acquaintances at the former workplace. Work for pay was not difficult to find. For a number of reasons, workplaces have an interest in hiring retired postrevolutionaries. As one explained:

> We are always people known to the workplace. They know us. They do not have to train us. We usually have worked in the line of work before. . . . So even before we start work, they are familiar with us. . . . [And] the workplace can freely keep us on or fire us—as it likes. This is very difficult to do with personnel hired formally or personnel listed in the authorized positions of the workplace (*bianzhi*). Most of our work is on limited-term projects and it is very easy for the workplace to tell us we are no longer needed because the project has been completed. . . . [And] we are good workers. We are conscientious. We can be counted on. We have a strong sense of responsibility. It is not the same if they hire young people. For the price, the workplace is getting a very good worker.[45]

Further, while pay for retired postrevolutionaries could exceed the differential supplement, it was apparently never as high as the salary

---

[43] Officials at the Ministry of Personnel termed it a *tu zhengce* (a locally developed policy). Chen Liang (Deputy Director of Special Retirement Division, Cadre Retirement Bureau, Ministry of Personnel) and Wang Wenbo (Director of Cadre Retirement Bureau General Office, Ministry of Personnel), interviewed in Beijing, 7 Nov. 1988.

[44] Interview subject no. 28.

[45] Ibid.

of cadres who had not retired. Retired postrevolutionary cadres interviewed reported that their pay was generally only somewhat higher than the supplement. Finally, all Chinese workplaces operate under strict restrictions on the number of regularly employed personnel. Retired cadres working for pay were classified as temporary workers and as such were not subject to these restrictions. Workplaces could hire them for less pay and without sacrificing other employees.

SUMMARY

For most cadres, veterans and postrevolutionaries, retirement has made a real difference in their relationship to regular work. Cadre retirement has been accompanied by an actual and perceived severance from regular work at the former workplace. At the same time, some form of work after retirement is common among cadres. This includes helping the former workplace with work, but it seems that in most cases this work is not "business as usual."

One of the interesting features of cadre retirement policy is its explicit encouragement of a continued work role for retired veteran cadres. This has undoubtedly been part of an effort to enhance the appeal of retirement. But as retired cadres with personal connections and influence to exploit in new positions began to do so, policy makers issued progressively stricter restrictions on the legitimate ability of retired veterans to work for pay. From the very beginning, retired revolutionary veterans were encouraged to promote the party's tradition of "serving the people" without material reward. By the end of 1988, this exhortation had become an official restriction on working for pay.

For some years, cadre retirement policy paid little attention to the activities of retired postrevolutionaries. It failed to provide support for leisure and educational activities comparable to that provided for retired veteran cadres. At the same time, policy makers did not actively regulate the activities of retired postrevolutionaries. One result of this has been an experience among retired postrevolutionaries that in many ways resembles the pre-retirement experience more closely than is true for retired veterans.

THIS BOOK and its conclusions mainly draw attention to a process, but our interest in outcomes is certainly not trivial. Has a norm of cadre retirement emerged? The existence of a norm is not, of course, an all-or-nothing matter, but a matter of degree. As Jack Gibbs has observed, any specification of a point at which a norm exists is essentially arbitrary.[1] Yet, unequivocally, if we take de facto lifelong tenure for cadres as the status quo ante, then more than a decade of effort by policy makers has indeed produced a major change in the cadre corps. Millions of cadres have retired. Other cadres have come to expect retirement at specified ages, whether they like it or not.

Further, voluntary enforcement of retirement by younger cadres looking after their interest in moving up seems to be generating its own momentum. Younger cadres have proved to be natural allies of policy makers in building a cadre retirement norm because they view their own promotion and the retirement of older co-workers as a zero-sum game. Without movement out of the limited number of cadre positions at all levels, there cannot be movement up and into them. Younger cadres are only punishing themselves if they do not enforce compliance with the policy to retire cadres. The result is a tacit and indirect, but widespread and widely sensed, voluntary enforcement of retirement by younger cadres. The principle at work here is the metanorm mechanism, introduced in chapter 1.

Younger cadres will eventually face retirement themselves. Though they may view the situation as zero-sum, the conflict of interest is only partial. Younger cadres today are setting in motion a machinery of social enforcement that will eventually put them too out of office. We can presume there will always be younger cadres willing to enforce retirement policy and, therefore, that the process is self-sustaining. It is fair to conclude that the process is fueling the emergence of a norm of retirement for the overwhelming majority of Chinese cadres.

Of course, there is not a single norm of cadre retirement but at least two. There are explicit exemptions for leaders, especially for leaders at the very top. In addition, cadre retirement does not mean stopping work altogether. Nor does it mean severing links with the former workplace. And for many cadres it does not mean a reduction

[1] Gibbs, *Norms, Deviance, and Social Control*, 7–21.

in income received as salary. Nonetheless, retirement does make a difference for most cadres, bringing about an actual and perceived severance from regular work at the former workplace.

THE PROCESS OF POLICY IMPLEMENTATION

Although policy makers did succeed in retiring large numbers of cadres and setting up a mechanism to drive the emergence of a cadre retirement norm, we know that many cadres did not retire at the ages stipulated or at the prices set in Beijing. Cadres targeted for retirement bargained with middlemen charged with implementation at the workplace and managed to obtain a better deal than that set out in party and government guidelines. Better housing, a pre-retirement promotion or salary raise, and a job for a son or daughter are things cadres routinely bargained for and won. Moreover, after employment substitution was abolished, many postrevolutionary cadres managed to resist retirement until local governments increased their pension incomes. In sum, very significant deviation from official policy took place during the process of its implementation. This deviation reflected the material interests of cadres targeted for retirement.

Clearly, policy makers in Beijing did not fully dominate the process of implementation. Targets of policy proved not to be the passive objects the term connotes. As to those charged with policy implementation, however, they proved truly to be middlemen: they played a role in shaping the characteristics of the final product as well as its price. Caught between pressures from above to streamline and rejuvenate the cadre corps and disinterest or reluctance from below to give up cadre positions, middlemen bent the rules and offered cadres more attractive terms. Policy makers at the top were forced to remake policy in response to countermeasures from below—prohibiting some, condoning and codifying others. Results were achieved in implementing policy, but at prices significantly higher than those contained in original policy initiatives.

Middlemen have a strong incentive to realize policy objectives set at the top. Boosting incentives to policy targets through privately negotiated deals made the task of implementation easier, as cadres were then more likely to retire. On the other hand, middlemen are evaluated in large part by policy outcomes. If private deals are too costly or deviate too much from official policy, middlemen suffer the consequences most severely.[2]

[2] See Manion, "The Behavior of Middlemen in the Cadre Retirement Policy Process."

Considering the incentive structure in which middlemen operate, the deviation observed in policy implementation may be fairly unproblematic. Policy makers in Beijing embarked on the project of cadre retirement with great uncertainty about likely responses. In such situations, it may make sense for policy makers to treat incentives they fix in official policy as essentially estimates to which policy targets and middlemen can be expected to respond. Policy makers can treat the process of implementation as a process of information gathering too: they can entrust the fixing of effective prices to middlemen and react authoritatively only when prices rise to unacceptable levels.

From this perspective, the deviation that takes place in the course of policy implementation may supplement inadequate information about what it takes to achieve new kinds of policy objectives. Indeed, Charles Lindblom has observed that leaders in the communist system consistently lack accurate and timely information because of their reliance on bureaucratic authority rather than pluralist politics or economic markets. The system has "strong thumbs and no fingers."[3] Accordingly, the deviation that we observe in policy implementation may be a useful supplement to a system that systematically produces poor information.

THE POLITICS OF BUILDING A NORM

Policy makers in Beijing are not political scientists testing abstract theories of norm building. They are, first and foremost, political power holders. At the same time as they promoted a policy of regular age-based exit from office for most cadres, they demonstrated a keen interest in holding onto their own positions of political power. Protecting their positions while presiding over a massive bloodless circulation of other elites required some maneuvering.

Considered in the framework of the ideas reviewed in chapter 1, the impact of political maneuvering at the top served only to *confound* the emergence of a norm. That is, the process of norm building failed to unfold neatly as theorized not only because the leaders in Beijing did not fully control the process but also because of specific policy measures they adopted to protect their own interests while promoting retirement for others. Measures they adopted were ambiguous, ambivalent, inconsistent, and discriminatory. They were

---

[3] Lindblom, *Politics and Markets*, 65–77.

quite contrary to some theoretical principles about how norms emerge.

Specifically, the *exemplary rules* discussed in chapter 1 help build norms because, in theory, they provide clarity, enhance salience, and grant legitimacy through the authority of the state. Yet the rules Chinese policy makers issued in official documents violated these principles in several respects. Initially, the documents were ambivalent and ambiguous. And at no time did they give any evidence of a serious intent to enforce.

Policy makers disagreed in 1978–81 about the urgency of veteran cadre retirement. This ambivalence was plainly reflected in documents. Government documents combined general principles with concrete measures to institutionalize retirement. Party documents contained a message with an emphasis on restoring to power veteran cadres who had been purged or demoted during the Cultural Revolution. Not until February 1982 did the Central Committee issue a partner document to the several State Council initiatives on cadre retirement. While restoration of veterans as a strategic policy was not irreconcilable with retirement, in practice the two policies contradicted one another.

Further, the documents issued in 1978–81 were ambiguous. None delineated an objective decision rule for cadre retirement. The basis for cadre retirement was not old age per se but two vague intervening variables: state of health and ability to carry a normal workload. Without age standards as the basic decision rule for retirement, such decisions could be made only through case-by-case deliberation on the applicability of these two criteria to individual cadres. Finally, at no time did the rules specify punishment for cadres who did not retire.

In sum, official documents identified cadre retirement as an important issue. But while they enhanced the salience of the issue, they also called attention to the ambivalence at the top about the urgency of the immediate problem. And ambiguity about exactly who was to retire suggested to older cadres that the issue did not necessarily apply to them. Rules changed in 1982, but new rules could not build on the effect of earlier ones. Instead, new party and government documents had to dispel misconceptions about the policy—misconceptions fostered by previous documents.

Protection of positions at the top also obstructed the smooth unfolding of other principles of norm building. For example, in theory the manipulation of beliefs through *argument* helps build a norm by establishing a foundation based on reason. The arguments are attempts to appeal to collective rationality: what is socially functional is presented as socially obligatory too. In this case study, the critique of lifelong tenure aired in the Chinese press followed the arguments to their logical conclusion by identifying retirement of top leaders as essential and crucial to retirement below. Not surprisingly, however, policy makers in Beijing were inconsistent in interpreting and applying these arguments. They set up a highly stratified retirement system that discriminated among cadres to reflect the existing hierarchy of power. For example, they fully exempted from retirement "a few dozen leaders" at the top.

Inconsistency in applying arguments against lifelong tenure to all cadres resulted in the confounding of another principle of norm building, namely, *exemplary conformers*. Exemplary conformers are supposed to provide evidence that conformity exists and to educate others about what kind of conduct is correct. The key in this theory is to promote exemplary conduct among salient groups or groups that tend to inspire emulation. In practice, while the party newspaper introduced hundreds of models of ordinary cadre retirement, top leaders did not step down in large numbers until 1985. And even these leaders often turned up in other positions. At the same time, many very old leaders remained in office. Policy makers in Beijing provided cadres below with personal examples consistent with lifelong tenure. These examples were at least as salient as the models of retirement in the party press.

Finally, ambivalence and discriminatory measures in cadre retirement also confounded the principle of building a norm through *association*. In theory, association works to help build a norm by explicitly linking up new policy with already existing beliefs and norms. It appeals to old norms to build new ones. Association can produce norms only when there is a common base of information and understanding and few conflicting principles from which to generalize. In the case of cadre retirement, policy makers drew on three existing traditions to build a norm free of the stigma of the political purge notion of exit from office. They revived special retirement status from the past and expanded its scope to all veteran cadres. They presented retirement to veteran cadres as a new work assignment. And they emphasized that retirement was a duty of communist party members who are bound to submit to the discipline of the organization.

These associations were problematic in a number of ways. First, because of initial ambivalence and emphasis on restoring veteran cadres to power, it was easy for revolutionaries to seize on a tradition that legitimated *not* retiring—the revolutionary ideal of public service. Deprived of the chance to work in the Cultural Revolution years and mistrustful of the younger generation of cadres that had risen during those years, veterans could and did rationalize that staying in power was their last chance to make a contribution before their health gave out.

Second, policy makers sought to destigmatize exit from office by granting special retirement status to veteran cadres. But as a consequence of elevating veterans at the expense of postrevolutionaries, policy makers created a new kind of stigma which attached itself to retired cadres ineligible for the status and rewards of special retirement. The discrimination implied in the tradition of revolutionary seniority became explicit and more salient than ever. Retired postrevolutionaries became obviously "second-class" retirees. In trying to solve one kind of problem, policy makers created another.

Viewed in light of the theories about how norms emerge, reviewed in chapter 1, the measures policy makers took to protect their political positions served to confound the growth of a norm. While these measures reflect abstract principles of how norms might emerge spontaneously, in their forms as mechanisms of norm building they did not unfold here as theorized.

THE LOGIC OF SMALL WINS

The ambiguity, ambivalence, inconsistency, and discriminatory measures we observe in the process described here may, however, have practical advantages not considered in theories about the spontaneous emergence of norms. The process described above as so problematic may present a different logic of norm building, one that accords with the pursuit of private interest by those at the top and below.

In a project of social transformation on the grandiose scale of norm building, ambiguity, ambivalence, inconsistency, and discriminatory measures have their advantages. They fragment the process and divide targets of the policy. The emergence of a norm in this situation operates by what Karl Weick terms "the logic of small wins."[4] He defines a small win as "a concrete, complete, implemented outcome of moderate importance."[5] A small win is not important by itself but small wins become important cumulatively as they pick up allies, deter opponents, and lower resistance to subsequent proposals. They set in motion forces that favor more small wins:

[4] Weick, "Small Wins," 40–49.
[5] Ibid., 43.

Small wins stir up settings, which means that each subsequent attempt at another win occurs in a different context. . . . Much of the artfulness in working with small wins lies in identifying, gathering, and labeling several small changes that are present but unnoticed, . . . changes that in actuality could be gathered under a variety of labels.[6]

Each attempt at a small win is a self-contained effort to solve a small piece of the problem, given the existing constellation of interests and resources. Policy makers need have no grand plan, only a sense of direction. Many of the logical connections between small wins are made ex post facto. These connections are political ones, with policy makers repackaging past wins under a common label so that they can move forward on the next win.

Small wins can work because they are initially perceived as disconnected, and disconnected units make stable building blocks. Weick cites the following fable to illustrate this principle:

Your task is to count out a thousand sheets of paper, while you are subject to periodic interruptions. Each interruption causes you to lose track of the count and forces you to start over. If you count the thousand as a single sequence, then an interruption could cause you, at worst, to lose a count of as many as 999. If the sheets are put into stacks of 100, however, and each stack remains undisturbed by interruptions, then the worst possible count loss from interruption is 108. That number represents the recounting of the nine stacks of 100 each plus the 99 single sheets. Further, if sheets are first put into stacks of ten, which are then joined into stacks of 100, the worst possible loss from interruption would be 27. That number represents nine stacks of 100 plus nine stacks of ten plus nine single sheets. Not only is far less recounting time lost by putting the paper into "subsystems" of tens and hundreds, but the chances of completing the count are vastly higher.[7]

Seen in this perspective, policy makers in Beijing maneuvered cadres toward a norm of retirement by decomposing the problem and dealing with only one component at a time. Because of the ambivalence and ambiguity at the top, the veteran cadres who were the most immediate targets of the policy were not threatened when it was introduced. All the while restoration of revolutionary cadres was going on, the idea of retirement was being codified and publicized.

Only in 1982 did policy makers adopt measures to implement cadre retirement effectively and then they challenged targets of the

[6] Ibid., 43–44.

[7] From Kuhn and Beam, *The Logic of Organizations*, 249–50.

policy selectively. They fully exempted those at the very top, only semiretired other leaders, and focused most on getting the majority of old veteran cadres out of office. This seems to have blunted active resistance, but not momentum for the emergence of a norm. The different applications of the idea of retirement to different groups created cleavages among targets of the policy and made opposition more difficult to articulate and organize. Cadres did not find themselves in shared circumstances. Different forms of retirement elicited different responses and demands. Cadres were not treated as a single group and they did not respond as such.

Gradually, however, policy makers began to destratify the system. They made it more uniform below the very top at the same time as they took steps to routinize retirement. In this sense, scattered small wins were combined. Now, even younger cadres know that retirement means their eventual retirement too.

Reassembly of small wins can work to build norms because small wins are like the short stacks of paper in the fable. Weick claims with optimism: "They preserve gains, they cannot unravel, each one requires less coordination to execute, interruptions such as might occur when there is a change in political administration have limited effects, and subparts can be assembled into different configurations."[8]

This logic of norm building is good news for political leaders because it suggests building a norm can accord with the usual practices of politics anywhere. Building a social norm from a public policy does not necessarily require comprehensive planning, logical consistency, or complete agreement among policy makers. In fact, such an approach can be a real detriment because lines of battle will be drawn clearly and early enough in the process to halt it or slow it down. And as policy makers cannot fully direct the process as it unfolds, it makes little sense to map out and follow a total plan. Rather, flexibility is required to respond to situations presented by the countermeasures that emerge from below.

CORRECT CONDUCT THROUGH SOCIAL CONFLICT

The one mechanism described in chapter 1 that seems uniquely to have unfolded as theorized is the *metanorm* mechanism. We see that younger cadres have a vested interest in enforcing the retirement of their senior co-workers. Policy makers in Beijing succeeded in mak-

[8] Weick, "Small Wins," 44.

ing policy work by exploiting an existing conflict of interest. They encouraged one group in society to police another.

I argued in chapter 1 that beliefs explain conformity to norms because to believe a social standard of propriety exists is to believe it is enforced by society and, consequently, to engage in enforcement and self-enforcement in most cases. But does the manipulation of social conflict, which is the core of the metanorm principle of building a norm, require the consideration of beliefs at all? I think so. For a number of reasons, beliefs remain important in understanding the success of metanorms in cadre retirement. Lifelong tenure was no weak principle but a strongly entrenched practice that had developed over decades. What are the prospects of success in a "naked" battle by self-interested younger cadres in such a context? Old communist cadres were and are by no means powerless. Veteran cadres especially have contacts and prestige that younger cadres lack. Younger cadres possess one important resource in this battle: the state is on their side.

But even though they have taken sides, policy makers in Beijing have no interest whatsoever in alienating old cadres. By promoting a notion that retirement is correct conduct, not simply a policy that older cadres must step down, policy makers have given younger cadres a public-minded rationale for enforcing retirement. At the same time, they have given older cadres a public-minded rationale for retiring. This has served as a resource for younger cadres in their role as unofficial enforcers of cadre retirement policy. It has also allowed older cadres to exit more gracefully, if not always more willingly.

More generally, it seems it cannot be in the overall interest of political leaders to solve policy problems by promoting and manipulating undisguised social conflict. It is costly to the authorities because it creates enemies. It can also be costly to society. Crucial to the efficacy of normative beliefs is their impersonal nature as matters of principle. They are informal rules, in principle directed not for or against any particular group although in practice often favoring one group over another.

Marxist views about "false consciousness" notwithstanding, there is at work here an obvious and not, I think, inherently sinister principle of norm building in situations with an underlying metanorm structure of conflict.[9] Beliefs can mask, reduce, and even dissolve social

[9] Such situations abound. In the United States, the prohibition of smoking in public places is a good example of a policy problem and emergent normative proscription with a metanorm structure. Nonsmokers find they are punishing themselves by not taking action against people who smoke in public places. Consequently, nonsmokers have an interest in enforcing a prohibition, whether it is a legal one or a newly perceived right to protection from passive smoking.

conflict if those with the most to lose are given reason to believe losing is the right thing to do.

OPPORTUNITIES AND CONSTRAINTS FOR LEADERSHIP

Norms and interests are often viewed as contradictory, rather than consistent or supportive, forces. Here, I have tried to develop a notion of norm-guided action consistent with self-interest. Quite apart from this, I also discovered the pursuit of private interests at the core of the process of building a norm of cadre retirement. While unwilling to reject fully the role of beliefs about correct conduct in the success of this process, I nonetheless find that a key mechanism driving the process is the manipulation of a conflict of interest between the generations in the cadre corps.

This generational conflict presented policy makers in Beijing with an opportunity to exercise leadership. The structure of the conflict was purely fortuitous, however. Many policy objectives cannot draw on the benefits of a metanorm structure of conflict.

And even benefiting from the metanorm structure, policy makers in Beijing proved to be highly constrained as they worked to realize their policy objectives. Again, the pursuit of private interests was at work—but here as a hindrance rather than as an aid. Cadres proved not to be passive targets of retirement policy. Instead, they bargained to get a better deal from middlemen charged with policy implementation. This bargaining process is especially significant when we consider who the policy targets are in the case studied here. They include most prominently those we might expect to be most responsive to appeals from the top: communist party members, many of them old revolutionaries. Least of all, perhaps, might we expect these citizens of the Chinese communist state to haggle when confronted with authoritative decisions from Beijing.

The disguised and undisguised widespread pursuit of private interests in the processes described here seems to confirm something fairly obvious that we already suspect about leadership in the post-Mao period.[10] For most of the years since 1978, Chinese communist economic policy has celebrated, on a scale bigger than at any time since the communists came to power in 1949, the pursuit of private

[10] See, for one example among many in American newspapers, Nicholas Kristof's article about the attempt to eradicate mah-jongg in Shanghai. *New York Times*, 25 Feb. 1992, A8.

material interests as a proper means by which collective interests can be realized. In promoting an environment of normative self-interest, leaders in Beijing have at the same time created for themselves constraints on the mechanisms they can manipulate successfully to realize specific policy objectives.

Appendix

Survey Methods

The basis for drawing inferences about Chinese politics is relatively weak. Available published data is meager, incomplete, and often contradictory. Political scientists do not have enough access to information and interviews at the top of the system to help us do good empirical studies of elite politics. And the study of politics at the grassroots is highly constrained by Chinese authorities. While research opportunities in other environments exist[1] and while conditions for research in the People's Republic of China did improve in the decade after 1978, the circumstances described above remained essentially the same. Since the protests and massacre of 1989, the situation has become much worse.

For these reasons, if we want to develop our understanding of Chinese politics, we must pay more than usual attention to promoting cumulativeness in the field. At a minimum, this obliges us to make explicit our sources and research methods. Only then can colleagues evaluate findings conveniently and situate them appropriately among conclusions drawn in other studies and based on other research strategies. To this end, I summarize here my survey research methods.[2] I also hope a practical description of my research experience will point up to other students of Chinese politics some of the pitfalls to avoid and opportunities to pursue.

MULTIPLE METHODS

Conditions for good survey research in the People's Republic of China are far from ideal. Many Chinese officials do not understand or do not believe our scholarly interest in conducting surveys that meet rudimentary accepted standards of social science. Samples avail-

---

[1] Mainland Chinese emigres in Hong Kong have been interviewed by social scientists since the 1960s. See especially Martin King Whyte's very useful discussion in "On Studying China at a Distance." A more recent discussion can be found in Andrew Walder's *Communist Neo-Traditionalism*, 255–69. And Andrew Nathan discusses interviewing Chinese emigres in Hong Kong and the United States in *Chinese Democracy*, 235–55.

[2] I discuss published sources used in the section on sources and methods in the Introduction.

able to us are usually not probability samples. Respondents often are unfamiliar with surveys other than those conducted for official purposes. As a result, they may be apprehensive about the consequences of complete and truthful responses. Finally, in addition to the language and cultural obstacles common to students of comparative politics, there is the handicap of being relative newcomers to using survey research to study Chinese politics.

To reduce the effects of some of these problems, I opted for a methodological pluralism in my survey methods, as in the study overall. Specifically, I combined exploratory, loosely structured interviews with a small sample of thirty-six retired cadres in Beijing, questionnaires with closed-category items distributed to a larger sample of 670 retired cadres in the northeast, and semistructured interviews with seventy-one younger employed cadres. In my view, any merit this study has as a methodological contribution to the field of Chinese politics surely derives not from the larger survey and quantitative analysis per se, but from the combination and the particular sequencing of interviews and the larger survey.

INTERVIEWS WITH RETIRED CADRES

I began by conducting interviews with thirty-six retired cadres, all in Beijing.[3] These interviews were loosely structured, most were arranged through informal contacts, and many were conducted in the private homes of subjects. Excepting questions about background characteristics, all questions were open-ended. The rationale for the interviews, their loose format, and the use of informal contacts as subjects and also to recruit other subjects fit together in what I view as an important preliminary step and complement to the larger survey of retired cadres.

My purpose in the interviews was in large part exploratory. At the time I began them, my understanding of the issues derived almost exclusively from official published sources. My research questions had yet to be honed. I was in no sense prepared to design a questionnaire containing unambiguous, specific items presented in the forced-choice format that facilitates objective coding for quantitative analysis. The unstructured format of the interviews allowed subjects to direct me to concerns that seemed to them important, many of

---

[3] By "interview" I refer to a situation in which I informed the subject that I was conducting research on cadre retirement, asked questions directed toward understanding cadre retirement, and openly took notes while subjects talked. I do not include discussions in which any of these conditions were lacking.

which were not prominent in official sources. For example, retired cadres interviewed drew my attention to the process of bargaining with middlemen at the workplace and told me about requests typically included in the process. I was able to draw on much of what I had learned in interviews, including the particular vocabulary used, to design the questionnaire. The interviews not only guided questionnaire design but also helped me make sense of some responses at a later stage of quantitative analysis.

The unstructured interviews also elicited the rich contextual description that eludes quantitative measurement. The qualitative data provided by interview subjects—including their gripes, anecdotes, and digressions, virtually unobtainable and certainly not encouraged in a more easily coded questionnaire—made the interviews intrinsically worthwhile. It also made my research and the presentation of it more interesting.

Given the exploratory and orienting aims of the interviews, reliability of response was a top priority. Most of all I needed subjects to provide frank and complete accounts. As I observed in the Introduction, retired cadres generally make very good interview subjects: most have plenty of time to spare, like to talk, and are articulate. And compared to those with positions to lose, they may feel less constrained about what they say. All the same, I relied little on interviews arranged through official channels, reasoning that official selection might be biased toward the ideal. Most interview subjects were known to me personally or were introduced through personal contacts who knew them. This personal connection between subjects and myself, sometimes quite tenuous, did not guarantee reliability but my Chinese contacts and I believe it greatly enhanced it.

Twenty-three of the thirty-six interview subjects were personal acquaintances or introduced through informal contacts. Almost all were party cadres. This is not altogether undesirable, as it is precisely this population of cadres that might otherwise prove difficult to access and it is from this population that one might otherwise expect low reliability of response. Interviews with thirteen other subjects were arranged institutionally, most through two veteran cadre centers. In some cases, cadres interviewed seemed to be unusually orthodox politically or to enjoy unusually good retirement benefits. Also, institutions tended to select cadres who were easy to contact. The former problem poses a threat to reliability of response. The latter is less serious. In fact, I welcomed the opportunity to meet the "regulars" at a veteran cadre center, as I personally knew no one in this category.

The interview format was loosely structured, for the reasons discussed above. I made every effort to allow discussion to flow naturally or logically rather than according to a strict preconceived agenda. Throughout the interviews, however, I bore in mind three general topics and associated clusters of subtopics. Question phrasing and order varied to take into account cues from subjects, but I usually managed to cover most of the topics. On cadre retirement policy, I asked about perceived rationale for the policy, perceived degree of success, opinions on the best way to implement the policy, and future outlook. On the process of retirement I asked about attitudes toward retirement, context and manner in which the subject's retirement was initially raised, actions of officials at the workplace in arranging retirement, discussion with co-workers and family members about retirement, and (after initial interviews) requests to the workplace before retirement. On post-retirement life I asked about routine activities, problems of adaptation, relations with the former workplace, and whether and how subjects kept up with current events and participated in political activities. In addition to these questions, all open-ended, I used a standardized form to record information on background characteristics. Some of these characteristics are summarized in Table A.1, which also describes background characteristics of retired cadres who responded to the questionnaire in the larger survey.

Interview procedures were essentially the same, regardless of whether the interview was arranged institutionally or through an informal contact. I introduced myself, my topic, the purpose served by the interview in my research, and I guaranteed the subject's anonymity. After discussion was well underway I asked for permission to take notes. In no case did I encounter objection or hesitation. Although many background characteristics were volunteered early in the interview, I brought out the standardized form only at the end of the interview so as to maintain an informal conversational style throughout. Interview protocols were written up from notes as soon after the interview as was feasible, usually on the same day.

Most of the informally arranged interviews took place in the subject's home, some with the contact present. In a couple of cases I interviewed two subjects (husband and wife) at one time. All the institutionally arranged interviews took place in institutional settings and were small conference-style interviews. These were clearly the mode of interview preferred by the officials in charge and perhaps also by the interview subjects, to whom I was a complete stranger, a foreigner, and a mere student. One such interview was attended by a cadre from the veteran cadre center arranging the interview, which I judge to have had a stifling effect on subject response. Other institutionally arranged interviews were not supervised in any way, except in the important sense that subjects supervise each other. Generally,

TABLE A.1
Background Characteristics of Retired Cadres Surveyed

Characteristic	Questionnaire Respondents	Interview Subjects
Retirement Status		
Specially retired	173	28
Regularly retired	72	8
Party Membership		
Communist	206	36
None or noncommunist	39	0
Revolutionary/Work Service		
Revolutionary Civil Wars	0	4
Anti-Japanese War	2	18
War of Liberation	171	6
< 1950 (but regularly retired)	22	5
1950–55	44	3
1956–60	6	0
Sex		
Male	208	19
Female	37	17
Age in 1987		
< 55	37	0
55–59	106	6
60–65	86	21
> 65	16	9
Years of Schooling		
0–6	66	12
7–9	125	5
10–12	26	8
> 12	19	11
Missing data	9	0
Administrative Rank		
Ministerial	0	2
Bureau	6	15
Division	10	11
Section or below	204	8
Missing data	25	0
Year of Retirement		
1978–81	69	3
1982–84	137	16
1985–87	35	17
Missing data	4	0

interviews with one subject lasted two to three hours, interviews with two subjects lasted three hours, and conference-style interviews lasted four hours.

QUESTIONNAIRES DISTRIBUTED TO RETIRED CADRES

The larger survey employed a self-administered mail-back questionnaire containing closed-category items only. It was distributed to 670 cadres in a small city in the northeast. My purpose was to investigate rather more rigorously and widely initial hunches, ideas suggested in the theoretical literature on norms, and insights developed during the interviews. Quantitative analysis of questionnaire responses provided me with a replicable check on my interpretation of qualitative data and a test of its generalizability. It also forced me to frame qualitative findings in unambiguous terms in order to figure out what I was looking for and understand what I found in the quantitative data.

That stated, conditions for survey research in the People's Republic of China are poor. Understanding and acceptance of this methodology were only beginning before the crackdown in 1989.[4] In my own case, Peking University lent its official sponsorship to the survey. However, content was not censored, although the questionnaire itself was examined for approval at three bureaucratic levels.

The selection of the locality in which to distribute my questionnaire was made on the basis of pure expedience. Quite simply, my Chinese colleagues and I had good contacts in this city. One of them transported the questionnaires back to the city, received approval for their distribution from the organization department there, and had the neighborhood committees hand-deliver the questionnaires to retired cadres. The city has a population of about 100,000, with less than 20 percent engaged in agriculture. As to selection of the sample within the city, I was concerned that any reliable sampling technique I suggested would be impractical or so troublesome as to invite a relaxation of standards and introduce major systematic bias. The virtual elimination of opportunities for officially directed sample bias was achieved by arranging distribution of the questionnaires to all retired cadres in the city, with actual distribution by individuals unconnected with any of the various organizations for cadre management. All personnel with an administrative rank and who had retired from a party

[4] See the excellent overview by Stanley Rosen and David Chu, "Survey Research in the People's Republic of China."

or government bureaucracy, public institution, public-sector enterprise, or noncommunist party organization and resided in the city comprised the sample.

Questionnaires were distributed to 670 cadres.[5] Only 250 completed and returned questionnaires,[6] a response rate of 37 percent that I continue to find disappointing.[7] Based on aggregate data on retired cadres in the city obtained later, it is clear that the response rate is much higher among specially retired cadres than among regularly retired cadres, much higher among cadres who retired before 1982 (most of whom are regularly retired) than among those who retired in 1982 and after, and much lower among cadres aged sixty-five or older (in 1987) than among cadres younger than sixty-five.

I have no confirmed explanation for the low response rate or for its distribution across subgroups. I do note, however, that distribution of the questionnaires more or less coincided with the 1986–87 student demonstrations, in which Peking University students figured prominently. The low response rate may have had to do with an unwillingness of older cadres to cooperate with Peking University. A more mundane explanation is suggested by the physical appearance of the questionnaire, which was not printed in characters of larger than normal size. Older cadres, who also tend to be less literate, may simply have found it too much of an effort to read the questionnaire. As I note in the Introduction, my worry initially was about how to react to a suspiciously high response rate if one materialized, which would have left me wondering about official intervention.

I began to design the questionnaire after having completed interviews with thirteen cadres. I revised it substantially three times, in consultation with Chinese colleagues and retired cadres. It contains forty-five closed-category items: fourteen items are background items and the remaining thirty-one are forced-choice items with a range of four to seven choices, from which the respondent was instructed to choose only one.

Seventeen of the nonbackground items concern circumstances before retirement and the retirement process. They include questions

[5] A comparison with aggregate data on cadre retirement in the city indicates the number retired at the time was in fact higher than 670. The aggregate data was not available at the time the survey was conducted. At worst, as many as eighty-eight retired cadres did not receive questionnaires. These would most likely be recent retirees.

[6] Five respondents had retired in poor health before 1978, and I did not include them in my analysis.

[7] The response rate is not low if compared with rates obtained in similarly conducted surveys in advanced industrial democracies, however. I consider it low given the suitability of retired cadres as survey subjects.

about attitude toward retirement, actions of officials at the workplace in arranging retirement, discussion of retirement with others, perceived level of understanding of policy, opinions on the policy, requests to the workplace before retirement, and perceived pressure to retire from co-workers. Fourteen of the nonbackground items are on circumstances after retirement. They include questions about activities, visits to the workplace, political participation, interaction with others, visits to the veteran cadre center, and adaptation to post-retirement life.

I tried to keep question wording simple. Also, in scalar items I generally did not provide a midpoint, but forced the respondent to choose a direction, although I did make available low-intensity choices in each scalar item. This practice gives an inaccurate measure for respondents who are truly neutral. In adopting it I presumed that most respondents in my sample and population of interest do in fact have a (non-neutral) position on the items presented—mainly because the items are not general or abstract issues about which respondents have given little thought. Rather, the items are highly specific questions about a recent important change in their lives. I also presumed that, even in circumstances of anonymity, Chinese respondents may find it more comfortable to select a midpoint choice, providing a response without providing an opinion.[8] I wanted to prevent this.

Second, on items that interviews had suggested touched on sensitive matters, I usually framed the item as a question about other cadres rather than about the respondent. This was the case, for example, on the issue of perceived pressure to retire from co-workers at the workplace.[9]

Finally, on the single issue of pre-retirement requests, I broke questionnaire design convention and asked a leading question. Interviews had indicated that requests were almost the rule, but were not discussed with others nor viewed as fully legitimated by official policy. Further, their content varied. In order to find out about content of requests, I used an item that presumed requests had in fact been made (although provided denial as a response option).[10]

[8] See the experiments and discussion in Schuman and Presser, *Questions and Answers in Attitude Surveys*, 161–78.

[9] And as I note in chapter 4, even this technique did not overcome resistance to respond. The items about pressure from co-workers have a higher number of missing observations than any other items.

[10] The question with its choice options was worded as follows. Before I retired I asked the workplace to help me resolve: salary problems; housing problems; son's or daughter's employment problems; other problems; I did not make any requests.

I have already indicated how the questionnaires were distributed in the sample city. Before they left Beijing I placed each in an envelope containing a stamped envelope addressed to my department at Peking University and sealed the outer envelope. The introduction to the questionnaire asked respondents to complete the questionnaire within two weeks and to post it in the envelope provided. I received all 250 in just over a month's time.

INTERVIEWS WITH YOUNGER CADRES

The first set of interviews and the larger survey gave me information and views about cadre retirement from the perspective of cadres who had been the main targets of retirement policy for nearly a decade. But if they were the losers in the retirement process, there were also winners—younger cadres, who stood to gain new positions with the retirement of their senior co-workers. I considered their perspective critical to my research. If social enforcers were to emerge to implement retirement policy as a norm, these younger cadres were the most likely initial candidates for the task. As described in chapter 4, I found younger cadres are indeed both keen observers and willing unofficial enforcers in the policy implementation process.

I conducted the interviews with younger cadres on a second research trip, in the fall of 1988. I interviewed seventy-one cadres from workplaces in nearly every province of the country, who had come to Peking University for two years of special cadre study to obtain the college graduate equivalence that would help qualify them for promotion. The sample consisted of all but a few cadres in the class. Only five (in the class and the sample) were women. Time considerations prevented me from completing interviews with the entire class.

The contact with the cadre class was made through official university channels. I had no acquaintance with the cadres prior to the interviews. In such a circumstance, I was surprised at the frankness of most subjects about a number of issues that might be considered sensitive—employment substitution, their perceptions of retirement and promotion as fully zero-sum, and the tactics they used to encourage older cadres to retire on time, to give a few examples. The cadres were young and had been apart from their workplaces for more than one year at the time I interviewed them. Some spoke to me of the comparatively relaxed environment at the university. These factors may have contributed to frankness.

One of my concerns with the sample of younger cadres was the diffusion of information among interview subjects. Cadres shared cramped dormitories and attended classes together. It was easy for cadres already interviewed to communicate to others whatever they recalled about the interview schedule. Indeed, given the novelty of the situation, it was natural to do so. Subjects told me that the interviews were in fact sometimes discussed informally among them. Obviously, I wanted to avoid a situation of consensus among interview subjects on a set of answers, whether these emerged by pre-arranged agreement or by more subtle peer group influences.

It may be fortunate for me, then, that younger cadres interviewed found the subject of retirement dull. Informal discussions were as likely to focus on the interview experience and question format as on question content. Also, the interview schedule comprised more than sixty items, many of which were forced-choice items with four or more answer options. While it is conceivable that interview subjects were able to recall subject areas, I think it unlikely that they could have recalled specific items or options.

The overwhelming majority of interview subjects were in their thirties and none was older than forty. For these cadres, retirement is decades away. This point has some implications relevant to the analysis. It is reasonable to suppose that somewhat older cadres, in their fifties, for example, are less enthusiastic enforcers of retirement policy. The weight of future costs (their retirement) is more salient for them than for younger cadres. And it is also true that cadres in their forties are more likely to reap the most immediate rewards in the form of promotion when older cadres retire. As a consequence, they are probably the most zealous enforcers of all. In short, I suspect the age group I interviewed included neither the most nor the least aggressive enforcers among younger cadres.

The interviews followed a schedule designed after I had almost completed analysis of responses from retired cadres. I asked fifteen open-ended questions and used forty-eight forced-choice items, repeating some of the items from the larger survey of retired cadres. Of the sixty-three items, thirteen are background items and twelve solicit opinions on retirement. Other items focus on the retirement process at the workplace and in the locality.

I arranged my interview times to facilitate the study schedule of the interview subjects. As this schedule was the same for the entire class, I set up blocks of interviewing time and cadres signed up at their convenience, usually on the day of the interview. Interviews were conducted in a small university meeting room. All cadres were interviewed individually and (so far as I know) privately. I and my research topic had already been introduced to the cadres as a group. I repeated these introductions to each cadre at the beginning of the interview and guaranteed the subject's anonymity. I also demonstrated the forced-choice format, apologized for its clumsiness in capturing their views, and explained its advantages in quantitative analysis.

I began with a few easy open-ended questions and then moved on to some of the forced-choice items, using response cards for all forced-choice items. No subject was familiar with this form of interview, some insisted on treating all forced-choice items as open-ended questions, but the majority managed to respond to most questions. As interview times were pre-scheduled, most interviews lasted an hour. None was longer than one-and-a-half hours.

IMPLICATIONS FOR ANALYSIS

The description above is of survey research in circumstances characterized by serious constraints and threats to reliability, validity, and generalizability. Why bother? Put another way, what are the implications for analysis?

Consider first the question of sample bias. Everything done in my research violated a fundamental tenet of survey research—probability sampling. Even in a sample of moderate size and where the locale is not contaminated by official selection according to criteria unknown to us, it is clear that we cannot presume sample features to be in any sense representative of the population of interest. Nor can we know its degree of unrepresentativeness.

This poses a serious threat to generalizability of findings. But it does not restrict us to a characterization of the research as a case study of one locality. If the sample is sufficiently varied along the dimensions of analytical interest and if cases in each of these dimensions are sufficiently numerous, it is not inappropriate to make some kinds of generalizations to the larger population of interest. I cannot turn to my sample data for a description of the retired cadre population along any single dimension—how cadres feel about retirement or how many cadres retired late, for example. Measures of central tendency based on data from nonprobability samples are generally not considered reliable estimates of population parameters.

But there is not necessarily a problem in subjecting data from nonprobability samples to inferential statistical analysis to test relationships between variables.[11] I can therefore generalize reliably about the relationship between amount of pension and willingness to retire,

[11] Researchers analyzing findings from the Soviet Interview Project confronted essentially the same issue. Most respondents in their sample are Jews, who are a small minority in the Soviet population. See the discussion in Anderson and Silver, "The SIP General Survey Sample."

between rank and time of retirement, or between willingness to retire and time of retirement. For example, my sample data is not useful on the issue of how early or late Chinese cadres retired, but it does provide a reliable basis for the general inference that high-ranking cadres retired later than ordinary cadres, other things equal. The proportions of cadres with high or low rank or who retired early or late may be significantly greater or smaller in my sample than among all retired cadres. Barring peculiar circumstances, however, the relationships are the same.

In short, nonprobability samples such as we are likely to encounter for some time in the future, to the extent that we are permitted to do survey research at all in the People's Republic of China, can be used and can be useful to us in testing relationships between variables. This is perfectly acceptable because, for the most part, social science is not about single-dimension description but about precisely such relationships.

Although we can test relationships even given a biased sample, we want to start out with some very good ideas about what kinds of relationships to look for. We want a theory about these relationships, something that explains the causal direction. This will not emerge from inferential statistics. And while there are many possible theoretical points of departure, ultimately we require a survey instrument in order to measure the hypothesized relationships.

In my case, before designing the questionnaire, I conducted exploratory, loosely structured interviews with cadres chosen because of a relationship (often indirect) with me. These interviews introduced relationships between variables that I had not previously considered and helped me develop measures. The conscious violation of probability sampling presumes a trade-off between probability sampling and reliability of interview subjects who were not anonymous to me. I have no evidence that retired cadres I knew or who were introduced through personal contacts were more frank and complete with me than they would have been in other circumstances. I do note, however, that cadres introduced by institutional contacts and interviewed in institutional settings were less forthcoming about sensitive subjects such as bargaining, employment substitution, and relations with co-workers than subjects I knew personally or who were introduced through others I knew personally and who were interviewed in private homes. I also heard more complaints in private homes than I did in institutional settings.

The particular combination and sequencing of interviews and the larger survey was of great help in my research. This is not only because the interviews with retired cadres helped me design the questionnaire. In addition, the interviews helped me make sense of some responses at a later stage of quantitative analysis, supplemented quantitative findings with their rich contextual description, and made my research experience more interesting and generally educational.

Works Cited

Newspapers and Periodicals

Banyuetan. Beijing.
Beijing Review. Beijing.
Daily Report: China. Washington, D.C.
Guizhou shehui kexue. Guiyang.
Guowuyuan gongbao. Beijing.
Ha'erbin yanjiu. Ha'erbin.
Hebei laodong renshi. Shijiazhuang.
Henan laodong. Zhengzhou.
Hongqi. Beijing.
Issues and Studies. Taipei.
Jiangxi laodong renshi. Nanchang. Neibu before 1988.
Lao tongzhi zhi you. Shenyang.
Laodong lilun yu shijian. Chengdu.
Laodong renshi bao. Beijing.
Laodong renshi zhengce zhuankan. Beijing. Neibu.
Laodong yu renshi. Changsha.
Laonianxue zazhi. Changchun.
Laoren tiandi. Beijing.
Liaowang. Beijing.
New York Times. New York.
Renmin ribao. Beijing.
Renshi. Taiyuan.
Shehui. Shanghai.
Shehui kexue. Lanzhou.
Shehui kexue. Shanghai.
Shehui kexue yanjiu. Chengdu.
Shehui kexue zhanxian. Changchun.
Shehuixue yanjiu. Beijing.
Tuixiu shenghuo. Changchun.
Xingzheng yu renshi. Shanghai. Neibu.
Xinhua yuebao. Beijing.
Zhongguo laonian. Beijing.
Zhongguo renshi guanli. Beijing.
Zhongguo shehui kexue. Beijing.
Zhongguo xingzheng guanli. Beijing.

Official Documents

Caizheng bu laodong renshi bu. Guanyu yange kongzhi fafang ge zhong butie jintie he kongzhi zixing tigao tuixiu daiyu wenti baogao. 10 Jan. 1987.
Guowuyuan gongbao, 1987, no. 5:195.

Communique of the Fifth Plenary Session of the 11th Central Committee of the Communist Party of China. 29 Feb. 1980. *Beijing Review* 23, no. 10 (1980):7–10.

Constitution of the Communist Party of China. 6 Sept. 1982. *Beijing Review* 25, no. 38 (1982):8–21.

Draft of the Revised Constitution of the Communist Party of China. 2 Apr. 1980. *Issues and Studies* 16, no. 9 (1980):85–109.

Guowuyuan. Guanyu anzhi lao ruo bing can ganbu de zanxing banfa. 2 June 1978. In *Zhonghua renmin gongheguo laodong fagui xuanbian*, edited by Laodong renshi bu zhengce yanjiu shi, 332–36. Beijing: Laodong renshi chubanshe, 1986.

———. Guanyu gongren tuixiu tuizhi de zanxing banfa. 2 June 1978. In *Zhonghua renmin gongheguo laodong fagui xuanbian*, 337–40. See Guowuyuan 2 June 1978, above.

———. Guanyu lao ganbu lizhi xiuyang de zanxing guiding. 7 Oct. 1980. In *Zhonghua renmin gongheguo fagui huibian 1980*, edited by Guowuyuan fazhi ju, 279–82. Beijing: Falu chubanshe, 1986.

———. Guanyu yange zhixing gongren tuixiu tuizhi zanxing banfa de tongzhi. 7 Nov. 1981. In *Zhonghua renmin gongheguo fagui huibian 1981*, edited by Guowuyuan fazhi ju, 294–97. Beijing: Falu chubanshe, 1986.

———. Guanyu fabu lao ganbu lizhi xiuyang zhidu de ji xiang guiding. 10 Apr. 1982. In *Lao ganbu gongzuo wenjian xuanbian*, vol. 1, edited by Zhonggong zhongyang zuzhi bu lao ganbu ju laodong renshi bu lao ganbu fuwu ju, 43–46. Beijing: Zhonggong zhongyang zuzhi bu lao ganbu ju laodong renshi bu lao ganbu fuwu ju, 1983. Neibu.

———. Guanyu renzhen zhengdun zhaoshou tuixiu tuizhi zhigong zinu gongzuo de tongzhi. 3 Sept. 1983. *Guowuyuan gongbao*, 1983, no. 20:931–33.

———. Guanyu fagei lixiu tuixiu renyuan shenghuo butie fei de tongzhi. 10 Jan. 1985. In *Guojia jiguan he shiye danwei gongze zhidu gaige wenjian huibian*, vol. 2, edited by Laodong renshi bu gongze ju, 3. Beijing: Laodong renshi chubanshe, 1986. Neibu.

———. Guanyu fabu gaige laodong zhidu si ge guiding de tongzhi. July 1986. In *Laodong hetongzhi shouce*, edited by Liu Qingtang, 20–22. Beijing: Kexue chubanshe, 1986.

———. Guanyu zhongyang guojia jiguan cong lingdao gangwei tui xia lai de tongzhi bu zai baoliu yuan bangongshi de tongzhi. 12 Feb. 1988. *Laodong renshi zhengce zhuankan*, 1988, no. 5:16.

Guowuyuan bangongting. Guanyu xian yi shang dang he guojia jiguan tui(li)xiu ganbu jingshang ban qiye wenti de ruogan guiding. 3 Oct. 1988. *Renmin ribao*, 25 Oct. 1988, 1.

Laodong bu renshi bu caizheng bu quanguo zong gonghui. Guanyu lituixiu renyuan shenghuo butie fei de tongzhi. 23 May 1988. *Laodong renshi zhengce zhuankan*, 1988, no. 8:30.

Laodong renshi bu. Guanche guowuyuan guanyu lao ganbu lizhi xiuyang guiding zhong juti wenti de chuli yijian. 10 Dec. 1982. In *Lao ganbu gongzuo wenjian xuanbian*, vol. 1, 47–55. See Guowuyuan 10 Apr. 1982.

————. Guanyu lixiu ganbu jiankang xiuyang de ji xiang guiding. 25 May 1983. In *Lao ganbu gongzuo wenjian xuanbian*, vol. 1, 90–92. See Guowuyuan 10 Apr. 1982.

————. Guanyu guanche zhixing "guowuyuan guanyu renzhen zhengdun zhaoshou tuixiu tuizhi zhigong zinu gongzuo de tongzhi" zhong ruogan wenti de yijian. 10 Feb. 1984. In *Lao ganbu gongzuo wenjian xuanbian*, vol. 2, edited by Zhonggong zhongyang zuzhi bu lao ganbu ju laodong renshi bu lao ganbu fuwu ju, 306–9. Beijing: Zhonggong zhongyang zuzhi bu lao ganbu ju laodong renshi bu lao ganbu fuwu ju, 1986. Neibu.

Laodong renshi bu caizheng bu. Guanyu tigao zhigong tuixiu fei tuizhi shenghuo fei de zui di baozheng shu de guiding. 28 June 1983. In *Zhonghua renmin gongheguo laodong fagui xuanbian*, 383. See Guowuyuan 2 June 1978.

Weisheng bu. Guanyu lizhi xiuyang ganbu yiliao wenti de guiding. 16 Jan. 1981. In *Lao ganbu gongzuo wenjian xuanbian*, vol. 1, 177–78. See Guowuyuan 10 Apr. 1982.

————. Guanyu tiaozheng lao zhuanjia yiliao zhaogu de tongzhi. 2 July 1981. In *Lao ganbu gongzuo wenjian xuanbian*, vol. 1, 181–83. See Guowuyuan 10 Apr. 1982.

————. Guanyu zhongyang guojia jiguan zai jing danwei siju zhang yi shang ganbu he zhuanjia yiliao zhaogu de buchong guiding. 13 Dec. 1984. In *Lao ganbu gongzuo wenjian xuanbian*, vol. 2, 229–31. See Laodong renshi bu 10 Feb. 1984.

Weisheng bu baojian ju. Guanyu lao ganbu lao zhuanjia waichu yiliao shouxu deng wenti de tongzhi. 8 May 1986. In *Lao ganbu gongzuo wenjian xuanbian*, vol. 2, 231–34. See Laodong renshi bu 10 Feb. 1984.

Zhonggong zhongyang. Guanyu jianli lao ganbu tuixiu [*sic*] zhidu de jueding. 20 Feb. 1982. In *Lao ganbu gongzuo wenjian xuanbian*, vol. 1, 1–13. See Guowuyuan 10 Apr. 1982.

————. Guanyu jin yi bu jiaqiang qingshaonian jiaoyu yu fang qingshaonian weifa fanzui de tongzhi. 4 Oct. 1985. In *Lao ganbu gongzuo wenjian xuanbian*, vol. 2, 21–33. See Laodong renshi bu 10 Feb. 1984.

Zhonggong zhongyang bangongting. Guanyu zhongyang wenjian yinfa -yuedu he guanli de banfa. 10 June 1985. In *Lao ganbu gongzuo wenjian xuanbian*, vol. 2, 118–22. See Laodong renshi bu 10 Feb. 1984.

Zhonggong zhongyang bangongting guowuyuan bangongting. Guanyu guanche zhixing lixiu ganbu shenghuo daiyu guiding de tongzhi. 3 June 1984. In *Lao ganbu gongzuo wenjian xuanbian*, vol. 2, 199–202. See Laodong renshi bu 10 Feb. 1984.

————. Guanyu fahui lixiu tuixiu zhuanye jishu renyuan zuoyong de zanxing guiding. 6 Oct. 1986. *Guowuyuan gongbao*, 1986, no. 19:856–58.

Zhonggong zhongyang bangongting zhonggong zhongyang zuzhi bu. Guanyu lixiu tuixiu ganbu yuedu wenjian wenti. 26 Aug. 1981. In *Lao ganbu gongzuo wenjian xuanbian*, vol. 1, 131–33. See Guowuyuan 10 Apr. 1982.

Zhonggong zhongyang guowuyuan. Guanyu shezhi guwen de jueding. 13

Aug. 1980. In *Lao ganbu gongzuo wenjian xuanbian*, vol. 1, 14–16. See Guo-wuyuan 10 Apr. 1982.

———. Guanyu yanjin dangzheng jiguan he dangzheng ganbu jingshang ban qiye de jueding. 3 Dec. 1984. In *Lao ganbu gongzuo wenjian xuanbian*, vol. 2, 8–15. See Laodong renshi bu 10 Feb. 1984.

———. Guanyu jin yi bu zhizhi dangzheng jiguan he dangzheng ganbu jing-shang ban qiye de guiding. 4 Feb. 1986. In *Lao ganbu gongzuo wenjian xuan-bian*, vol. 2, 17–20. See Laodong renshi bu 10 Feb. 1984.

Zhonggong zhongyang zuzhi bu. Guanyu jiaqiang lao ganbu gongzuo de ji dian yijian. 29 Dec. 1978. In *Lao ganbu gongzuo wenjian xuanbian*, vol. 1, 80–88. See Guowuyuan 10 Apr. 1982.

———. Guanyu anpai he zuzhi hao lixiu tuixiu tuizhi dangyuan zuzhi shenghuo. 30 July 1981. In *Lao ganbu gongzuo wenjian xuanbian*, vol. 1, 128–31. See Guowuyuan 10 Apr. 1982.

———. Guanyu tuoshan anpai tuichu xianzhi de lao ganbu de yijian. 2 June 1982. In *Lao ganbu gongzuo wenjian xuanbian*, vol. 1, 192–95. See Guo-wuyuan 10 Apr. 1982.

———. Guanyu queding jianguo qian ganbu canjia geming gongzuo shijian de guiding. 27 Sept. 1982. In *Lao ganbu gongzuo wenjian xuanbian*, vol. 1, 104–11. See Guowuyuan 10 Apr. 1982.

———. Guanyu fahui zhongyang guojia jiguan lixiu lao ganbu de zuoyong de yijian. 11 Oct. 1982. In *Lao ganbu gongzuo wenjian xuanbian*, vol. 1, 196–201. See Guowuyuan 10 Apr. 1982.

———. Guanyu banli lao ganbu lizhi xiuyang shouxu de tongzhi. 30 Oct. 1982. In *Lao ganbu gongzuo wenjian xuanbian*, vol. 1, 218–20. See Guo-wuyuan 10 Apr. 1982.

———. Jiu sheng shi lao ganbu gongzuo zuotanhui jiyao de tongzhi. 25 Apr. 1983. In *Lao ganbu gongzuo wenjian xuanbian*, vol. 1, 89–97. See Guowuyuan 10 Apr. 1982.

———. Guanyu zhuajin banli lixiu shouxu de tongzhi (dianbao). 12 Nov. 1985. In *Lao ganbu gongzuo wenjian xuanbian*, vol. 2, 122. See Laodong ren-shi bu 10 Feb. 1984.

Zhonggong zhongyang zuzhi bu laodong renshi bu. Guanyu zhongyang guo-jia jiguan lao ganbu ju (chu) zhize fanwei de shixing banfa. 31 Dec. 1982. In *Lao ganbu gongzuo wenjian xuanbian*, vol. 1, 222–23. See Guowuyuan 10 Apr. 1982.

Zhonggong zhongyang zuzhi bu weisheng bu. Zhongyang guojia jiguan zai jing danwei lixiu lao ganbu he zhiming renshi zhuanjia yiliao baojian zanxing banfa. 2 June 1982. In *Lao ganbu gongzuo wenjian xuanbian*, vol. 1, 183–86. See Guowuyuan 10 Apr. 1982.

Articles and Books in Chinese

Bao Jirui. "Tantan zhongshenzhi wenti." *Guizhou shehui kexue*, 1981, no. 1:29–34.

Cao Zhi, ed. *Zhonghua renmin gongheguo renshi zhidu gaiyao*. Beijing: Beijing daxue chubanshe, 1985. Neibu.

Chen Yeping. "Baozheng dang de shiye jiwang kailai de zhongda juece: xuexi Deng Xiaoping wenxuan zhong guanyu xin lao ganbu hezuo jiaoti sixiang de tihui." *Hongqi*, 1983, no. 16:2–6.

"Dadao lituixiu nianling ganbu yao ruqi banli lituixiu shouxu." *Lao tongzhi zhiyou*, 1987, no. 7:28.

Deng Xiaoping. "Zai zhongyang guwen weiyuanhui di yi ci quanti huiyi shang de jianghua." *Xinhua yuebao*, 1982, no. 9:65–68.

Gao Fang. "Feichu ganbu zhiwu zhongshenzhi de weida yiyi." *Renwen zazhi*, 1980, no. 4:7–10.

Gong Fuzhong. "Zhaogu xing tiba bu zu qu." *Jiangxi laodong renshi*, 1987, no. 3:39.

"Gongren keyi lixiu ma?" *Zhongguo laonian*, 1985, no. 10:17.

"Guanyu fagei lixiu tuixiu tuizhi renyuan linshi shenghuo butie de tongzhi." *Henan laodong*, 1988, no. 3:23.

"Guanyu gei tuixiu zhigong jiafa buzhu fei de tongzhi." *Henan laodong*, 1987, no. 2:16, 22.

"Guanyu gongren tuixiu tuizhi shi xiang de wenda." *Banyuetan*, 1981, no. 23:10–11.

"Guanyu tuixiu ganbu guanli gongzuo de zanxing guiding." *Renshi*, 1988, no. 6:14–15.

Guojia tongji ju shehui tongji si, ed. *Zhongguo laodong gongze tongji ziliao 1949–1985*. Beijing: Zhongguo tongji chubanshe, 1987.

Ha'erbin shi shehui kexue yanjiu suo shehuixue yanjiu shi. "Ha'erbin shi lixiu ganbu zhuangkuang diaocha baogao (shang)." *Ha'erbin yanjiu*, 1984, no. 3:35–47.

———. "Ha'erbin shi lixiu ganbu zhuangkuang diaocha baogao (xia)." *Ha'erbin yanjiu*, 1984, no. 4:21–30.

Hongqi bianji bu. "Jigou gaige shi yi chang geming." *Hongqi*, 1982, no. 6:2–5.

Hu Guohua, and Tang Hua. "Yi xin de fangshi luxing zeren." *Liaowang*, 1984, no. 14:9–11.

Hu Jinbo. "Lituixiu ganbu ying tongyi guanli." *Renshi*, 1988, no. 4:13.

Huang Baowei. "Lao ganbu xuanba zhongqingnian ganbu zhong de lishi zeren." *Lilun yu shijian*, 1981, no. 8:32–33.

Jia Dezhang. "Lue tan wo guo xianxing yanglao zhidu." *Shehuixue yanjiu*, 1986, no. 3:71–77.

Jia Fuhai, Cheng Jie, and Wei Yi. "Lue lun zhongshenzhi." *Shehui kexue*, 1980, no. 4:10–15.

Jiao Shanmin. "You guan renshi zhidu gaige de jige wenti." In *Laodong gongze renshi zhidu gaige de yanjiu yu tantao*, edited by Laodong renshi bu ganbu jiaoyu ju, 279–94. Beijing: Laodong renshi chubanshe, 1985. Neibu.

Jilin shi di si renmin yiyuan Jilin sheng meikuang gongren wenquan yiyuan. "150 ming chengshi tuixiu gongren, ganbu de xinli diaocha." *Laonianxue zazhi* 2, no. 1 (1984):51–52.

"Kefou tiqian banli lixiu?" *Lao tongzhi zhi you*, 1987, no. 11:9.

Lao ganbu shouce bianxie zu, ed. *Lao ganbu shouce*. Shenyang: Liaoning kexue jishu chubanshe, 1988.

Laodong renshi bu ganbu jiaoyu ju, ed. *Laodong renshi tongjixue*. Beijing: Laodong renshi chubanshe, 1985.

Li Juemin. "Lixiu lao ganbu manyi chengdu fenxi." *Lingnan xuekan*, 1989, no. 4:97–102.

Li Rui. "Xin xingshi yu ganbu gongzuo." *Xinhua yuebao*, 1985, no. 2:31–35.

Lin Lenong, and Geng Kun. "Tuixiu zhigong kaocha." *Shehui kexue zhanxian*, 1983, no. 3:101–8.

Liu Yongchuan. "Dui Beijing shi 106 ming lixiu ganbu xiankuang de diaocha baogao." In *Shoudu laoling zhanlue wenti yanjiu*, edited by Beijing shi laoling wenti weiyuanhui Beijing shi renmin zhengfu yanjiu suo, 155–66. Beijing: Beijing shi laoling wenti weiyuanhui Beijing shi renmin zhengfu yanjiu suo, 1986. Neibu.

Liu Zhong. "Zhigong tuixiu fei de zhifu biaozhun jidai yanjiu." *Laodong lilun yu shijian*, 1988, no. 4:6–7.

Peng Xiangfu, and Zheng Zhongbin. "Shitan feizhi ganbu zhiwu zhongshenzhi." *Lilun yu shijian*, 1980, no. 5:8–11 and excerpt in *Renmin ribao*, 3 June 1980, 5.

Pi Chunxie, and Zhang Huanguang. *Xiandai gongwuyuan zhidu yanjiu*. Beijing: Zhongguo guangbo dianshi chubanshe, 1988.

Qian Lihua, and Lu Zhengfang. "Wushi duo sui jiguan ganbu guanli de duice." *Zhongguo xingzheng guanli*, 1987, no. 12:19–21.

Shen Mengpi. "Guojia gongwuyuan de tuixiu tuizhi zhidu." In *Guojia gongwuyuan zhidu jianghua*, edited by Liu Junlin and Dai Guangqian, 226–52. Beijing: Nengyuan chubanshe, 1989.

Shi Ming. "Hai shi bu ti 'yure' hao." *Lao tongzhi zhi you*, 1987, no. 1:24.

"Shi wei pizhuan shi wei zuzhi bu 'guanche zhixing zhongyang zuzhi bu guanyu ganbu lixiu shouxu tongzhi de yijian.' " *Xingzheng yu renshi*, 1986, no. 3:18–19.

Song Renqiong. "Renzhen jiejue gongzuo mianlin de xin keti." *Hongqi*, 1980, no. 16:2–9.

Su Baotang, and Lin Yi, eds. *Guojia gongwuyuan zhidu jianghua*. Beijing: Laodong renshi chubanshe, 1988.

Wang Fa, and Li Manyin. "Wei xian gaige ganbu lixiu tuixiu zhidu chujian chengxiao." *Hebei laodong renshi*, 1987, no. 9:13.

Wang Jisheng. "Tuixiu, lixiu lao ganbu de xinli de mouxie yanjiu." *Laonianxue zazhi* 3, no. 1 (1985):40–43.

———. "Tuixiu, lixiu lao ganbu zhili yinsu yu fei zhili yinsu de yanjiu." *Laonianxue zazhi* 3, no. 3 (1985):59–64.

———. "Tuixiu, lixiu ganbu xinli fanying de tantao." *Laonianxue zazhi* 3, no. 4 (1985):14–17.

———. "Li, tuixiu laoren de xinli weisheng yuanze." *Laonianxue zazhi* 6, no. 4 (1986):19–20.

———. "Lixiu he tuixiu zhidu de xinlixue yiyi." *Laonianxue zazhi* 8, no. 1 (1988):25–26.

Wang Laihua. "Laonianren shehui jiaowang de zhuyao tezheng ji bianhua quxiang." *Shehuixue yanjiu*, 1986, no. 3:21–26.

Wang Xingming. "Chuyi ganbu tuixiu zhidu de gaige." *Renshi*, 1988, no. 2:4–6.

Wang Zhaohua. "Guanyu ganbu 'sihua' he ganbu zhidu gaige de ji ge wenti." In *Laodong gongze renshi zhidu gaige de yanjiu yu tantao*, 104–28. See Jiao 1985.

Wen Kang. "Ganbu zhidu de yi xiang genben xing gaige: tantan feizhi zhongshenzhi de wenti." *Qunzhong*, 1981, no. 5:8–11.

Wu Fang. "Lixiu ganbu 'lao you suo wei' de tedian, fangshi he fazhan qushi." In *Shoudu laoling zhanlue wenti yanjiu*, 179–91. See Liu 1986.

Wu Liping. "Ganbu zhidu shang yi xiang zhongda de gaige." *Hongqi*, 1980, no. 11:6–10.

"Xian yure bu ke zhuiqiu gao bili." *Zhongguo laonian*, 1984, no. 3:29.

Xiao Guangming et al. "Lun feichu ganbu lingdao zhiwu zhongshenzhi." *Jiangxi daxue xuebao*, 1980, no. 4:20–28.

"Xinyang xian dui lituixiu renyuan xianqi banli shouxu." *Henan laodong*, 1988, no. 4:33.

Xu Fan. "Ganbu yanjiu." *Jingji yanjiu cankao xiaoxi*, 1988, no. 7:1–16.

Yan Jiaqi. "Lun feizhi 'zhongshenzhi.' " *Xin shiqi*, 1980, no. 3:5–7 and excerpt in *Renmin ribao*, 12 June 1980, 5.

———. *Zhongshenzhi yu xianrenzhi*. Shenyang: Liaoning renmin chubanshe, 1984.

Yang Chenggang. "Gongxian yu shanyang." *Laodong lilun yu shijian*, 1988, no. 4:8–9.

Yi Zhimin, Li Ruhai, and Hu Zhenmin, eds. *Guojia gongwuyuan gailun*. Beijing: Zhongguo renmin daxue chubanshe, 1989.

Zhao Shouyi. "Jianli you zhongguo tese de ganbu lixiu tuixiu zhidu." In *Renshi zhidu gaige wenxuan*, edited by Renshi zhidu gaige wenxuan bianji zu, 130–33. Beijing: Laodong renshi chubanshe, 1983. Neibu.

Zhonggong Hunan sheng wei zuzhi bu. "Zhengque shixing lao zhong qing san jiehe de yuanze." *Hongqi*, 1987, no. 6:46–50.

Zhonggong zhongyang zuzhi bu lao ganbu ju laodong renshi bu lao ganbu fuwu ju, eds. *Lao ganbu gongzuo wenjian xuanbian*. Vols. 1 and 2. Beijing: Zhonggong zhongyang zuzhi bu lao ganbu ju laodong renshi bu lao ganbu fuwu ju, 1983 and 1986. Neibu.

Zhonggong zhongyang zuzhi bu yanjiu shi, ed. *Zuo hao xin shiqi de ganbu gongzuo*. Beijing: Renmin chubanshe, 1984.

Zhu Di. "Lun ganbu de xinlao jiaoti." In *Laodong renshi zhidu gaige wenxuan*, edited by Han Qing and Qiu Furong, 74–86. Changsha: Hunan renmin chubanshe, 1987.

Zhu Gaozhang. "Guangzhou shi lixiu tuixiu laonianren de shehui, xinli ji jiankang zhuangkuang de diaocha baogao." *Laonianxue zazhi* 8, no. 1 (1988):6–8.

Articles and Books in English

Achen, Christopher H. *The Statistical Analysis of Quasi-Experiments*. Berkeley and Los Angeles: University of California Press, 1986.

Akerlof, George A. "A Theory of Social Custom, of Which Unemployment May Be One Consequence." *Quarterly Journal of Economics* 94, no. 4 (1980):749–75.

Anderson, Barbara A., and Brian D. Silver. "The SIP General Survey Sample." In *Politics, Work, and Daily Life in the USSR: A Survey of Former Soviet Citizens*, edited by James R. Millar, 354–71. Cambridge: Cambridge University Press, 1987.

Axelrod, Robert. *The Evolution of Cooperation*. New York: Basic Books, 1984.

———. "An Evolutionary Approach to Norms." *American Political Science Review* 80, no. 4 (1986):1095–1111.

Banister, Judith. *China's Changing Population*. Stanford: Stanford University Press, 1987.

———. "The Aging of China's Population." *Problems of Communism* 37, no. 6 (1988):62–77.

Bardach, Eugene. "Implementation Studies and the Study of Implements." Paper presented at the Annual Meeting of the American Political Science Association, Washington, D.C., 28–31 August 1980.

Bardach, Eugene, and Robert A. Kagan. *Going by the Book: The Problem of Regulatory Unreasonableness*. Philadelphia: Temple University Press, 1982.

Barnett, A. Doak. "Social Stratification and Aspects of Personnel Management in the Chinese Communist Bureaucracy." *China Quarterly*, no. 28 (1966):8–39.

———. *Cadres, Bureaucracy, and Political Power in Communist China*. New York: Columbia University Press, 1967.

Bennett, Gordon. *Yundong: Mass Campaigns in Chinese Communist Leadership*. Berkeley: Center for Chinese Studies, University of California, 1976.

Bialer, Seweryn. *Stalin's Successors: Leadership, Stability, and Change in the Soviet Union*. Cambridge: Cambridge University Press, 1980.

Bianco, Lucien. *Origins of the Chinese Revolution, 1915–1949*. Stanford: Stanford University Press, 1971.

Blackwell, Robert E. Jr. "Cadres Policy in the Brezhnev Era." *Problems of Communism* 28, no. 2 (1979):29–42.

Bodde, Derk, and Clarence Morris. *Law in Imperial China: Exemplified by 190 Ch'ing Dynasty Cases*. Philadelphia: University of Pennsylvania Press, 1967.

Brzezinski, Zbigniew. *The Permanent Purge*. Cambridge, Mass.: Harvard University Press, 1956.

Burns, John. "China's *Nomenklatura* System." *Problems of Communism* 36, no. 5 (1987):36–51.

———. "Civil Service Reform in Contemporary China." *Australian Journal of Chinese Affairs*, no. 18 (1987):47–83.

———. "Chinese Civil Service Reform: The 13th Party Congress Proposals." *China Quarterly*, no. 120 (1989):739–70.

Campbell, John Creighton. "Democracy and Bureaucracy in Japan." In *Democracy in Japan*, edited by Takeshi Ishida and Ellis S. Krauss, 113–37. Pittsburgh: University of Pittsburgh Press, 1989.

Cancian, Francesca M. *What Are Norms?: A Study of Beliefs and Action in a Mayan Community*. Cambridge: Cambridge University Press, 1975.

Cell, Charles P. *Revolution at Work: Mobilization Campaigns in China*. New York: Academic Press, 1977.

Chan, Anita, Richard Madsen, and Jonathan Unger. *Chen Village: The Recent History of a Peasant Community in Mao's China*. Berkeley and Los Angeles: University of California Press, 1984.

Chang, Parris H. "Political Rehabilitation of Cadres in China: A Traveller's View." *China Quarterly*, no. 54 (1973):329–40.

Ch'en Yung-sheng. "Peiping's Current Cadre Policy." *Issues and Studies* 19, no. 1 (1983):14–30.

Ch'u, T'ung-tsu. *Law and Society in Traditional China*. Paris: Mouton, 1961.

Cialdini, Robert H. *Influence: How and Why People Agree to Things*. New York: Morrow, 1984.

Davis, Deborah. "Unequal Chances, Unequal Outcomes: Pension Reform and Urban Inequality." *China Quarterly*, no. 114 (1988):223–42.

Davis-Friedmann, Deborah. *Long Lives: Chinese Elderly and the Communist Revolution*. Cambridge, Mass.: Harvard University Press, 1983.

———. "Chinese Retirement: Policy and Practice." In *Current Perspectives on Aging and the Life Cycle*. Vol. 1. *Work, Retirement and Social Policy*, edited by Zena Smith Blau, 378–413. Greenwich, Conn.: JAI Press, 1985.

Deng Xiaoping. "On the Reform of the System of Party and State Leadership." *Beijing Review* 25, no. 40 (1983):14–22 and no. 41 (1983):18–22.

Elmore, Richard. "Instruments and Strategy in Public Policy." *Policy Studies Review* 7, no. 1 (1987):174–86.

Emerson, John Philip. *Administrative and Technical Manpower in the People's Republic of China*. U.S. Department of Commerce, Bureau of Economic Analysis, Foreign Demographic Analysis Division, International Population Reports Series P-95, no. 72. Washington, D.C.: Government Printing Office, 1973.

Fang Hsueh-ch'un. "The Problem of Peiping's Ageing Leadership Cadres." *Issues and Studies* 16, no. 5 (1980):27–35.

———. "Personnel Changes in the CCP's Central Leadership." *Issues and Studies* 21, no. 12 (1985):27–54.

Forster, Keith. "The Reform of Provincial Party Committees in China: The Case of Zhejiang." *Asian Survey* 24, no. 6 (1984):618–36.

———. "Repudiation of the Cultural Revolution in China: The Case of Zhejiang." *Pacific Affairs* 59, no. 1 (1986):5–27.

Gibbs, Jack P. *Norms, Deviance, and Social Control*. New York: Elsevier, 1981.

Gill, Graeme. "Institutionalisation and Revolution: Rules and the Soviet Political System." *Soviet Studies* 37, no. 2 (1985):212–26.

Gold, Thomas B. "After Comradeship: Personal Relations in China since the Cultural Revolution." *China Quarterly*, no. 104 (1985):657–75.

Graebner, William. *A History of Retirement: The Meaning and Function of an American Institution, 1885–1978*. New Haven: Yale University Press, 1980.

Hardin, Russell. "The Emergence of Norms." *Ethics* 90, no. 4 (1980):575–87.

———. *Collective Action*. Baltimore: Johns Hopkins University Press, 1982.

Hart, H. L. A. *The Concept of Law*. Oxford: Clarendon Press, 1961.

Hayek, Friedrich A. *Law, Legislation, and Liberty*. Vol. 1. *Rules and Order*. Chicago: University of Chicago Press, 1973.

Henderson, Gail E., and Myron S. Cohen, M.D. *The Chinese Hospital: A Socialist Work Unit*. New Haven: Yale University Press, 1984.

Hough, Jerry F. *Soviet Leadership in Transition*. Washington, D.C.: Brookings Institution, 1980.

Hsieh, Pao Chao. *The Government of China*. New York: Octagon Books, 1966.

"International Working Women's Day." *Beijing Review* 24, no. 11 (1981):6.

Johnson, Chalmers A. *Peasant Nationalism and Communist Power: The Emergence of Revolutionary China, 1937–1945*. Stanford: Stanford University Press, 1962.

———. "The Reemployment of Retired Government Bureaucrats in Japanese Big Business." *Asian Survey* 14, no. 11 (1974):953–65.

———. *Japan's Public Policy Companies*. Washington, D.C.: American Enterprise Institute, 1978.

Kataoka, Tetsuya. *Resistance and Revolution in China: The Communists and the Second United Front*. Berkeley and Los Angeles: University of California Press, 1974.

Kau, Ying-mao. "The Urban Bureaucratic Elite in Communist China: A Case Study of Wuhan, 1949–65." In *Chinese Communist Politics in Action*, edited by A. Doak Barnett, 216–70. Seattle: University of Washington Press, 1969.

Kaufman, Herbert. *The Forest Ranger: A Study in Administrative Behavior*. Baltimore: Johns Hopkins University Press, 1960.

Kolakowski, Leszek. *Main Currents of Marxism: Its Origins, Growth and Dissolution*. Vol. 2. *The Golden Age*. Oxford: Oxford University Press, 1978.

Kracke, E. A. *Civil Service in Early Sung China, 960–1067*. Cambridge, Mass.: Harvard University Press, 1953.

Kubota, Akira. *Higher Civil Servants in Postwar Japan: Their Social Origins, Educational Backgrounds, and Career Patterns*. Princeton: Princeton University Press, 1969.

Kuhn, Alfred, and Robert D. Beam. *The Logic of Organizations*. San Francisco: Jossey-Bass, 1982.

Kyvig, David E. "Sober Thoughts: Myths and Realities of National Prohibition after Fifty Years." In *Law, Alcohol, and Order: Perspectives on National Prohibition*, edited by Kyvig, 3–20. Westport, Conn.: Greenwood Press, 1985.

Lautz, Terrill Edward. "The Politics of Retirement in Republican China, 1911–1949." Ph.D. diss., Stanford University, 1976.

Lee, Hong Yung. "The Politics of Cadre Rehabilitation since the Cultural Revolution." *Asian Survey* 18, no. 9 (1978):934–55.

———. "China's 12th Central Committee: Rehabilitated Cadres and Technocrats." *Asian Survey* 23, no. 6 (1983):673–91.

———. "Deng Xiaoping's Reform of the Chinese Bureaucracy." In *The Limits of Reform in China*, edited by Ronald A. Morse, 19–37. Boulder, Colo.: Westview Press, 1983.

————. *From Revolutionary Cadres to Party Technocrats in Socialist China*. Berkeley and Los Angeles: University of California Press, 1991.

Lewis, David K. *Convention: A Philosophical Study*. Cambridge, Mass.: Harvard University Press, 1969.

Lewis, John Wilson. *Leadership in Communist China*. Ithaca, N.Y.: Cornell University Press, 1963.

Li, Chi. "The Changing Concept of the Recluse in Chinese Literature." *Harvard Journal of Asiatic Studies* 24 (1962–63):234–47.

Li Ying-ming. "The Recent Changes in the Peking Leadership." *Issues and Studies* 21, no. 12 (1985):65–75.

Lieberthal, Kenneth. *Central Documents and Politburo Politics in China*. Michigan Papers in Chinese Studies, no. 33. Ann Arbor, Mich.: University of Michigan, Center for Chinese Studies, 1978.

————. "China in 1982: A Middling Course for the Middle Kingdom." *Asian Survey* 23, no. 1 (1983):26–37.

Lindblom, Charles E. *Politics and Markets*. New York: Basic Books, 1977.

Lui, Adam Yuen-chung. "The Ch'ing Civil Service: Promotions, Demotions, Transfers, Leaves, Dismissals and Retirements." *Journal of Oriental Studies* 8, no. 2 (1970):333–51.

MacFarquhar, Roderick. *The Origins of the Cultural Revolution*. Vols. 1 and 2. *Contradictions Among the People, 1956–1957. The Great Leap Forward, 1958–1960*. New York: Columbia University Press, 1974 and 1983.

Manion, Melanie. "The Cadre Management System, Post-Mao: The Appointment, Promotion, Transfer and Removal of Party and State Leaders." *China Quarterly*, no. 102 (1985):203–33.

————. "The Behavior of Middlemen in the Cadre Retirement Policy Process." In *Bureaucracy, Politics, and Decision Making in Post-Mao China*, edited by Kenneth G. Lieberthal and David M. Lampton, 216–44. Berkeley and Los Angeles: University of California Press, 1992.

Mather, Richard B. "The Controversy over Conformity and Naturalness during the Six Dynasties." *History of Religions* 9, nos. 2 and 3 (1969–70):160–80.

Metzger, Thomas A. Foreword to *Moral Behavior in Chinese Society*, edited by Richard W. Wilson, Sidney L. Greenblatt, and Amy Auerbacher Wilson, ix–xxv. New York: Praeger, 1981.

Meyer, Alfred G. *Leninism*. Cambridge, Mass.: Harvard University Press, 1957.

Mills, William, deB. "Generational Change in China." *Problems of Communism* 32, no. 6 (1983):16–35.

Mote, Frederick W. "Confucian Eremitism in the Yuan Period." In *The Confucian Persuasion*, edited by Arthur F. Wright, 202–40. Stanford: Stanford University Press, 1960.

Munro, Donald J. *The Concept of Man in Early China*. Stanford: Stanford University Press, 1969.

————. *The Concept of Man in Contemporary China*. Ann Arbor, Mich.: University of Michigan Press, 1977.

Nathan, Andrew J. *Chinese Democracy*. Berkeley and Los Angeles: University of California Press, 1985.

Oksenberg, Michel. "The Institutionalisation of the Chinese Communist Revolution: The Ladder of Success on the Eve of the Cultural Revolution." *China Quarterly*, no. 36 (1968):61–92.

———. "Local Leaders in Rural China, 1962–65: Individual Attributes, Bureaucratic Positions, and Political Recruitment." In *Chinese Communist Politics in Action*, 155–215. See Kau 1969.

———. "Methods of Communication within the Chinese Bureaucracy." *China Quarterly*, no. 57 (1974):1–39.

———. "The Exit Pattern in Chinese Politics and Its Implications." *China Quarterly*, no. 67 (1976):501–18.

Olson, Mancur. *The Logic of Collective Action: Public Goods and the Theory of Groups*. Cambridge, Mass.: Harvard University Press, 1965.

Opp, Karl-Dieter. "The Evolutionary Emergence of Norms." *British Journal of Social Psychology* 21, no. 2 (1982):139–49.

Pepper, Suzanne. *Civil War in China: The Political Struggle, 1945–1949*. Berkeley and Los Angeles: University of California Press, 1978.

"Proportion of Elderly is Increasing." *Beijing Review* 31, no. 41 (1988):39–40.

Pye, Lucien W. *The Dynamics of Chinese Politics*. Cambridge: Oelgeschlager, Gunn and Hain, 1981.

Rosen, Stanley, and David Chu. "Survey Research in the People's Republic of China." Washington, D.C.: United States Information Agency, Office of Research, 1987.

Schelling, Thomas C. *The Strategy of Conflict*. Cambridge, Mass.: Harvard University Press, 1960.

Schram, Stuart. *The Political Thought of Mao Tse-tung*. Rev. ed. New York: Praeger, 1969.

———. *The Thought of Mao Tse-tung*. Cambridge: Cambridge University Press, 1989.

———, ed. *Chairman Mao Talks to the People: Talks and Letters, 1956–1971*. New York: Pantheon, 1974.

Schuman, Howard, and Stanley Presser. *Questions and Answers in Attitude Surveys: Experiments on Question Form, Wording, and Context*. Orlando, Fla.: Academic Press, 1981.

Schurmann, Franz. *Ideology and Organization in Communist China*. 2d ed. Berkeley and Los Angeles: University of California Press, 1968.

"Selecting Young Cadres for Leading Posts." *Beijing Review* 24, no. 31 (1981):3.

Sherif, Carolyn W., Muzafer Sherif, and Roger E. Nebergall. *Attitude and Attitude Change: The Social Judgment-Involvement Approach*. Philadelphia: Saunders, 1965.

Sherif, Muzafer. *The Psychology of Social Norms*. New York: Harper and Brothers, 1936.

Skinner, G. William, and Edwin A. Winckler. "Compliance Succession in Rural Communist China: A Cyclical Theory." In *A Sociological Reader on Com-*

plex Organizations, 2d ed., edited by Amitai Etzioni, 410–38. New York: Holt, Rinehart and Winston, 1969.

Sugden, Robert. *The Economics of Rights, Co-operation and Welfare*. Oxford: Basil Blackwell, 1986.

———. "Spontaneous Order." *Journal of Economic Perspectives* 3, no. 4 (1989):85–97.

Teiwes, Frederick C. *Provincial Party Personnel in Mainland China, 1956–1966*. New York: East Asian Institute, Columbia University, 1967.

———. *Politics and Purges in China: Rectification and the Decline of Party Norms, 1950–1965*. Armonk, N.Y.: M. E. Sharpe, 1969.

———. *Elite Discipline in China: Coercive and Persuasive Approaches to Rectification, 1950–1953*. Canberra: Contemporary China Institute, Australian National University, 1978.

Townsend, James R. *Political Participation in Communist China*. Berkeley and Los Angeles: University of California Press, 1967.

Tseng Yung-hsien. "The New Leadership in Mainland China." *Issues and Studies* 18, no. 6 (1983):15–42.

Ullmann-Margalit, Edna. *The Emergence of Norms*. Oxford: Oxford University Press, 1977.

Van Slyke, Lyman P. *Enemies and Friends: The United Front in Chinese Communist History*. Stanford: Stanford University Press, 1967.

Vogel, Ezra. "From Revolutionary to Semi-Bureaucrat: The 'Regularisation' of Cadres." *China Quarterly*, no. 29 (1967):41–44.

Walder, Andrew G. *Communist Neo-Traditionalism: Work and Authority in Chinese Industry*. Berkeley and Los Angeles: University of California Press, 1986.

Weick, Karl E. "Small Wins: Redefining the Scale of Social Problems." *American Psychologist* 39, no. 1 (1984):40–49.

Weimer, David L., and Aidan R. Vining. *Policy Analysis: Concepts and Practice*. Englewood Cliffs, N.J.: Prentice-Hall, 1989.

Wesson, Robert G. *The Aging of Communism*. New York: Praeger, 1980.

White, Tyrene. "Postrevolutionary Mobilization in China: The One-Child Policy Reconsidered." *World Politics* 43, no. 1 (1990):53–76.

Whitson, William. "The Field Army in Chinese Communist Military Politics." *China Quarterly*, no. 37 (1969):1–30.

———. *The Chinese High Command, 1927–1971: A History of Communist Military Politics*. New York: Praeger, 1973.

Whyte, Martin King. *Small Groups and Political Rituals in China*. Berkeley and Los Angeles: University of California Press, 1974.

———. "On Studying China at a Distance." In *The Social Sciences and Fieldwork in China: Views from the Field*, edited by Anne F. Thurston and Burton Pasternak, 63–80. Boulder, Colo.: Westview Press, 1983.

World Bank. *World Development Report 1991*. New York: Oxford University Press, 1991.

Index